MASTERING ONLINE RESEARCH

A COMPREHENSIVE GUIDE
TO EFFECTIVE AND EFFICIENT SEARCH STRATEGIES

MAURA D. SHAW

WRITER'S DIGEST BOOKS

www.writersdigest.com
Cincinnati, Ohio

Visit our websites at www.writersdigest.com and www.wdeditors.com for information on more resources for writers. For more fine books from Writer's Digest Books, please visit www.fwbookstore.com.

To receive a free weekly e-mail newsletter delivering tips and updates about writing and about Writer's Digest products, register directly at our Web site at http://newsletters.fwpublications.com.

11   10   09   08   07   5   4   3   2   1

Distributed in Canada by Fraser Direct, 100 Armstrong Avenue Georgetown, Ontario, Canada   L7G 5S4, Tel: (905) 877-4411; Distributed in the U.K. and Europe by David & Charles, Brunel House, Newton Abbot, Devon, TQ12 4PU, England, Tel: (+44) 1626 323200, Fax: (+44) 1626 323319, E-mail: postmaster@ davidandcharles.co.uk; Distributed in Australia by Capricorn Link, P.O. Box 704, Windsor, NSW 2756 Australia, Tel: (02) 4577-3555

Library of Congress Cataloging-in-Publication Data

Shaw, Maura D.

  Mastering online research : a comprehensive guide to effective and efficient search strategies / by Maura Shaw.

     p. cm.

  Includes index.

  ISBN-10: 1-58297-458-6 (pbk. : alk. paper)

  ISBN-13: 978-1-58297-458-3

  1. Internet searching. 2. Computer network resources. 3. Web sites--Directories. 4. Internet research. I. Title.

  ZA4230.S53 2007

  025.04--dc22

                              2007011286

Edited by Michelle Ehrhard
Designed by Claudean Wheeler
Cover Design by Grace Saunders and Claudean Wheeler
Production coordinated by Mark Griffin

[DEDICATION]

To Joe, always and forever.

[ABOUT THE AUTHOR]

Maura D. Shaw is the author of over a dozen published books, both fiction and nonfiction. She has worked in scholarly and trade publishing for more than thirty years, as managing editor for the Yale University Press and the University of Chicago Press Journals Division, as senior editor and electronic products manager for the print and online editions of the *Encyclopedia Americana*, and as senior development editor for a multifaith religious publisher. She has been closely involved with Internet resources since the early 1980s and spends the majority of her life in front of her computer, nearly oblivious to the beautiful Vermont countryside where she lives with her husband, Joe Tantillo, and two dogs.

TABLE OF CONTENTS

CHAPTER 7:
SEARCHING FOR PEOPLE AND PLACES   168

CHAPTER 8:
ACCESSING SPECIAL SEARCH AREAS   196

CHAPTER 9:
SEARCHING FOR IMAGE, AUDIO, AND VIDEO FILES
224

CHAPTER 10:
RESEARCH SKILLS FOR WRITERS 256

CHAPTER 11:
PERMISSIONS AND COPYRIGHT ISSUES 285

CHAPTER 12:

CONCLUDING YOUR RESEARCH   314

GLOSSARY

INDEX

INTRODUCTION

I'm glad I live in the age of the internet. I've become so accustomed to researching any and every subject that I no longer can imagine my life without it. I pursue serious and frivolous research on the Web, I shop, I look up addresses and phone numbers and old friends. I keep up with news and with history. I'm convinced that internet access saved my mother's life, because I was able to look up her atypical symptoms of a heart attack on a medical website and rush her to the emergency room. The World Wide Web was the greatest advance of the twentieth century, and it keeps on improving.

Writing this book gives me an opportunity to share the techniques and tips that I've learned over many years of working on the internet, running thousands of searches and analyzing websites, search results, and hyperlinks. Much of what I learned as far back as ten years ago still applies, but everything runs faster and better now. It's a great time for you to learn how to navigate the world of cyberspace.

This book will help you to master the skills and shortcuts of online research so your searches will be satisfying and the challenges enjoyable. You'll learn to love the thrill of the chase after pieces of information that somebody out there knows and you don't.

If you've never done much more than enter a search word or two in the Google or Yahoo! search box, you're in for a treat. You can find just about anything out there with the right search tools. And you'll learn practical methods to evaluate the websites you find for reliability, timeliness, relevance to your search, and other parameters.

In the *New York Times* on November 6, 2006, an article by Tom Zeller Jr. appeared concerning the internet pranksters who manipulated search results on the major search engine websites just prior to the U.S. election, in order to bring up certain politicians' websites when users searched for words such as "miserable failure." The use of the internet for political campaigning was a new phenomenon at the levels it reached at that time. But what was shocking to me was the report that ordinary internet users remain incredibly naïve about the results from search engines. "Numerous studies have shown that precious few sleuths go beyond the first page of search results. 'If it's not on the first page, it might as well be invisible,'" the newspaper quoted Danny Sullivan, editor of the online Search Engine Watch, as saying.

The article went on to state that the Nielsen Norman Group, which surveys internet behavior, found in 2005 that fewer than 1 percent of searchers used advanced search options. Even scarier was the statistic from the Pew Internet

& American Life Project that "only 38 percent of searchers were aware of a distinction between paid and unpaid results among search returns."

Once you've delved into this book and practiced your skills online, you'll be part of that intelligent, sophisticated, and effective 1 percent of internet searchers. Welcome!

CHAPTER 1

THE INTERNET DEFINED

Back in the early 1990s, you could buy a guide to the World Wide Web that was the size of a Manhattan phone directory, cost you about fifty bucks, and gave you hundreds of annotated websites organized by topic. Today you would need a forest's worth of paper to publish such a guide, and it would be out of date before the first page was printed. The explosion of websites means that the writer, teacher, researcher, or student who wants to search online has to learn how to draw out the best information from among hundreds of millions of electronic pages.

Sound challenging? It is—but it's fun, too. By following the tips and techniques in this book, you will soon be able to navigate the Web with ease. Mastering the art of online research will free you to pursue your creativity and open your mind to inspiration.

Just like learning to drive a car, you've got to practice basic internet skills until they become second nature—and then you can take off anywhere.

Some of you may already be proficient in using the internet for news, shopping, entertainment, and finding out general information about a multitude of topics. Others may have conquered the challenges of using e-mail but have been reluctant to venture out past the prescreened information sources offered by internet providers such as America Online (AOL). Still others may be starting from an even more basic level of computer use. If you don't yet have an internet service provider, talk to your friends and colleagues to find out which service would work best for you in your local area. This book offers helpful information for all of you, at a level that I hope will be approachable and easily put into practice.

All the techniques in this book are usable whether you are working on a PC or a Mac computer system. Mac users simply will substitute the simultaneous control key/mouse click whenever you are asked to right-click to bring up a menu.

As you gain familiarity with the techniques of "drilling down" through multiple pages on a website, following hyperlinks to other related sites, using web subject directories, evaluating the reliability of a website, and refining your search queries and results, you'll be amazed at the information that you can uncover.

WHAT CAN YOU FIND OUT THERE?

We're going to approach the nitty-gritty of internet research under the assumption that you're a word-oriented person—a beginning writer or a published one, a history buff or a journalist, a teacher or a student. You're looking to learn to use the research tools on the Web comfortably, without altering your mindset into that of a computer software engineer. You just want to learn how to find stuff. That's a perfectly fine goal. And the information you'll turn up will help you in your endeavors, and make it easier to work creatively and professionally. The lovely thing about the internet is that we don't all have to be computer wizards to use it.

When folks first started using the internet, they could access it only through large institutions and universities. The technology had been developed by the military for communication purposes, and there was no such thing as a user-friendly software operating system like Microsoft Windows or Vista. In the late 1970s when I first signed on to an e-mail program while working as an editor at Yale University, I had to learn a computer-compatible language called W-Script (named for the University of Waterloo in Canada where it was developed) in order to send e-mails to people at other large universities. I was so nervous typing on the terminal that my hands were clammy, and I had to walk three blocks across campus to the Computer Science department in order to get a printed copy of a message. Some years later, people working on developing internet sites had to learn another new language, HTML (HyperText Markup Language), to create websites and post their content. That restricted the internet world to those who could translate their documents into HTML or could afford to hire people to do so. Fortunately it wasn't too long before new, simplified programs were developed to allow less technical users to post their information on websites—and then the World Wide Web became the superhighway it is today.

This extremely condensed version of internet history is only meant to encourage you in approaching the twenty-first century's internet with confidence. No clammy hands; no need to learn a code—you can search the Web and pinpoint exactly what you are looking for. There are, of course, a few technical tips that will help you to evaluate a site, but, as you read this book, you'll learn to decode those with no problem.

So what can you find out there? Practically everything, if you know how to look.

Notice that the operative word here is "how"—not "where"—to look. The skill that will help you find everything is learning how to search speedily and efficiently. You can approach your search in different ways, using a broad sweep or a narrow target method. We'll go into those specific methods later in the book, building skills and knowledge in each successive chapter.

There are websites available for just about any topic a researcher or writer could need. Simply think of a question you want answered, and within a few seconds or minutes—voilà! You have a list of possibilities to evaluate, a wide variety of resources you can tap into from your own computer. It's called the *World Wide* Web for a reason!

TERMS TO KNOW

The World Wide Web may not be very old, but it has accumulated a vast store of terminology. New words and elements are added constantly. Can you hope to keep up? Probably not. No single person can—and still claim to have a life. But you can learn enough to understand and master the art of online research. We'll start with the simplest terms. (If you already know the basics, feel free to skip this section.)

Web, internet, and websites: When you embark upon online research, you will encounter two terms often used interchangeably, although they do not mean exactly the same thing: *World Wide Web* and *internet.* The World Wide Web refers to the community of websites that link to one another via the internet pathway. All websites are connected to the internet using a commonly accepted communication language and rules, called a protocol. The internet is actually the utility by which you can access the Web. The internet refers to the technical components and information pathways that allow you to communicate online with other users. Even the term *online* can be defined to mean having a connection to the internet.

When you are connected to the internet, you can access the websites on the World Wide Web. A *website*, put simply, is a group of files organized into pages displaying text and images, identified by a unique computer location called an IP or Internet Protocol address (more on that on page 17). Websites are hosted on *servers*, which are computers dedicated to handling the traffic of electronic information traveling back and forth on the internet.

Internet providers, such as AOL, Comcast, Earthlink, Verizon, and hundreds of others, make it easy for consumers to post their websites on the servers using various software programs. Large commercial and institutional websites will usually have their own servers.

You can easily navigate the Web by using the connections available on the internet, called *hypertext links* or *hyperlinks* or just plain *links*. Whether the link is displayed as a button or bar, a clickable image, or an underlined word in the text of a web page, it will link to a page on another website that receives the message at its IP address, which is not visible to you. In many cases you can see the web page link's *URL* (Universal Resource Locator), which is an address that shows you the *domain name* (registered owner of the website) and other valuable information. We'll analyze what you can learn from a URL on page 16.

Browsers: Accessing the internet is accomplished through a software application called a *browser,* which is installed on your computer. You can choose from several popular browsers, including Microsoft's Internet Explorer, Mozilla's Firefox, Netscape, Opera, and Blackberry. Each allows you to access and interact with the internet in similar ways.

The opening page of a website appearing on your browser screen is most commonly known as a *home page.* When you visit a website, often the home page will be the first page you see. If not, there is usually a navigational tool (a button or link) that is marked "Home." On this main page, you will find menus and links to take you to additional pages on the site. Some websites open with a *splash screen* (as in "making a splash" of the website's identity), which can be either static or interactive with a multimedia presentation. If you don't want to wait for all the bells and whistles, look for a small clickable link that says something like "skip intro." In chapter four, we will go into detail about the information you can find on a website's home page.

Home page displayed on a browser

Your browser allows you to access web pages on the World Wide Web by entering the URL into a small address window at the top of the browser screen. You can enter the address directly if you know it, or you can go to a search engine to find the website.

Internet connections: Connecting to the internet is made possible by several different technologies. Some people still use the first available method, a modem (receiver) with a dial-up connection through a phone line. Others use a cable modem, which brings the connection through the same lines that deliver cable television and radio station signals. Still others use a broadband connection that uploads and downloads data to satellites orbiting above our heads. Using devices called network routers or wireless routers, the internet connection can be delivered to several different computers in the same house. Gadget-lovers use mobile technology with a wireless network referred to as *wifi*, which can deliver e-mail, data, multimedia, and so on to their mobile devices and laptops. The delivery system you use depends on how much money you are willing to spend and the area you live in. Here on a mountainside in Vermont I can't install a satellite dish because the trees and the mountain block the sky, but that wouldn't be a problem on the plains of Kansas.

Search engines: A *search engine* basically is a coordinated group of programs: It uses a *webcrawler* (a robotic program) to visit millions of web pages to retrieve data that is then compiled into an indexed database that can be searched for matches to the queries you send to it, which it then delivers in a results list of clickable links to websites that match your search criteria. Questions are called *queries* and *search strings* in this online world, and the websites that are turned up in response are called *results* and *hits*.

Chapters two and three explain the details of search engines and how to create the best queries that will get search results efficiently and quickly. Basically, a *database* contains records of all the information about the contents of a website, which are searched using complicated programming code to find the best records that match the criteria you've requested in your query. Queries are composed of *keywords*—terms that describe most specifically what you want to find.

Search engine webcrawlers also rely on specific keywords called *meta-tags* that are placed in the website's coding so search engines can pick up on them. The meta-tags describe the site's content and include terms likely to match a high level of search queries, to drive traffic (visitors) to the site. As search engine technology has advanced, meta-tags are much less significant in the search process.

To be specific, a *search engine* is the programming application that directs the search and returns its results; a *search site* is the operating website that owns or licenses the programming software (such as Google.com). A *search system* can refer to either the search site or the choice of search method that you use—either a basic keyword search or an advanced search (both methods will be explored thoroughly in chapters two and three). Another type of search engine is called a *metasearch engine*, because its programming is designed to search the results of your query run on a group of other search engines, then sort and display the best and most relevant results from among them.

Another term you will encounter is the *subject directory*, an alternate method for doing online research. This was the first format for organizing information on the Web, a hierarchically organized list of subject categories evaluated and selected by human editors. You can *drill down* through layers of categories and subcategories, each of which contains multiple websites, until you find what you're searching for. Chapter five explains this process in detail.

WORKING ON THE WEB

Conducting research on the Web requires knowledge of a few more terms. All these will be shown in context in the following chapters, so this is just a small starter to increase your "web savvy"—in itself a funny web term, meaning you know how to understand and work with the language and logistics of cyberspace. By the end of this book you will be web savvy, honest!

One attribute that computer folks strive to instill into their software application programming, websites, even hardware, is that of being *robust*. A robust website has lots of valuable, reliable content and many useful features to help users exploit that content to their best advantage. Robust search engines do the job and don't break down. Robust websites don't crash or show up without their visual images in place. A robust database has everything you're looking for stored in accessible records.

Keyword searches: As you begin to search online for answers to your research needs, you will be using a combination of search methods. A *basic keyword search* will find results for simple words and phrases. An *advanced search* will look for keywords that are joined with other query requirements specified by you, such as the words being in a particular order or language, or appearing on a particular kind of site such as an educational site. Most large search engines are not case-sensitive in their searches; that is, they ignore whether a word is typed in capital or lowercase letters. The best method is to type all query words in lowercase letters, unless you are using an advanced search technique that specifies "case-sensitive" and "exact match."

Inadvertent misspellings of your keywords could be a problem in online searches; however, recognizing users' fallibility or sloppiness, search engines display the correct spelling of a word as an alternative at the top of the results list. If you search for "Ghandi," you'll see a message on Yahoo! asking, "Did you mean Gandhi?" Most search engines also will assume your mistake was unintentional and give you the results for the correct spelling anyway. You'll still pick up all those folks with web pages who never did learn to spell the Mahatma's name properly. (If you're searching deliberately for an oddly spelled word, just ignore the message.)

You will want to search for the same keywords on more than one search engine to make sure that you've obtained all possible results. Opening more than one browser window at a time will allow you to work more efficiently. Keeping track of multiple browser windows can be a bit tricky. I usually minimize those I am not actively looking at (click on the little box with the minus sign at the top right of the browser window to keep the window active as a small tab at the foot of your screen). Sometimes I work with two or more windows open, switching back and forth, and also travel to previous and next pages within one website by using the "Back" and "Forward" buttons on the browser toolbar at the top. Recently there's been an improvement in manipulating and organizing multiple screens, though. The newest versions of the Microsoft Internet Explorer browser and the Mozilla Firefox browser have a new feature called "tabbed browsing," which lets you add a tab at the top of the toolbar for each web page you visit in a research session. You can immediately open the web page by clicking on the tab, instead of using the browser's "Back" arrow button. Switching among a few instantly accessible web pages can be very useful. And you can quickly close all the open tabs with a single click, rather than one by one.

When you are looking at a web page of a site that interests you, use the scroll bar on the right-hand side of the screen to move down to the foot of the page. There are no standard "page" lengths on the internet, of course. You can guess how long a page is by how quickly the gray scroll bar on the right side of the window moves down the page. If you've scrolled past screenfuls of material and the scroll bar is still hovering near the top of the screen, it's a very long page indeed. Just drag the scroll bar quickly to the bottom with your mouse.

Commerce is a huge part of paying for the free searches online, making advertising commonplace on the World Wide Web. On almost any website, paid advertisements run along the sides and bottom of the page. Search results pages from Google, Yahoo!, and other search engines also display *sponsored results* on the left of the screen that are paid for by advertisers, and are separate from the results from keywords. Although many ads and banners are annoying and garish, some of the sites advertised can be helpful to your research. Small sites often support the expenses of making their content available online by accepting paid advertising. Not all of the products or services are pertinent to the subject matter of the site, but sometimes you will find that the advertising opens up a new angle of approach for your research, or another audience who might be interested in your work.

Downloads: The use of downloads on the Web is becoming more widespread as computers and mobile devices such as cellular phones and handheld units become more firmly integrated with the internet. Downloading files of music, videos, movies, and entertainment is not precisely what we include as "online research," but that same technology allows users access to a continuous stream of news alerts, updates of favorite websites and blogs, and other data. You can be connected to the real world through the online world in real time, 24/7, if you wish. The newest technology, called an RSS feed (or XML feed), allows websites to continually update information delivered to your computer or mobile device. The term *RSS* stands for Really Simple Syndication, a software application that uses the standard coding language of XML to easily allow websites to transmit content that can be read and displayed by an RSS feed reader installed on your computer. The feed readers are widely available and offered free or at minimal cost. Most up-to-date browsers such as Mozilla Firefox and Internet Explorer versions 7 and up include an RSS feed reader as one of the features.

One caution to searching on the Web, especially when you get into image searches: The more websites you visit, the more vulnerable you are to users who do not have your best interests in mind. Before you get started, please make sure your internet security protection is up-to-date.

THE SECRETS OF URLS

Every one of the millions of pages on the World Wide Web is identified by a unique address called a Universal Resource

Locator, or URL. (People occasionally pronounce the acronym as "earl," but the usual pronunciation is to sound out the letters separately as you would for IBM.) Every URL follows a specific internet protocol (rules for the transmission of data) in its format that allows all different kinds of networks to read the address and retrieve information for the searcher. Underpinning the URL is the IP or Internet Protocol address, a series of numbers that indicate the site's location on a network and even on a specific device such as a server or desktop computer. This IP address anchors the delivery of the data packets (information) sent back and forth between web servers. However, you don't have to know all the structure of the protocol to glean a lot of information about a website from an examination of its URL.

The website addresses represented by the URLs provide the directions for the search engines or the hypertext links to find one another across the vast cyberspace of the Web. The URL of the page you are looking at is displayed in a small box in the toolbar on your browser—in Microsoft Internet Explorer, for example, the box is labeled "address." That's where you type the URL if you want to access a site directly without using a search engine or a hyperlink. You've probably done that hundreds of times without considering the different components of the address that you're typing.

STRUCTURE OF A URL

Let's take apart a few URLs and see what they can tell us about the sites to which they point. The "http://" that precedes every website address stands for HyperText Transfer Protocol (HTTP) and is the signal that marks the rest of the address as accessible via the internet. For convenience, we'll omit that standard prefix from most of the URLs discussed here. *HyperText* is an early term for the data transfer, originally intended to imply its incredible speed for sending text (though by today's standards it would seem slow). The HTTP protocol runs on the foundation of TCP/IP (Transmission Control Protocol/Internet Protocol), a program that—to put it in the simplest terms—makes everything on the internet work.

Every website follows a convention in naming, for a good reason. The protocol was established so that any computer on the internet could talk to any other one. Simply put, in retrieving a page that a searcher requests, the "host" computer (called a server) sorts through the components of the URL to find the exact page location requested. The pages on every website are arranged in a hierarchical "tree" that organizes the HTML (or XML, another coding language) pages into levels. The levels are separated in the URL address by vertical slashes (and sometimes there are many levels, if a website is large and robust). At the very end is the designation of the type of file being accessed. For example, ".html" is a standard web page coded in HTML that will assemble together its page elements of text and graphics in your browser window, loading them piece by piece (some systems use the suffix ".htm"), and ".pdf" is a portable document format, which reproduces the visual appearance of a document already fully assembled as a static image.

That's about as complicated as we need to get for our purposes, except for the pages built "on the fly" that we'll look at on page 23.

UNDERSTANDING URLS AND DOMAIN NAMES

The most straightforward URL, such as www.bartleby.com, is a domain name, or registered business or personal name, followed by the ubiquitous "dotcom." Bartleby.com (named for Melville's famous scrivener) is one of the first and best sources for researching authors and their works, containing the full text of many significant works of literature. For example, from www.bartleby.com (the top-level domain) you can link to a page called www.bartleby.com/people/WhitmnW.html to find searchable works, quotations, a portrait, and an encyclopedia article on Walt Whitman. The site also offers the complete searchable text of Whitman's best-known works, including several successive editions of *Leaves of Grass*.

Many people—such as writers, who command a definite presence on the internet—register their own names as domain names (mine is www.mauradshaw.com, for instance). Others use the web page hosting services of their internet providers, which makes it a little more difficult to decode their URLs. One such site is www.home.earthlink. net/~clyons55/. You can't tell from the URL what this site contains. That's because the website is a personal home page hosted by the internet provider Earthlink. What's the clue? The tilde (~) before the personal name. When a URL contains that little wavy symbol (it's located on the far left of your keyboard), you can expect that whatever follows it is a sub-address for a secondary website maintained by the primary website. Nonetheless, you will often find valuable, creditable information on these personal pages.

Not everyone who shares information on a topic of interest wants to pay for and maintain a unique website identified with a domain name. Many people are content to create personal web pages hosted by their internet service providers as part of the service package. But unless the individual has made the effort to attract the attention of the search engines and web crawlers, the web pages won't appear in your search results. The website hosted by "clyons55," however, is a bona fide resource called Writing Road, which has a weekly newsletter, chat room, helpful links, interviews, book reviews, and so on, and it will appear on a results list for a search for "writers groups" or similar keywords.

Sometimes you can access a website directly by entering the company name as its URL without going through a search. If you type www.pepsi.com, that will bring you to the Pepsi-Cola home page, but if you look at the URL in the browser window, you will see www.pepsi.com/home.php. The words following the slash indicate that you've been redirected to another site automatically, on the assumption that you were searching for the home page of the Pepsi *beverage*. This redirect is accomplished by a scripting language ("php," which is short for personal home page tools) that brings you to a dynamic page called PepsiWorld. If you were looking for information on Pepsi's corporate history, you'd have to do a search to find the home page for the Pepsi-Cola *company*, www.pepsico.com.

If a website has moved to another host location or otherwise changed its URL, users will often be redirected to the new address automatically, with a notice of the change appearing on an interim screen. If it's a site you visit often, make sure to change the address in your Favorites or Bookmarks file.

There's another rule about the naming of website pages, which is useful to know. Because some special characters are used in the programming codes that underlie what you see on the screen, they have been declared off-limits for use in URLs. The list includes a question mark, an exclamation point, and some others. For example, if you want to visit the Yahoo! website and include the exclamation point as part of its name, you will instead see the dreaded "The page cannot be displayed" error screen. A space cannot be used to separate distinct words, either. URLs get around these restrictions by using an underscore (_) to replace the space. So you might see an address like this one for the Fire Department website in the city of Troy, New York: www.troyny.org/city_services_fire.html. The underscores make it much easier to read than "cityservicesfire."

Domain Levels

When you look at the URL www.bartleby.com/people/WhitmnW.html, you can see the levels of the web pages as they are arranged hierarchically. When you click on the Walt Whitman hyperlink from the Bartleby.com home page, the computer then goes to a file named "People" that contains all the authors whose work appears on the site, and then to a more specific level of file that is devoted to the poet Walt Whitman alone. In fact, these "files" may point to enormous databases that are called by these human-scale names. If you go to the site and search for the edition of *Leaves of Grass* published in 1900 (Whitman kept on revising the poems for each new edition), you would notice in the URL address that this particular edition is assigned the number 142 in the database (www. bartleby.com/142). That kind of information is very helpful when comparing different editions of a text online—you can always look at the URL to see which edition is onscreen.

URL Suffixes

Another piece of information you can glean from a URL is the country from which the website originates. For some U.S.-centric reason having to do with where the major development of the internet took place, websites originating in the United States do not carry a suffix to identify them. Other countries do. For instance, the website for the agent who handles popular novelist Maeve Binchy's work (www.christinegreen.co.uk/) makes it clear that she operates out of her office in the United Kingdom, specifically London. If her office had been located in Sydney, Australia, she would have had ".au" at the end of the address. The country designations are extremely useful when you are surveying a long list of search results.

In addition to the .com websites, other suffixes are used to represent sites hosted by internet service providers (.net); organizations that are non-commercial or non-profit (.org); sites maintained by the national, state, and local government (.gov); and sites hosted by educational institutions (.edu). Newer designations are also being used, such as .tv and .biz.

State and local government websites sometimes bury their URLs in a heap of acronyms. A website from the state of Maine

Mastering Online Research

(www.maine.gov/dhhs/beas/profile/) contains a recent data profile of Maine's older population that includes great statistics, but you would never guess it by looking at the URL. You might recognize the acronym for the Department of Health and Human Services in the URL, but you might have a harder time figuring out the Bureau of Elder and Adult Services. And you probably wouldn't know that "profile" indicates data collected from Maine's senior citizens. The data profile on this web page matched the keywords in the search query. If you don't find what you are looking for on the page, just delete that part of the address from the end of the URL and click to go to the main page for BEAS, the next level of the URL. From the BEAS home page, you can search the entire website and find many specific links.

Dynamically Generated URLs

As mentioned earlier, some web pages are dynamically generated, that is, they are constructed "on the fly." The information and graphics displayed on the page are brought together specifically to fulfill the requests in your search—they do not exist as a complete page of HTML or XML until the host computer follows complex programming commands to retrieve and process the data before showing it onscreen. Shopping sites are powered by this technology, as well as online newspapers and encyclopedias and many other sites, because it allows the site to display exactly what you've requested from their multiple databases of images, text, product features, hyperlinks, pricing, and so forth. But when you see one of these URLs in your browser window, it might look like a crazy jumble of letters, numbers, and characters, like this one: www.cherokee.org/home.aspx?section=story&id=EzczD82v4/Q. This page is displayed using active server page technology (the "asp" in the URL) to find the exact data in the database that matches the results of my search. The URL above is a page on the official site of the Cherokee Nation that shows former chief Wilma Mankiller reading to a group of schoolchildren. As a researcher, you don't need to be able to read this code, but it's useful to know what comprises the URL.

Now, when you review your Google or Yahoo! search results list, you'll be able to tell more about the website from the URL that appears below the brief text description and the name of the page. You'll know who sponsors the site, whether it's a commercial site or an educational institution, the country in which it originates, and so on. After a glance at the URL, if it's not a likely prospect for your research, you can move on to the next entry in the results list without actually visiting the web page. More detailed information about how to evaluate websites for content and reliability appears in chapter four.

KEEPING TRACK OF VALUABLE SOURCES

When you begin to work with a list of search results, you may quickly feel overwhelmed by the massive amount of information. Pages upon pages to read, links linking to other links, and through them to yet more links—all of them enticing—but clearly too much to print out on paper. Remember, the advantage of online research is that it's—um—online.

BROWSER BOOKMARKS

If you want to access websites with lengthy names such as www.beautifuleasygardens.com/ more often than once, you would have an unwieldy number of keystrokes to type. That's one reason why the "Bookmarks" or "Favorites" tools were developed for browsers. The bookmark captures the URL of the web page and saves it.

Bookmarks are easy to learn to use, and now you have more choices for where and how you can access them. All browser bookmark utilities work in just about the same way. On the Internet Explorer browser, bookmarks are called "Favorites." On the AOL browser, they are called "My Favorite Things." The Netscape browser was the first to use the name "Bookmarks." Firefox also uses "Bookmarks" and offers a well-organized window to manage bookmark files.

When you visit a web page that you want to be able to access again without searching, use the bookmark feature to save its URL to a file on the hard drive of your computer. Simply click on the browser toolbar. On Internet Explorer, for example, you can click on the word "Favorites" and a popup window will open with the command line "Add to Favorites." Click that and another small popup window will open, where you can give a title to the web page and choose which file folder in your Favorites file you would like it to be stored in.

To retrieve the favorite site, click on "Favorites" on the browser toolbar to open the popup window containing the list of your saved sites, then click on the title to go directly to the web page itself.

Newer versions of Internet Explorer also have a yellow star icon on the toolbar that makes it even simpler to access the "Favorites"—that icon will also allow you to access your RSS feeds (more on that in chapter eight) and to search the history of the sites you have visited. By clicking on the star icon with the plus sign, you can instantly add "Favorites" to your list.

Take the time to learn how to organize the bookmarks into folders and subfolders that are meaningful to you. Everyone has different views on data organization, and I won't attempt to recommend any particular system here. My method has been to simply transfer my old research habit of stuffing notes into a separate folder for each chapter of a book into saving bookmarks into a folder designated for each book project as a whole. It's quicker and easier to scan the alphabetical list of bookmarks than it was to sort through scraps of paper and old envelopes in my paper files, so I've given up the chapter-by-chapter divisions in the bookmark folders. Bookmarks are easy to manage in folders—if you don't know how to do so, check your browser's "Help" feature for instructions.

TOOLBAR BOOKMARKS

Even if you're using the Microsoft Internet Explorer as a browser, you can manage your bookmarks by using a Google or Yahoo! toolbar instead of using the Internet Explorer Favorites utility. The search engine toolbars are easily downloaded and installed on your browser page. AOL has a bookmark feature on its downloadable toolbar that is compatible with Internet Explorer, but at present it's available only for PCs, and not for Macs.

What's the advantage to using a Google or Yahoo! toolbar to save, manage, and access your bookmarks? It's a big one—your bookmark files are stored on the Web, so they're accessible from any computer or mobile device, any time, anywhere, when you're signed in to your free Google or Yahoo! account. Bookmarks stored on your home computer's hard drive are only accessible on that machine.

This might be enough reason for you to install either the Google or Yahoo! search engine toolbars on your browser. It's also very handy to have the search window on the toolbar for instant searches. (I have both toolbars on my Internet Explorer browser, and I also keep Mozilla's Firefox browser at the ready, too.) If you use the e-mail service on Google or Yahoo! you can check your e-mail on the toolbar as well. You can transfer all your existing "Favorites" from your Internet Explorer browser to the toolbar bookmarks file by going to the Google "Help" page and following the links and instructions to import your "Favorite" files into the Google program. Yahoo! helps you to do the same.

Installing Toolbars

Google and Yahoo! make it very easy to install their search engine toolbars on your browser. Go to the Google home page and click on the "More" links until you find the page that lists all the Google features and products—then choose "Google search toolbar." The web page that comes up has a clickable bar marked "Install Google Toolbar" and gives the minimum requirements for computers running Internet Explorer. If you're not already a registered Google member, you can open your free account before downloading the toolbar. If you use Firefox as your browser, you can click on a different link to install a Firefox-compatible toolbar. Once you've accepted the terms of usage, the toolbar will appear on your browser.

The Yahoo! toolbar is installed in the same way, after you have signed in with your Yahoo! ID to your free account.

SOCIAL BOOKMARKS

A discussion of bookmarks wouldn't be complete without mentioning the new technology of social bookmarking. In some respects, it is similar to using the toolbar bookmarks discussed on the previous page, which are stored on the Web, but social bookmarking really is about sharing your favorite bookmarks with others in the online community. By storing your bookmarks on a website specifically designed for bookmark and file sharing, you can allow anyone to access them, and you can use tags (like keywords) to identify their content or what's important to you about them. You can also keep bookmarks in a private section where no one can see them.

The most often accessed social bookmarking website is www.del.icio.us, created by Joshua Schachter in 2003 to allow friends to share web pages. It was acquired in 2005 by Yahoo! and continues to grow in popularity. If you're planning to work on a research project with other partners, it might be just the right thing for you. Check it out—it's fun and free.

MORE TIPS FOR ONLINE RESEARCHERS

In addition to using bookmarks, I also keep a Microsoft Word file called "notes" open as I search the internet, to have a quick place to copy and paste a URL and make a quick note to myself about why it's valuable or where it fits into the manuscript.

If I turn up a website that contains specific information that I know for certain I'll be using in my article or book, I sometimes print the page so I'll be certain to have it when I need it. Some websites disappear and some links break. If I am planning to use an exact quotation from a piece online, rather than print the page, I will often copy the text into a Microsoft Word document and add the source citation—that method captures the keystrokes and I won't have to retype it from a hard copy. In general I tend to avoid clicking the print button—not only do I care about the trees, but I also don't like to waste ink. As you conduct searches and decide how to best manage the results, you'll develop your own way of working.

This chapter has introduced you to the basic organization of the World Wide Web—its history, its sense of community, its speedy race to embrace the technology of the future. In the chapters that follow, you'll learn to master the skills needed to fully participate in this incredibly rich source of information. The more you can use your intuition and engage your curiosity, the better your results will be.

CHAPTER 2

CONDUCTING BASIC SEARCHES

Remember the old saying about trying to find "a needle in a haystack"? It's a pretty apt description of what it's like to search for a specific piece of information on the internet—except that in this case, you have a chance of finding it. Think of the needle as the piece of information and the haystack as the billions of web pages out there on the World Wide Web.

Dr. Matthew Koll, a research fellow for America Online, used this haystack analogy in his keynote address to the fall 1999 meeting of the Association of Information and Dissemination Centers. Koll was talking about the ways that search engines address the task of retrieving information. If you stop to consider what each of the following tasks is requesting, you'll be amazed that human minds could engineer software to successfully fulfill these requests within fractions of a second. A human searcher considering the same points on Koll's list might well give up after the first one.

Using Koll's list, the search engine must consider the best way to find:

- A *known* needle in a *known* haystack
- A *known* needle in an *unknown* haystack
- An *unknown* needle in an *unknown* haystack
- *Any* needle in a haystack
- The *sharpest* needle in a haystack
- *All* the needles in a haystack
- Affirmation of *no needles* in the haystack
- Things *like* needles in any haystack
- A new needle *whenever* it shows up
- *Where* the *haystacks* are
- Needles, haystacks—*whatever.*

Isn't this an elegant concept? Each statement is a challenge in itself. It's the epitome of relationship—one-to-one, one-to-many, many-to-many, many-to-one, and many-to-none.

In practical terms, search engines make it possible to retrieve documents and images from the billions of available pages on the World Wide Web. And as the Web itself has evolved, search engines have continually refined the ways in which they process and store information. Because the focus of this book is to help you master the practical aspects of online research, we won't go into great detail about how search engines were developed and what kinds of technology they employ. You can search for that information on the Web, or you can check out a couple of the many books published on the subject, if you have a need to know. It's more important for you to learn how to make the most of your search techniques than to wrap your mind around the technical aspects.

So we'll look briefly at how search engines function today and then move on to the really fun part of writing queries to find the needles in the haystack.

INTRODUCTION TO SEARCH ENGINES

Basically, a search engine stores information gathered from multiple websites and then indexes it for future retrieval by a search query. As we learned in chapter one, the gathering is done by automated web browsers, called webcrawlers or spiders, that follow links from one site to another. Can't you just see those critters spreading out all over the virtual web, ensnaring bits of data and trundling them back home to be devoured? The nomenclature of the Web is clever and reflects the creativity and humor of the computer scientists and engineers who built it. The first tool for searching, back in 1990, was called Archie (short for "archives"), the next was called Gopher (as in "go-fer"), and then came Veronica and Jughead (characters from the Archie comics), which indexed the data found and stored by Gopher. To keep yourself entertained when you're working on the Web, allow yourself a chuckle once in a while at the ingenuity of the folks behind the scenes.

One function of the search engine is to analyze how the contents of each web page should be indexed so a search query entered by a human researcher would turn up useful results. There is an entire area of computer science devoted to search engine optimization, and one of its principles is "the rule of least astonishment." The people writing the search engine programs are asked to consider what results the human user will expect to see, relying on common sense. If you type two keywords into a search box, for example, you could reasonably expect to see those same two words appear in all the pages that fill the results list. The rule goes on to say that if a conflict exists between the possible results that could be displayed by the search engine (or, more generally, the action that could be taken), the programmer should choose the most humanly logical result.

The information captured from the web page is stored in a database. Different search engines store information in slightly different ways, and you may find you prefer the results from one search engine over another. For instance, running a search for "popcorn history Aztec" on both the Google and AltaVista search engines brings up the same website, the Encyclopedia Popcornica at www.popcorn.org, but provides varying descriptions in the results list. The Google results list takes you directly to the short section on the Aztecs, while AltaVista gives you more of an outline of the entire page, with subheadings. The keywords appear in bold type.

GOOGLE SEARCH RESULTS

Early Popcorn History

Encyclopedia Popcornica: Early Popcorn History ... Popcorn was integral to early 16th century Aztec Indian ceremonies. Bernardino de Sahagun writes: "And. ...

www.popcorn.org/encyclopedia/epanhist.cfm

ALTAVISTA SEARCH RESULTS

Early Popcorn History

Encyclopedia Popcornica: Early **Popcorn History**. Biblical accounts of "corn" stored in the pyramids of Egypt are misunderstood. The "corn" from the bible was probably barley. ... Encyclopedia Popcornica: Early **Popcorn History**. Early **Popcorn History** | Recent **History** | **History** of **Popcorn** Popper ... food for the **Aztec** Indians, who also used **popcorn** as decoration for. ...

www.**popcorn**.org/encyclopedia/epanhist.cfm

Note the subtle differences between the results. I prefer Google's results, which seem quicker in determining relevance, but that's because I'm always working on a tight deadline.

The technique of indexing done by a search engine has evolved over the past several years, and certainly it will continue to do so. The proliferation of pages has made it difficult for robotic webcrawlers to keep up with visiting and revisiting all the sites to update content information, and faster ways will continue to be developed to handle the exponential growth of the Web. Some of the earlier practices, such as websites individually applying to be listed by a search engine, have gone by the wayside—a new website with legitimate content will automatically be found and indexed by the webcrawlers within a couple of weeks, once it has been linked to other sites that the webcrawler visits.

The use of searchable meta-tags, long relied upon by *webmasters* (the electronic product managers of a site) to get their websites noticed by search engines, has been phased out and replaced with new technology. Using meta-tags, the webmaster inserted key words or subjects to be found by the webcrawlers. The practice has declined because some unethical people stuffed their meta-tags with popular key words that had nothing to do with their particular site and unfairly bumped their sites up to the top of otherwise legitimate results lists. A similar

Mastering Online Research

spam tactic was employed for text-content searches, in which an entire dictionary would be posted on a site in order to match any word for which someone searched. Now meta-tags have become somewhat suspect, unless they are used within an *intranet* (an internal site within a particular company for employee use, without the threat of external tampering).

Instead of (or, in some cases, in addition to) meta-tags, webcrawlers are capturing the titles and subheads of websites, significant words in the text content, and the links going into and out from the website, which help determine its popularity and recognition as a useful site. All of this data and more is indexed in a database to make it accessible by the search engine's query program and is continually updated to reflect changes made to individual websites. Is your human mind boggled yet?

When you enter a search term in the search box on the Google, Yahoo! or other search engines, you are creating a search string or query. When you type "space shuttle," for example, the search engine will turn those two words into a query to process, giving it a computer-readable format such as http://www.google.com/search?hl=en&q=space+shuttle&btnG=Google+Search.

You can see that "space" plus "shuttle" are still there. And the results will bring in photos from NASA, news coverage, shuttle mission profiles, and a bunch of information that you might find appropriate. (You'll also be offered the opportunity to buy space shuttle kites and toys, of course.)

The web search engine matches the string "space+shuttle" against its database to give you the results that most closely match your criteria, which in this case is rather broad. The order of the list in which the results are returned, however, is determined by sophisticated algorithms that assign certain levels of significance to specific criteria to determine a "page rank" of relevance to the search query. These algorithms are proprietary to each search engine and are continually being refined to prevent deliberate interference with the search results by outsiders.

The algorithms work the magic that allows a search for "popcorn history Aztec" to display results at the top of the list that are readily useful, rather than being buried in the other ninety-seven thousand-plus results. Even if you switch the search to "history Aztec popcorn" or "Aztec popcorn history," you'll get just about the same results in the same ranking. That's because you are conducting a simple word search for these three words: Any website containing all three words (not two out of three, but all three) will appear in the list. And the algorithm with its criteria for weighing the websites' relevance makes sure that you're seeing the cream of the crop, so to speak.

That's sufficient information on the mysterious ways in which web search engines operate. Let's move on to learn to optimize your time spent on the internet with basic searches and queries.

HOW TO USE QUERIES TO GET RESULTS

Queries are search strings of words designed to bring back the best possible results for an online researcher. The search engine indexes the data in an online document and your query

Mastering Online Research

matches itself against that data to give you the most closely related results. That's a pretty clear statement of the simplest query process. As you become more knowledgeable about advanced searches and how they work, your queries will become more targeted and thus more productive. But we'll take things at an easy pace in this chapter.

Search engines differ in the way they process requests and deliver results, but most of the major search sites employ similar query techniques. What works on the Google website usually will work on Yahoo!, for instance, as well as other smaller search engines. The appearance of the web pages may differ, but the underlying technology is consistent.

For example, the search engine called AlltheWeb.com offers a user-friendly advanced search window, but since its acquisition by Yahoo!, its data is now drawn from Yahoo!'s indexes—so the content of the results list will be the same as a Yahoo! search even though the way the query is entered is different. In fact, Yahoo! has added AlltheWeb's advanced search functionality to the Yahoo! site—so you might prefer to use the main Yahoo! search. It's up to each individual researcher to decide which search engine is most comfortable and intuitive for searching. Throughout this book we'll rely primarily on the Google and Yahoo! search engines for examples, because their searches are designed for the average user, not for the computer specialist, and those two companies are most likely to retain their dominance and popularity on the Web.

One constant about the internet is how quickly it changes. The searches described here may produce slightly different results if used at a later time; however, the techniques remain useful, even if the particulars differ.

THE BASICS ON BASIC WORD SEARCHES

Basic word searches are the simplest form of a search query. You enter a word or two into the search box on the main page of the search engine or the search box on your browser toolbar. The trick is to figure out which exact words will net you the results closest to what you want. Though that may seem obvious, it's helpful to really zero in on what you're looking for before you begin a search. Spend a little time thinking about the words most often used to describe the topic, person, or place in which you're interested. Start with a general search using basic keywords to identify the scope of your topic.

Example of a Simple Search

A general search can be undertaken for any topic or research interest. If you want to find information on the diamond-cutting industry, for instance, you might not know exactly where to begin if it's a new topic for you. To get useful results, you'll need some basic information on the diamond industry, which then will allow you to refine your search techniques to use the correct terminology and the optimum geographic locations. You can begin by doing a basic word search.

A simple search term might be "diamond cutting." It's more specific than merely the word "diamond" but still broad enough to cast a wide net. By typing the words "diamond" and "cutting" in the search box, you are asking the search engine to find all the documents that have both words in the text on the web page.

The results lists from the Yahoo! and Google searches contain a couple of sites that have information on diamond cutting in Florida—that might be an interesting start. There are also several websites that offer historical background on the industry and descriptions of the methods of cutting diamonds. You can ignore all the commercial advertisements for diamond jewelry sellers, or you can check out some of the most recognized companies to see if they include an informational web page on the processing of rough diamonds.

If none of the websites from this simple search are sufficient for your research, in themselves, they could still provide a very basic introduction to the topic that would help to refine your searches.

The next logical step might be to try another search using an alternate term that would relate to diamond cutting. Perhaps "lapidary," a word that is used to refer to an artisan who works with gemstones, would have interesting results. As it turns out, most of the "lapidary" results have to do with rock hounds and gemstone enthusiasts. Diamond cutters are so specialized that they aren't considered lapidaries. But in other basic searches, the substitution of an alternate term can be very effective.

Clearly, if you want to gather in-depth information about the diamond-cutting industry, you'll need to learn about the more sophisticated and targeted search techniques that we will explore on page 46. But are there instances where a single keyword search can be useful? Yes, indeed.

SINGLE KEYWORD SEARCHES

If you are looking for someone or something with an unusual name, it might be possible to get great results on the first try with a single word. Searching for "Blackbeard" will turn up a treasure chest of information on the famous pirate, his ship, his haunts on the North Carolina coast, and links to pirate lore from several centuries. Similar one-word searches are very successful for the third-century Greek mathematician Archimedes and contemporary rock legend John (formerly Cougar) Mellencamp, using the musician's distinctive last name. A search for "Krakatoa" will get you lots of information about volcanic eruptions, and you can spell it in either of its generally accepted forms (the common, anglicized Krakatoa or the preferred Krakatau) because the search engines will recognize the alternate spellings. In many cases the search engine will actually ask you if you would like to search on another spelling of a word—a polite way of handling the mistakes in typing and spelling that could skew a search without the user realizing it.

Tips on Using Keywords in Basic Searches

You can use keywords to broaden, narrow, or change the focus of your search. The keyword searches on most of today's search engines operate in similar ways, so the following tips and suggestions are applicable to just about any basic search you want to conduct.

Use any form of your keyword. When choosing keywords, think about the various forms of the word or words and use the one you believe to be most closely related to your research.

Does it matter whether you use the singular or the plural form of a word? Is it better to use a shortened form of the word, as in a stem word without the ending? Will the results depend on whether the words are capitalized or lowercase?

The short answer to those questions is no, if you are using major web search engines such as Google, Yahoo!, or Ask .com. Their technology anticipates your needs.

Commonly, the ability to search for variant forms of a single word is called *truncation*, which means that only the stem of a word is entered as the search term, without the endings that mark the word as singular or plural, or that narrow down its definition. (The term is used in mathematics and in programming in a different but related way.) For example, if you enter the keyword "theat" into a search engine that uses truncation, you would get results for "theatre," "theater," "theatrical" (and all their plural forms), "theatricality," and the original "theat." Truncation was an important tool in the earlier years of searching on the Web, and it still is used on some websites (especially library resources, educational databases, and archival sources) to search within their own databases, collections, and archives. Check the site's "Help" page before you do a search on a proprietary search engine to see whether truncation and wildcards (more on these on page 46) are supported. Today, however, truncation has been superseded by the more sophisticated search engine optimization technology. Google and Yahoo! searches, for instance, use stemming technology to search for all words related to the stem of the search keyword, when appropriate. It's a smart technology. If you search for "bear," the results will also include "bears" automatically. You no longer have to worry about whether the singular or plural form will bring in more results (previously, the singular form would have, because the plural "bears" contains the singular form). Stemming will find "canaries" as well as the keyword "canary," because it's programmed to understand the complicated rules of pluralizing English words.

So how will you obtain the best, most relevant results in your search? The answer to this question is a list of tips:

Use word combinations to narrow your search. Adding significant words to your keyword will reduce the number of results that are unhelpful to your research project. The above search for "canary" could be better targeted by adding the words "Islands" or "bird" to your search string—depending on which canary you have in mind.

Use a common term to net more results than a less common term. For instance, "swimsuit" is a better search term than "bikini," which is used not only for swimwear but also for place names and software programs, not to mention those adult sites that use the term.

Use synonyms for your keyword or narrow your scope with more specific terms. People who host websites have different ways of referring to the same topic—should you search for "youth sports" or "kids' sports" or "children's sports"? Or if it's Little League baseball you're looking for, is that a sufficiently broad keyword query to get good results? In this case, the terms "youth," "kids'," and "children's" are recognized by the search engine as having the same or similar meaning. Searching for one term (combined with "sports") will bring up all three. "Little League baseball" is a much more specific query and will bring up sites with only those words, whereas "youth sports" will include links to Little League information.

Try searching for the most common term first, and then run another search on the same search engine with an alternate term. If you are researching capital punishment, search for "capital punishment," and then search for "death penalty." You can also add another defining word such as "pro" or "anti," which will help to limit your results to one side of the argument or the other.

Search for other, related terms used in your topic area. If you are researching mining history or the mining industry, you might want to search for words such as "black lung," "asbestos," "union organizers," "mineral deposits," and other terms you will pick up during your beginning research. These related words bring up websites that would be overlooked by a keyword search using only your keyword. Don't spend a lot of effort on these ancillary searches, but in a quick search you might pick up something interesting that doesn't appear on the most commonly visited pages.

Enter your search words in logical, commonsense order to find the best results. The search engines are sensitive to syntax and will attempt to group the words into logical search terms. The most significant word can be at the beginning of the string if it makes sense: "Mom gifts Mother's Day" gets better results if you're really looking to buy or make gifts for

Mom than does "Mother's Day gifts Mom," which focuses on the Mother's Day holiday first and gifts second.

More Notes on Basic Searches

Here's a quick way to search using the Google and Yahoo! search engines while your browser is open to a web page. Simply highlight any words in a web page and right-click on them with your mouse. (Mac users, click on your mouse and the Control key simultaneously.) Choose a Google search from the small menu that pops up and a results list for those search words will fill your screen. Choose a Yahoo! search (an icon will appear as soon as you highlight the word or phrase) and a small popup screen of search results will appear. Try it—this is one search method that takes longer to describe than to perform.

The Google search engine has some proprietary features you might find helpful as practice in defining your searches to bring up the most relevant results. On the main Google search page, below the entry box, you'll see a button labeled "I'm Feeling Lucky." This button automatically takes you to the number one web page returned for your query, which presumably has the most relevance to your query. An "I'm Feeling Lucky" search, according to the Google slogan, means "less time searching for web pages and more time looking at them."

Let's see how this works for a word with multiple, very different associations. For example, if you enter the word "Sojourner" in the search box and click on the "Lucky" button, you will bring up a magazine entitled *Sojourners: Faith, Politics, Culture*, which is perhaps a surprise. If you didn't know about the magazine, the expected result might be something on either Sojourner Truth, the nineteenth-century abolitionist, or *Sojourner*, the NASA research vehicle. Entering "Sojourner Truth" brings up a specific match of one library website—but you would have much broader choices for research if you conducted a standard Google search for her name. If you enter "Sojourner vehicle," the "Lucky" search reverts to a normal Google search, and those multiple results confirm that *Sojourner* was a six-wheeled robotic roving vehicle sent to gather information on Mars. I find the "I'm Feeling Lucky" tool to be more of a novelty than a serious research tool, but while you are getting to know the techniques of searching, you can use it to practice targeting precise search terms and get instant feedback on your accuracy.

Another nifty Google proprietary feature can be accessed if you have installed the Google toolbar on your browser. The toolbar search box has a feature that automatically fills in a drop-down menu with suggested search words based on the letters as you type them. For instance, typing the letters "mo" brings up a choice of "mo*vies*," "mo*rtgage calculator*," "mo*zilla*," "mo*nster*," "Mo*torola*," "mo*nster.com*" and so on. Adding the letter "r" changes the drop-down menu instantly to "mo*rtgage calculator*," "mo*rpheus*," "mo*rtgage rates*," "mo*rtgages*," "Mo*rgan Stanley*," and so on. Clicking on any of the words will enter them in the Google search box and launch the search. This is an interesting feature; it's also useful, especially if you're not sure how to spell the term you want to search.

When you're pressed for time, these simple word searches can be especially helpful. If you can target the one or two words that will immediately bring up the needed information, you can zip in and out of a site in seconds. I've used this technique in the middle of dinner party discussions, excusing myself from my guests for only a couple minutes while I check a fact that could add to the conversation. (As a polite host, I reserve such absences for a burning need to know.) I use the Google toolbar search to speedily access names and dates of movies, or the year in which some obscure British colony achieved independence, or the truth behind the legend of Zorro. Granted, this is a frivolous use of the technology, but once you've been bitten by the online research bug it's hard to keep away from it.

MOVING BEYOND BASIC QUERIES

In this section we will look at ways to add to the basic search string of keywords in order to further refine your search. Research queries start from the simplest single-word searches and increase in complexity. When the basic search reaches its limit, you can move on to the advanced search techniques described in chapter three.

WILDCARDS

As mentioned, a few (but not all) search engines in their basic search function allow you to use a wildcard in your search term to expand the search beyond the specific form of the word that you entered. A *wildcard* is a character representing other letters or numbers not provided within a search string of a word or phrase. The most commonly used wildcard is the asterisk (*), which usually represents zero or several other characters. A single missing character is represented by the wildcard of a question mark (?).

Adding the asterisk to the stem of a word will return results that contain the stem with all possible endings: Typing "librar*" will return websites containing "library," "libraries," "librarian," and so on. The usefulness of the wildcard search has been diminished by the newer functionality of search engines that automatically insert the rest of the word for you and ask if that's what you're looking for ("librar" defaults to "library," for instance).

However, the wildcard asterisk is not defunct. Using the asterisk between two search words, with a space on either side, will tell even the most innovative search engine to look for a word that occurs in between the two other words. Typing "color * dye" in a Google search box will bring up websites in which "color hair dye" or "color tie die" or "color fluorescent dye" are listed.

Although interesting, this is not a very useful research tool—if you don't know whether you want to find out about hair dye or DNA research techniques, you're in big trouble! The wildcard asterisk can be helpful, though, in finding someone's full name: "John * Smith" will give you all those guys who try to distinguish themselves by their astonishing middle names. It can also be inserted between words in an "exact phrase" search, where the search query must be matched exactly in the results. The asterisk will bring in words to fill in the phrase, such as "four score and *ago." Try it for finding the exact title of a book that you *almost* remember.

PHRASE SEARCHES

Another very useful basic word search technique is searching for a specific phrase by enclosing the words within quotation marks in the search box. The quotation marks tell the search engine to look for an exact match to the string of words within the quotation marks. Major search engines also allow phrase searches to be entered on their advanced search menu page, in the search box labeled "the exact phrase."

You can use this technique to request the search engine to find results in which the words are in the exact order typed, which can make all the difference in the results. Let's say you were looking for information on what conditions lead to river runoff. You could enter "river runoff" without quotation marks, and your results would include any web page that the search engine has indexed as containing both the words "river" and "runoff"—nearly six million results. By enclosing the two words in quotation marks, the results list displays about 158,000 results. From those websites you can further define what your specific interests in river runoff are and narrow your results. "Hudson River runoff" within quotes returns only nine results, for instance, whereas the same search without quotation marks returns about 527,000. (The Hudson River does not have a severe problem with runoff water, as it happens.)

An even handier use of this search engine feature is to find specific passages from online documents—whether lines of poetry, inspiring quotes, titles of books, or any unique string of words. This kind of search is fun to play with, a valuable tool, and one of the easiest searches at which you can be instantly successful. Let's take a few examples.

A line of poetry or prose or the fragment of a title, for instance, can lead you to the complete online text of a work. Enter "jumping frog" within quotations and among the first hits are the full text version of Mark Twain's "The Celebrated Jumping Frog of Calaveras County." Two sites from the University of Virginia Library's Etext Center might appear to be the same, but if you look carefully you will see that one is the original 1865 version of the story ("Jim Smiley and His Jumping Frog") and the other is the revised and retitled version published in 1867.

The inspirational or folksy messages people are always forwarding in e-mails often lack the credits for the original authors. If you want to quote a line or two from one in an article or on a website, it would be a good idea to give the credit to whoever wrote it. A popular poem for adoptive mothers sometimes called "In My Heart," for instance, appears on postcards, wall plaques, pillows, and other articles and is frequently e-mailed, often without attribution. Searching for one of its most distinctive lines "nor bone of my bone" brings up websites aplenty, with several correctly attributing the complete poem to Fleur Conkling Heyliger, who wrote it for her adopted daughter. The fact that the 1952 copyright is still held by the *Saturday Evening Post* magazine is another matter, but we'll learn about permissions and copyright laws later in chapter eleven.

A distinctive line of poetry can be searched to find its author and also literary criticism and scholarly research pertaining to it. One of my favorite lines from Allen Ginsberg is the "animal soup of time." Type that phrase within quotation marks and you'll find links to the full text of his most famous poem, "Howl," as well as literary essays and articles on the Beat poets. Type the two words "animal" and "soup" without quotation marks and you'll get recipes for dog soup and a pairing of two Marx Brothers films, *Animal Crackers* and *Duck Soup*.

You can enclose a bit of dialogue within quotation marks as a search query as well. Rhett Butler's "Frankly, my dear" gives results for *Gone With the Wind* in film and print versions, although the line in the book is just "My dear, I don't give a damn." If you try Scarlett O'Hara's famous "Tomorrow is another day," however, you'll be led off into websites for a newer movie by that title.

The phrase search can be rewarding if you're looking for unusual strings of words or well known lines from literature—but if you want to look at sites connected to *Gone With the Wind*, a more specific query for the film or book itself will be a better use of your research time.

COMMON OR "STOP" WORDS

In order to make searches run faster, most search engines are programmed to ignore certain common words. These words appear so frequently in the English language that searching for them would bring up an overwhelming number of results, most of which would not be useful. Each search engine or proprietary database has its own list of such words; primarily they are articles (*a, an, the*); prepositions and conjunctions (*and, in, over*); very common words such as where and how; and sometimes single digits and single letters.

To search for web pages about a book titled *The Wind in the Willows*, for instance, you only need to type "wind willows" and results for Kenneth Grahame's beloved children's book will appear. That's a shortcut I often use—I've become accustomed to searching on only the main words of a title, sometimes with an author's first or last name as well. Similarly, you could enter "gone wind" and get a decent search results list for *Gone With the Wind*, but if you enclose the two words within quotation marks as a phrase search, the results are very poor indeed.

The Google results list provides a comment at the top of the screen to notify you when it has excluded a word from your search. Just for fun, you can try searching for "in and out," two prepositions separated by a conjunction, which might return no results if the particular search engine ignores these words. In a Google search, the top results lead to a California burger chain called In-N-Out Burger, which has a fan following and even an article in Wikipedia.com. The Google page helpfully notes for you that the word "and" was not necessary to your search, because it is automatically assumed to exist between the search words. Entering just the words "in" and "out" without quotation marks, though, only retrieves one site devoted to the burger chain, its homepage (www.in-n-out.com), and searching for the two words enclosed within quotation marks ("in out") brings up a lot of results from office supply websites selling in/out sign up boards.

Running the same search terms on Yahoo! provides similar results, although the sites include more popular media links, such as the movie *In & Out* starring Kevin Kline and more financial resource sites (for "in and out" trading) earlier in the results list.

On their advanced search pages, many search engines will allow you to specify a search on a stop word. According to its online "Help" pages, the Google basic keyword search permits you to add a plus sign (+) in front of a word to add it to the search string. To find websites on the film *Star Wars: Episode I*, you would type "Star Wars Episode +I." However, search engine technology evolves rapidly, and a phrase search with "Star Wars Episode I" (within quotation marks, no plus sign) results in the same number of hits as a phrase search without the plus sign. Yahoo! also allows users to add a plus sign before a stop word to include it in a basic search.

USING BOOLEAN OPERATORS

Some searches cannot be accomplished with simple one- or two-word queries, as we saw in the previous example of "diamond cutting" on page 38 To further enhance search capabilities, search engines use an application of logic known as *Boolean operators* to filter the search and provide more accurate results. These operators are the words AND, OR, and NOT, which are used to connect the search words in specific relationships. They were first defined by George Boole, a nineteenth-century British mathematician who worked out a system to formulate the precise queries upon which the Boolean search is based.

To craft successful search queries, it's extremely important to understand how the Boolean operators differ from one another. If you use the advanced search menus on the largest search engines you may not need to actually type the AND, OR, or NOT operators into the search box, but as you think about your query, those operators are the foundation for organizing the order and inclusion or exclusion of keywords. Their operating principles are clearly visualized in the diagram below.

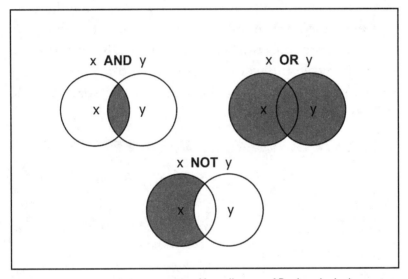

Venn diagram of Boolean logical operators

Fortunately the largest search engines have incorporated Boolean logic into their basic and advanced search features with easy-to-use formats for entering your search terms. Some allow you to type the operators directly into the basic search box, using either the words in capital letters (Yahoo!) or the corresponding symbol (Google—a plus sign for AND, a minus sign for NOT; the functionality for OR is not available outside the advanced search menu). I would recommend, however, that you use the simpler method of entering your search terms in the advanced search menu page. We will explore those advanced search options in detail in chapter three.

The AND operator. The Boolean logical operator AND instructs the search engine to find documents that contain every one of the keywords you have specified. On the advanced search menu, AND is expressed as "all of the words." You may realize that you already have been using the Boolean operator AND in any search that contains more than a single word. Search engines automatically add that operator between the words, expressed as a plus sign in the search string. (That's how we searched for "space+shuttle" on page 35.)

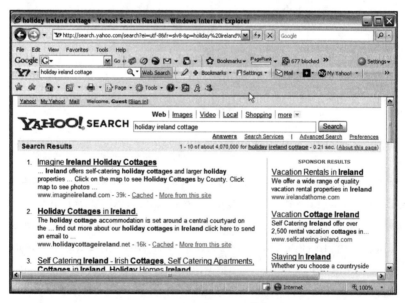

Yahoo.com search results page

Mastering Online Research

Using the automatic AND operator, a search in Yahoo! for "vacation Ireland farmhouse" will bring you good results if you want to plan a vacation. But remember, when you are deciding on the keywords, to think of synonyms or alternate expressions and include those, too. It's especially important if you are researching global information. Since "vacation" is an American term, you might expect better results with the European term "holiday," and adding the familiar Irish term "cottage" to "farmhouse" provides even more useful results.

The OR operator. The Boolean logical operator OR tells the search engine to find documents in which at least one of the keywords appears. It is expressed on the advanced search menu as "any of these words" and is used to retrieve documents in which one term may be used interchangeably with another. A search in Yahoo! for "dog biscuit OR cookie" will bring up the web pages that contain the word "dog" and also either "biscuit" or "cookie." Even though you don't type the AND between "dog" and "biscuit OR cookie," the search engine inserts it logically for you.

The NOT operator. The Boolean logical operator NOT is handy for reducing the number of results in a search for a term that has several meanings, because it tells the search engine to ignore the word following the operator. On the advanced search menu it is expressed as "none of these words." If you were searching for websites on the 1938 movie *Holiday*, for example, you wouldn't find any in the top ten results—the list is dominated by the hotel chain Holiday Inn, travel websites, and pages on the celebration of holy days (holidays). If you use an AND search for "holiday" AND "movie," your results won't improve substantially, since "holiday movies" is an enormous subject category on its own. Searching by excluding will work best here, using the NOT operator: "holiday NOT inn NOT holy."

PROXIMITY SEARCHES

Some search engines continue to offer a feature that retrieves results based on how close together your chosen search terms appear in the website text. In the earlier years of the World Wide Web, this function was more necessary; today's sophisticated algorithms have made it less relevant. Yahoo! searches can still use the proximity operator NEAR, although it is not possible to specify the number of words that separate the keywords. Occasionally, the proximity search can be helpful. If you enter the search string "killer NEAR mold," for example, your results list will contain ten times fewer results than if you searched only for "killer mold." In this case, fewer hits are better because they are more targeted to the problem of killer mold. Of course, searching directly for the scientific name of the toxic black mold, *Stachybotrys chartarum*, would bring up even more specific results—but not being a mycologist I wouldn't know that name unless I first found it on a "killer mold" results list.

OTHER SPECIAL OPERATORS

In addition to Boolean operators, search engines support other kinds of special operators that modify the search or direct it to be performed on some elements other than the HTML document text. Most of these special operators have been included as part of the advanced search menu on the Google and Yahoo! sites or appear as clickable links on search pages. The operator "allintitle:" will search only the titles of websites. The operator "related:" will list web pages that are similar to a specified web page. For instance, the query "related:www.mapquest.com" entered into the Yahoo! search box brings up about thirty other websites that are similar to Mapquest.com—mapping services, map libraries, travel planning map sites, and so on. The same functionality is available on a basic Google search for "mapquest," if you click on the hyperlink "Similar pages" that appears beneath each search result on the list.

The "define:" operator is most easily used by clicking on the "definition" hyperlink at the top right of the Google search results screen, which brings up definitions of the search term from Answers.com. However, if you do enter the search operator followed by a term to be defined (for example, "define: adjutant") in the search box, the results will give you definitions from several different online sources and a few related terms. How else could you discover that "adjutant" was the name of an Indian stork as well as a military officer?

We will look at the other operators in chapter three, in the context of learning how to use the advanced search menus on the Yahoo! and Google search engines, where the input of search words is less cumbersome. Should you find it useful, you'll be able to search for keywords within the titles of web pages, or for all other websites linked to a particular one, or for all websites containing your keywords within a specific domain (say, the keyword "homeschool" only on .edu domain names). The possibilities for finding what you need on the internet are endless.

CHAPTER 3

CONDUCTING ADVANCED SEARCHES

The examples and information in the previous chapters have already primed you for success in conducting advanced searches. You're familiar with the idea of making each keyword count in a search string; you understand the principles of including and excluding certain words for maximum results; and you have experimented with both Yahoo! and Google searches to see which feels most comfortable to you. You probably have explored a few other search engine websites, too, to see for yourself how they differ in delivering results lists. So now you're ready to get serious about online research using advanced techniques.

We have already looked at many of the functions on the advanced search pages, but there are a few others that can be accessed only through the advanced search menus. The drop-down menus on the most popular search engines will seem familiar if you are in the habit of using the drop-down menus on Microsoft Word and other software programs—or if you shop online. When you see an entry box with a little gray square on the right side, just click on the downward arrow to reveal the scrolling menu of choices in that entry box, and then click on your selection. It will appear in the entry box.

The Google and Yahoo! websites have similar features on their advanced search pages. Since the Google search engine is larger, we'll use that for examples. Unless otherwise indicated, descriptions of Google's features also are true of Yahoo! (wherever their differences are significant, we'll look at the features separately). After using both search engines, you might decide that Yahoo! is a bit simpler to use and that it contains all the functions you need, without a lot of bells and whistles. The Yahoo! search engine's database is not as large as Google's, but you may find what you need just as efficiently. On the other hand, Google's development teams are constantly working to add the most innovative features to its search engine, and if you're excited by trying out new technology, you might enjoy the Google Labs and other search capabilities being tested in the beta stage of development. Many of those new features go on to become part of the standard Google search. Several of the features are likely to appeal primarily to users who work with the technical aspects of computer software and hardware.

ADVANCED SEARCH FEATURES

The Google advanced search has many features that will speed your research work and help you narrow your search to obtain optimal results. The search engine supporting the

Google search contains the largest database of information on the World Wide Web and is constantly updated.

The advanced search feature opens from the main browser window at www.google.com. Click on the "Advanced Search" hyperlink on the right of the search box at the top to bring you to the search screen. You'll see an illustration of the search screen below, but in order to learn about the many features, you'll want to explore the web page itself on your computer.

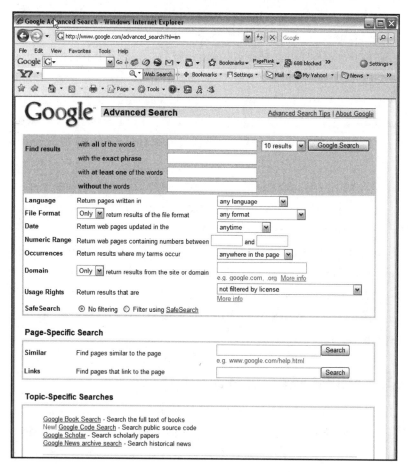

Mastering Online Research

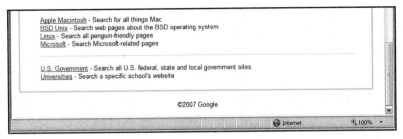

Apple Macintosh - Search for all things Mac
BSD Unix - Search web pages about the BSD operating system
Linux - Search all penguin-friendly pages
Microsoft - Search Microsoft-related pages

U.S. Government - Search all U.S. federal, state and local government sites
Universities - Search a specific school's website

©2007 Google

Internet   100%

Google.com advanced search screen

On the Yahoo! website, accessing the advanced search page is a similar process—click on the button on the Yahoo.com home page marked "Web Search," and you will go to the Yahoo! main search page, where the "Advanced Search" hyperlink appears on the right of the search box. If you have the Yahoo! toolbar installed on your browser, you can click on the "Web Search" toolbar icon to access the search page.

The advanced search page is organized in sections. The wording differs only slightly on the Yahoo! search page.

FIND RESULTS

The search entry boxes in the "Find Results" section of the advanced search page are labeled with user-friendly terms that are actually the Boolean logical operators discussed in chapter two. It's easier and faster to enter your keywords into these tidy search boxes on the "Find Results" feature than to mess with typing spaces and plus or minus signs in the basic search page entry box.

"With *all* of the words." This automatically inserts AND between every keyword you enter and will search for documents containing all of the words. "Green tea ice cream" gives you a list of search results for recipes and vendors of this Japanese treat. That's pretty simple, really no different from using a basic keyword search. A more specific request for "Kelly's last stand" gives you a list of about 560,000 search results, many related to the Australian outlaw Ned Kelly's 1880 armored shootout with the law, but it also brings up web pages containing information about the U.S. manhunt for George "Machine Gun" Kelly in 1933. Searching specifically for "Ned Kelly" delivers two million results, the top of the list displaying links to the 2003 movie of the same name. Yahoo! also suggests other search strings at the top of the results list (next to the icon of a light bulb, for "bright ideas"), which could be very helpful in pinpointing exactly what you're looking for: "Ned Kelly biography"; "Ned Kelly pictures"; "information on Ned Kelly"; and "Ned Kelly DVD." Check out those optional searches whenever you use the Yahoo! search engine. They'll help you refine your query as it relates to their search parameters.

"With the **exact phrase.**" This choice searches for the words in the order in which you type them. A search for "sixteen men on a dead man's chest" will turn up websites with the lyrics for the well-known pirate shanty, along with advertisements for the second *Pirates of the Caribbean: Dead Man's Chest* film. However, a search for a very common phrase might need to have another search term to limit the results. Say you wanted to find the origin of the phrase, "It ain't over 'til it's over"—searching on that exact phrase will bring up numerous appearances of the phrase, in book ti-

Mastering Online Research

tles, movie titles, song titles, political articles, and so on. But the famous New York Yankee who coined it is not found in the first thirty results. Adding the name "Yogi" in the search box for "all of these words" handily brings up web pages about Yogi Berra's often-quoted saying. If you couldn't remember Yogi's name but knew the quote had something to do with baseball, you could use "baseball" in the search box instead.

*"With **at least one** of the words."* This uses the OR operator to search for documents containing any one or more of the words you enter. Searching for "briefcase," "satchel," and "attaché"—all synonyms for the case that carries business papers—also brought back Satchel Paige the ballplayer and Attaché the software program within the first ten results. In Yahoo! the OR operator is described as "**any of these words**," which means exactly the same thing as the Google phrase. If you wanted to find information on the film industry in India's most populous city, you might search for Bollywood OR Bombay OR Mumbai. The city changed its name back to its pre-colonial original some years ago, using both versions of the name will ensure that you capture all the references to the city, because many documents still use the anglicized Bombay. Adding Bollywood (the popular name for the Indian cinema industry based in Bombay) to the OR search will bring up specific film industry information and help to target your research to those kinds of sites.

*"**Without** the words."* This uses the NOT operator to exclude from the search whatever words you enter in this box. Using

the "attaché" example, if you enter the same search words as above ("briefcase," "satchel," and "attaché") in the "**at least one** of these words" entry box and also enter "Paige" in the "**without**" entry box, the results list will omit the web pages in which Satchel Paige appears. Logically, this search does not function if there are no search words in either of the search boxes to provide results from which to eliminate the word specified as "without." In Yahoo! the phrase is "none of these words."

On the right side of the Google advanced search screen, you'll see a drop-down box that allows you to set your preference for how many results are delivered per results page screen. The default is ten per page, but as you become more experienced in online research, you may want to change the number to twenty or thirty. The Yahoo! advanced search screen has the same function, but the drop-down box is at the bottom of the page.

LANGUAGE

The World Wide Web naturally contains millions of pages in languages other than English, and the Google and Yahoo! websites have the ability to search in many different languages. The default language is "any language," but using the drop-down menu on Google you can select from among three dozen modern languages. You can specify "English" if you prefer, but that might be limiting your research capabilities. You might find images on a French website, for instance, and with the help of an online dictionary translate the captions without too much difficulty. Many internationally oriented organizations and institutions post their websites in a choice of languages as well. The Yahoo! search page offers a display of boxes to check for whatever languages you want to include in your search.

Note: If the search results include websites in languages that contain characters not part of the display fonts (typefaces for alphabets) accessible by your browser on your computer, you will see only placeholder characters (often little empty squares) rather than the text of the website. Anyone seriously researching Japanese or Sanskrit content, for example, will require those special fonts to be available so that the web pages generated in those languages will appear correctly when displayed in HTML or XML. More recent computer operating systems such as Windows XP and Mac OS X include Asian and other language font files that can be activated by using the Regional and Language Options settings on the control panel (some languages are automatically installed), and most browsers support the language fonts. Some websites also display text in other alphabet fonts by using static graphic image files of the words rather than HTML-generated text.

FILE FORMAT

The "File Format" option allows you to specify what kinds of files you want to be included in your online search. The default is "any format." Using two drop-down menus, you can choose to search "**Only**" for a particular type of file or you can choose to eliminate a type of file from your search "**Don't** return results of the file format **Microsoft PowerPoint**" will tell the search engine to ignore any web pages that have the file extension ".ppt" to indicate that they were created in the Microsoft PowerPoint program. The file formats you can choose from on Google are the most commonly posted on the internet:

- Any format
- Adobe Acrobat PDF (.pdf)
- Adobe Postscript (.ps)
- Microsoft Word (.doc)
- Microsoft Excel (.xls)
- Microsoft PowerPoint (.ppt)
- Rich Text Format (.rtf)

The Yahoo! search page also allows you to search for HTML (.htm and .html), RSS/XML (.xml), and plain text format (.txt).

The default setting is to return results of searches on all file formats. If you are conducting a specific search involving mathematical or scientific topics, though, you might find it useful to generate a results list of pages that contain Microsoft Excel files, which are normally tables and spreadsheets. It really depends on what you're looking to do with the data you acquire.

DATE

Limiting your search by choosing from the "Date" drop-down menu (called "Updated" in Yahoo!) might be a useful feature if you are researching a time-sensitive topic, such as a news event or a scientific breakthrough. This search parameter allows you to search only websites that have been updated in the past three months, six months, or one year. The default on the drop-down menu is "anytime," which will include

Mastering Online Research

web pages that are orphaned (abandoned by their creator but still live on the host server), defunct, or rarely updated. If you are researching a topic in which opinions and recommendations change frequently, you might want to check out the results of your keyword search by rerunning the search for updates "**within the past 3 months**." A search for "food pyramid," for instance, will bring in articles and studies on earlier versions of the U.S. government recommendations; modifying the search using the "Date" feature screens out most sites that do not incorporate the newer guidelines released in 2005.

Cached pages: Search engine webcrawlers routinely visit web pages to keep them up-to-date. You can easily check the date on which the Google webcrawlers last visited the site to index any new material or changes by clicking on the hyperlink "Cached" appearing below a search result on the list. That link will take you to a page where Google lists the last date on which the page was visited by a webcrawler and also allows you to see the version of the page as it was stored by the Google indexing database, called the "cached" page (*cache* means a hiding place for safekeeping). Sites that have not been indexed by Google, and sites whose owners have requested that they not be included as caches, do not show the hyperlink. You can compare the cached page to the current live web page by clicking on the "Current page" hyperlink if you want to see what information or images have been updated or removed from the page. Yahoo! also offers a hyperlink to its cached pages but does not furnish the date the page was last indexed.

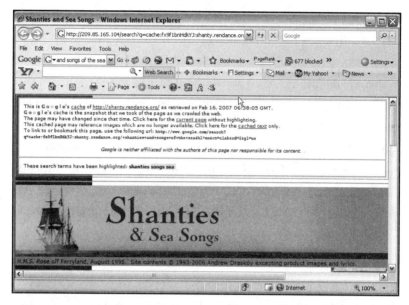

Google.com cached page

NUMERIC RANGE

The Google website offers an advanced search that will screen web pages using a numeric range of dates or other relevant numbers. You can enter a range of two numbers (one in each entry box), and the Google search will return results of pages between that range. If your number refers to a unit of measurement, it's necessary to specify that unit—if you're comparing trucks of certain weights, for instance, you would enter "truck ton" in the "**all** of the words" search box and ".5" and "4" in the numeric range boxes. If you are interested in a particular period of an actor's career, you could use this search to narrow the results. A search for actor Russell Crowe with the numeric range "1999" and "2002" will focus results on that period of time, during which he starred in the film

A Beautiful Mind. I haven't found this feature to be of great usefulness in the types of searches I run, but others may.

This feature is not presently available on the Yahoo! advanced search page.

OCCURRENCES

The "Occurrence" search feature allows you to specify the number of times your search terms appear in the documents retrieved. This can be an efficient way of returning highly specific results—and it permits searching in different areas of the websites, not only in the text of the page. This feature is not available on the Yahoo! advanced search.

From the drop-down menu on the "Occurrences" search you can filter choices for "Return results where my terms occur" by selecting:

- Anywhere on the page
- Anywhere in the title of the page
- Anywhere in the text of the page
- Anywhere in the URL of the page
- Anywhere in links to the page

As an example, let's follow what happens when you run the same search using each of the different selections. The search keywords "tin pan alley" in a basic Google search will return more than 950,000 results. Only a handful of the top ten entries are directly related to the American popular music development known as Tin Pan Alley.

Entering "tin pan alley" in the advanced search box for "**all** of the words" will bring results of websites that contain all three of these words, the same as a basic keyword search. If you specify "anywhere on the page," it's not much different from the results for a basic search, because the Google engine looks at the whole page on any website where the three search terms appear.

If you narrow the search by selecting search "anywhere in the title of this page" you will get results where the three words appear in the title of the webpage—which narrows the list down to about 10,400 websites. All of these websites will have "tin pan alley" coded within the HTML (or other coding language) tags that indicate the title of a page. The weakness of this search is that, while it will give you web pages pertaining to Tin Pan Alley, it will overlook any pages that might contain textual information about the musical genre yet have a title something like "Irving Berlin, George M. Cohan, and Ira Gershwin"—all Tin Pan Alley composers—because the specific search terms do not appear in the title. However, if you were looking to revisit a web page that you remembered as having "Tin Pan Alley" in its title, this tool might help.

Searching for "tin pan alley" using the "anywhere in the text of the page" will retrieve over one million results, over a broader sweep of reference, from dog kennels to rock bands of that name. How can such a search technique be useful, then? It's not much different from either an "exact phrase" search or a basic keyword search for all of the words. However, this search parameter (also called the "allintext:" modifier) searches only the page content. It does not search the URL or page title, so the results list will not show pages that contain the search terms only in the web address or title but not the text. That can help eliminate false results. However, it would be more useful if the Occurrences feature ranked the results by the number of times that your search terms occurred in the pages.

The drop-down menu also allows you to search only on words that appear within the URL address by choosing "anywhere in the URL of the page." This feature has rather limited value, and you would want to look closely at the resulting URLs before taking the time to visit them (although one niche use is for demographers and researchers involved in trend analysis to see how often a particular term is coming up in URLs across the web). Most of the 2,380 URLs containing either "tin-pan-alley" or "tin+pan+alley" are commercial websites that insert the phrase from their own databases for ordering products. For example, the popular music vendor CD Universe offers a CD of Tin Pan Alley music, which probably will not be of much help to someone researching the history of the composers. You can look at the URL on the search results list and determine its content by what the filenames reveal: www.cduniverse.com/search/xx/music/pid/5811303/a/**Tin+Pan+Alley**+Selection.htm

Similarly, from the URL you can tell that the article on Tin Pan Alley from the Concise Encyclopedia Britannica is retrieved from the Britannica's own database, as you can see from the article number and title appearing in the URL: http:// concise.britannica.com/ebc/article-9380806/**Tin-Pan-Alley**. You might want to visit this web page—but you probably could have located it much more simply with a basic keyword search.

The web page retrieved from Answers.com contains the keywords in its URL and is titled "Tin Pan Alley: Information from Answers.com." However, if you look at the entire URL (www.answers.com/topic/**tin-pan-alley**-1960-album-by-ray-agee) you will see that this web page only pertains to a specific musical album by Ray Agee called "Tin Pan Alley."

The last entry on the drop-down menu for "Occurrences" allows you to search for your keywords in the hyperlinks that are contained within websites. Remember that there are complicated algorithms that determine the results of Google searches—some of the links that turn up as results for the "anywhere in links on the page" have the keywords "tin pan alley" in the name of the link as it appears in the text, rather than in the URL of the link itself. In terms of searching through hyperlinks, you may find the techniques in chapter five more useful.

DOMAIN

This feature allows you to search for a keyword or phrase only on a particular website domain, the URL of which you must specify in the search box. Using the drop-down menu, you can choose "Only" to return results from the specified site or domain, or to exclude that website or domain from the search by selecting "Don't." Using this feature requires prior knowledge of the site or domain you want to target. An example of this kind of search would specify "Only" to search the website from Carnegie Mellon University for the exact phrase "game theory," which returns about 2,100 results from that prestigious university. Stanford University offers even more results. The likelihood of finding web pages with cutting-edge academic research on game theory is increased by running this type of filtered search.

Yahoo! offers the capability to search by specific standard domain types. You can choose the default ("Any domain"), or you can run your search on only ".com," ".gov," ".edu," or ".org" domains. These searches look at the URLs of the websites and return only results that contain your designated choice as the top-level domain name. For example, if you entered the search term "food pyramid" and selected "only .gov domains," your search results would be targeted to government websites that provide information on this nutrition program from the U.S. Department of Agriculture. Yahoo! also allows a specific website to be searched for your keywords. Entering "www.foodnetwork.com" in the "Domain" search box with "artichoke" in the keyword search box will result in lovely recipes for artichokes from cable television's most popular chefs.

USAGE RIGHTS

This Google search feature might be of some value if you are planning to use the content of your research in another format, such as on your own website or in a book or article. (Be sure to check out the accepted rules regarding permission and copyrights for online material provided in chapter eleven.) If you know you're looking for reproducible content or free software, you can request the Google search to return results of web pages that are free to use, share, or modify, when specified by their rights owners. The web documents' various usage restrictions can be searched separately with the drop-down menu choices:

- **Not filtered by license.** (This will return all results, regardless of usage rights.)
- **Free to use or share for personal use.** (This permission is specified by the website's owner, and you should read the website's own statement to see if there are any requirements for source citations or reproduction.)
- **Free to use or share, even commercially.** (This means that you can use the material in a work that will be used commercially—for instance, an advertisement—or be sold.)
- **Free to use, share, or modify for personal use.** (The key term here is "modify," which means you have permission to rewrite the material or, if it's software, to revise the code.)
- **Free to use, share, or modify, even commercially.** (This allows you to create a new, altered version of the material for commercial purposes.)

A search for the exact phrase "IE 7" on sites that are "free to use or share" results in links to several blogs and download sites where you can obtain Microsoft's test version of the browser Internet Explorer 7. This kind of filtered search, however, is used primarily for technical aspects of website construction and maintenance, whereby users share software applications freely among themselves to encourage innovation.

On the Yahoo! advanced search page, there is a similar feature called "Creative Commons search." This also allows you to search for web content that can be used for commercial purposes or adapted or modified without requesting permission. Copyright owners who wish to allow others to use and modify their material without formal permission can register with the nonprofit group Creative Commons and specify which rights they want to reserve, if any. The rights will be indicated clearly on their websites. Yahoo!'s search feature, which searches pages that have content with a Creative Commons license, is still in a beta testing stage, but you can explore it by clicking on the "Learn More" link on the search page. Many of the Creative Commons license holders are within the science and technology sectors and are interested in sharing ongoing research.

Creative Commons search on Yahoo.com advanced search page

SAFESEARCH

The ability to choose to filter out adult-oriented and explicit sexual content may be valuable to you. The "SafeSearch" feature attempts to eliminate explicit sexual content and inappropriate, offensive web pages from your search results. On the Google "Preferences" page (accessed from the main search page) you can select the level of protective filter: "Moderate filtering" (the default, which screens for explicit images only) or "Strict filtering" (which screens image searches and complete web searches); "No filtering" turns off this function entirely. The Google advanced search page and the Yahoo! advanced search page offer only two options, "Filter" or "Do not filter."

The "SafeSearch" filter applies only to the particular search you are running and needs to be selected each time. If you would like to block explicit content for every search, you can go to the "Preferences" link on the main search page and set your personal default to always use the "SafeSearch" filter.

Using this filter is a matter of personal preference. I usually do not use it, but neither do I share my computer with young children. Of course neither Google nor Yahoo! can guarantee that an offensive site won't slip through in a search, but the companies do take the filtering seriously. If you click on the "SafeSearch" link on the advanced search screen, you can read Google's explanation of the feature to help you decide.

PAGE-SPECIFIC SEARCH

If you've found a web page that is especially helpful to your research—whether in content, keywords, or other elements such as bibliographies—you can request the Google search to find other pages that are either similar to that page or that link directly to it, presumably because they are closely related.

Say you wanted to find websites created by fans of best-selling novelist Tom Clancy. By running a Google search on "Tom Clancy" you've found a fan site at www.clancyfaq.com, and you'd like to find others. Simply enter this URL into the search box for "Similar," and you'll find about thirty similar web pages on Tom Clancy. If you then click on the "Similar pages" hyperlink appearing in one of the results that is obviously a fan page (check its URL), you get a great selection of pages from devoted Tom Clancy fans.

The "Links" search works with a specified URL and finds web pages that contain links to that page. For instance, entering www.stephenking.com in the search box will return over two thousand results of web pages that link to this official website for Stephen King.

The Yahoo! advanced search page does not offer either of these features.

TOPIC-SPECIFIC SEARCH

The Google website is continually adding to its Google brand features, and the advanced search screen contains hyperlinks to a few of them at the foot of the page. Some of the search features are still in the beta testing stage, which means there might be a few glitches or bugs in the way they return results. But try some of the features for yourself and see if you like the results. Google Book Search (search the full text of books) and Google Scholar (search scholarly papers) look especially intriguing. The Google News Archive search allows you to search historical news archives and display a timeline of results on your search topic. You can also search U.S. government news content from federal, state, and local agency sites including press releases, and search specific university sites, listed alphabetically. Computer buffs might enjoy searching the topics for Apple Macintosh, Unix, Linux, and Microsoft information.

COUNTRY

Yahoo! offers this specialized feature on its advanced search page. The default for this search parameter is "any country." You can choose to limit the search to the websites hosted in any of twenty-seven countries by selecting from the drop-down menu. For instance, if you were researching legal precedents in English law, it might be helpful to limit the search to websites in the United Kingdom. Be careful of setting your search parameters too narrowly, however, because you might miss some really good websites in our increasingly global internet.

SUBSCRIPTIONS

Yahoo! offers a search function (still in the beta testing stage at the time of this writing) that will allow you to use the Yahoo! advanced search to include content from a selected group of websites that require subscriptions. Many of them, such as *Consumer Reports* and the *New England Journal of Medicine*, are accessed by paid subscription only. Click on the "Learn More" link below the list of supported subscriptions for up-to-date information on the service.

ADVANCED SEARCHES USING OTHER SEARCH ENGINES

In practical terms, you probably don't need to go any further afield than the Google and Yahoo! search engines. They are well designed, dependable, and easy to use, and they cover most of what's out there on the World Wide Web. However, in the modern world we are accustomed to having a lot of choices, so it's worth looking at advanced search options on a couple of other search engines.

There aren't as many independently developed search engines on the Web as there once were. Over the past few years, the larger internet search companies voraciously acquired smaller companies. Some niche companies had their databases integrated into those of the larger search engines, while others had their sophisticated search programming expanded and applied to the larger scope of the major companies. The underlying motivation for the expansion of the search engines on the internet is financial. Small, privately maintained databases or collections of hyperlinks couldn't command the amount of advertising revenue necessary to compete, so they dropped out of the competition. Still, there are a few remaining search engines that offer great functionality and are easy to use. We'll look at them briefly here, but be sure to check them out for yourself.

ASK.COM

One of the niceties of the internet for quite a few years was a search website called AskJeeves.com, which accepted questions phrased in plain English and translated them into search queries. It was named for the character Jeeves, a British "gentleman's gentleman" who, in the humorous novels of P.G. Wodehouse, served his master Bertie Wooster with great devotion, wit, and wisdom in the early decades of the twentieth century. In 2006, Jeeves took a well-deserved retirement, and the website search engine was renamed Ask.com. It's one of the most comprehensive, user-friendly search engines, and well worth your time in becoming familiar with its capabilities.

When you enter a search term in the search box on Ask .com, the proprietary algorithm searches the web for that term and returns results that are divided into several categories. At the top of the results screen is a site Ask.com considers to be the most helpful overall, called "the smart answer." If you're searching for "Ireland," for instance, a box containing the flag of the Republic of Ireland, vital statistics about the country, and links to weather, time, travel information, maps, and other information appears at the top of the screen.

The next search results list (below the paid advertising results appearing in a screened box) is ranked by relevance, again determined by Ask.com's proprietary algorithm. What's exciting is the icon of a pair of binoculars next to each result. If you click on the binoculars, you'll see a preview of the web page, in a small image (called a thumbnail image). It's easier and quicker to look at that little web page than to deconstruct the URL to figure out what the website is, or to click on each link. If the page looks interesting, a simple click on the preview image will bring you there. (In the new Internet Explorer 7 browser, the preview image pops up when you roll over it with your cursor, and clicking on the binoculars brings you directly to the full web page.)

On the right side of the results screen, where most search engines display their paid advertising clients' websites, Ask .com instead offers ways to narrow or expand your search or to look for related sites. The results list for "Ireland," for example, allows you to choose new targeted searches on maps, culture, and history, or even to distinguish between the Republic of Ireland and Northern Ireland. To expand your search, you can select Irish names, Irish food, and even the Blarney Stone, as well as other countries that are members of the European Union. The "related names" search in this case merely turns up "St. Patrick," but if you searched for "Scotland" you could pick up the "Loch Ness Monster" and "William Wallace" of *Braveheart* renown.

In addition to its web search capabilities, Ask.com offers search results from an encyclopedia, a dictionary, image collections, and blogs (more on those in chapter seven). Ask

Mastering Online Research

.com also provides web search results to other search sites such as Lycos.com, a major web portal that licenses content from other sources.

GIGABLAST.COM

The Gigablast web search engine was developed to handle up to two billion pages of web data, and it licenses its search functionality to various metasearch engines, which we'll look at on page 83. If you want to conduct more than a basic keyword search on Gigablast.com, you can access the advanced search page. It allows many of the search modifiers that Yahoo! and Google search engines use, including Boolean logical operators. The results returned at the top of the web page as "Giga Bits" are most helpful; they give results for topics that are percentage-rated for relevance to your search term. For instance, a search for "diabetes type 2" generates a dozen Giga Bits such as "81% diabetes mellitus" and "77% symptoms," which you can click on to see all the results for that specific topic. You also may find it useful to browse the hyperlinked categories that appear beneath some of the Gigablast results. Using the Gigablast website for a direct search is not my preference because the results pages are overstuffed and visually confusing. You can access the Gigablast search technology and its enormous database on other search engine sites such as MSN.com, where the results are displayed in more clearly organized pages.

WISENUT.COM

Some smaller search engines operate somewhat like satellites of their larger website search engines. WiseNut.com is actually using the LookSmart.com database, but its own search features are manipulated to bring up results in a slightly different organization. If you search for "Peter Pan" on WiseNut.com, for example, you will see a results page that includes a category-specific list of websites relating to the search term, including bus companies by that name and tickets to theatrical shows. It's a little less busy than the same search results page on LookSmart.com, and it may be preferable if you like the smaller scale search and find it more manageable.

WINDOWS LIVE SEARCH

A recent entry into the field of search engines is Windows Live Search, developed by Microsoft as part of its Windows Live package of features. Check out the website at www.live.com and click on the "Options" and "Advanced" hyperlinks at the top right to see what's available for search parameters. In addition to the usual advanced search capabilities—"Images," "Maps," "People," "Businesses," and even "Classifieds"—Live Search also has a few new tricks to offer. If you click on the "More" link you will see the beta search features such as "Local," "QnA," "Video," "Academic," "Books," and others. Most of them are in beta versions, but before long the features will be standard.

Windows Live is intended to take full advantage of the speed of wireless communication and to be used across the various devices relied upon by the electronically savvy consumer. If you do an ordinary keyword search for "border collie," for instance—which brings up typical results and a helpful list of related searches in the top right column of the results page—and then click on the "Feeds" search hyperlink, your results page will display websites that offer continuous RSS feeds on border collies, your original search term. Likewise, clicking on the "Maps" search will bring up a map of the United States with locations of border collie breeders and rescue organizations. It will be exciting to see where this new level of searching will lead.

OTHER RELATED SEARCH SITES

Like Gigablast.com, LookSmart.com licenses its database and search capabilities for use by other online search sites that then present the search results in slightly varying ways. The graphics and organization of the results differ, but the information is based on the LookSmart technology. You can use the LookSmart.com website to search directly, if you wish. I don't recommend the site to the serious researcher because the results seem driven by commercially sponsored advertising—relevant, but often promoting a particular product or service.

Additionally, there are large corporations such as InfoSpace.com that share their technology and database services among several partner search sites (such as Dogpile.com and Webcrawler.com) and among other types of search sites such as Switchboard.com and various business and personal directories. InfoSpace is very strong in the delivery of information for "yellow pages" and "white pages," which we will explore in chapter seven.

HOW TO USE METASEARCH ENGINES

Metasearch engines are so called because they combine the results of search queries that are run on a group of individual search engines. Only the highest ranked results are then displayed to you. Each metasearch engine has its own method of ranking the results by relevance and popularity (the number of hits or "votes" a site receives).

The biggest advantage to using metasearch engines for your online research is also the biggest drawback. The keywords you enter into the search box will be "forwarded" for searching on many different search sites, and the top few results will be delivered by the metasearch engine. You are at the same time casting a wide net over a variety of search engines and narrowing your search because only a handful are returned as relevant results from each of them.

Metasearch engines can be very helpful when you are first beginning your general research into any topic. The results that come from a variety of search engines can help you to define your search more directly. You may be lucky and find exactly what you're looking for in a metasearch results list, and it may be sufficient to simply follow the hyperlinks through that single website or use its internal site search feature.

Keep in mind that the metasearch engine technology does your initial screening of results *for* you. Instead of five thousand websites you may see only sixty, and the closest match to your search query may not be among those. As you gain more experience in evaluating web resources, most metasearch engines may no longer be your best search choice.

DOGPILE.COM

Dogpile.com, one of the most popular metasearch engines, has been online since the mid-1990s, although now it is part of a larger corporation called InfoSpace. When Dogpile first launched, its web design and navigation system were dominated by images of squirming happy puppies. The metaphor continues with Arfie, the iconic Dalmatian who "fetches" the information for you. Today's site is graphically more sophisticated but you'll still get a "dogpile" of search results.

If you enter the word "schooner" into the basic search box, Dogpile will search for the term in the Google, Yahoo!, msn.com, and Ask.com search engines. In addition to displaying the eighty or so results, Dogpile also provides a list titled "Are You Looking For?" on the right side of the page to suggest other search terms related to "schooner." That can be quite helpful.

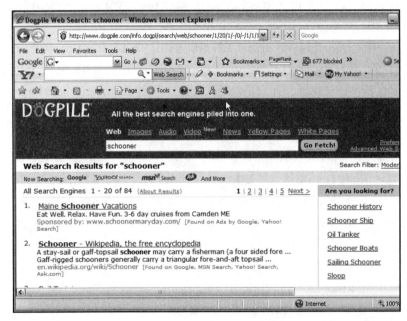

Dogpile.com search results page

The results of the Dogpile search contain a mix of sponsored and non-sponsored websites, as well as other results that appear because the sites have purchased paid placement on one of the search engines that Dogpile included in the search. The mix of those results is determined by Dogpile's metasearch technology and can vary depending on the number of hits those individual websites have recorded prior to your search query. For instance, the results list for the "schooner" search contains many websites that offer schooner cruises or rentals, as well as websites about the history of schooners and sailing and about some notable schooners such as the *Clearwater* on the Hudson River and the *Amistad* slave ship. You can even find out about short-haired American schooner cats and the westward journeys of the prairie schooner wagons.

To the right of the URL for each result in the list appears the source of the web page retrieved. That's very handy. For instance, the first result is a link to Maine schooner vacations sponsored by a windjammer cruise outfit, and the link clearly identifies the site as a sponsored link found by ads appearing on the Yahoo! and Google search engines. The next result is an article on schooners in Wikipedia.org, which was retrieved through searching the Google, Yahoo!, msn.com, and Ask.com databases. Several other results show historic schooners that are maintained by various historical, cultural, and educational organizations.

Clicking on the link to "schooner history" on the right side of the page brings up a list of results more specifically oriented to the history of the tall ships. Few of these results are sponsored or paid links, and thus are more directly helpful to the search. Many of these results were found by Dogpile in the larger web subject directories, LookSmart.com and About.com. Searching in web directories, which have the wonderful advantage of being compiled by human editors rather than by robotic webcrawlers, will be explained in chapter five.

You might enjoy using Dogpile as you become accustomed to conducting searches on the Web. It offers the same kinds of advanced search techniques as the single search engines, including the Boolean logical operators, date range, language, and various standard filters. It's a little easier to learn how to use those advanced techniques when you're evaluating the results from only one search engine, though—what happens to the results list when you tweak the search queries is more obvious when the search is entirely drawn from one search domain (for example, Yahoo!) than when the results come from four or five search engines.

The advanced search techniques on Dogpile are accessed on the "Preferences" page and the advanced web search page; both hyperlinks appear on the right of the "Go Fetch!" button. The "Search" filter that screens explicit sexual content is set at a "moderate" level by default, but you can raise or lower the level of filtering by selecting it on the "Preferences" page. Dogpile also allows you to specify whether you want the search to correct misspellings of your search words automatically. If you choose to disable this option on the Preferences page, then Dogpile will still ask you if you meant to spell the word differently on the results page. Most search engines do this for you as a default service. If you're searching for a highly unusual spelling of a common word (for instance, in a sixteenth-century document), you might want to turn off the spelling correction in Dogpile.

You can specify the number of results displayed per page for each kind of search in Dogpile—different numbers for images, web documents, audio files, and so on. You can also request that your search terms be highlighted in bold type when the results are displayed. And if you want your search results list to open in a new browser window, just click on that option.

CLUSTY.COM

Another metasearch engine that has plenty of punch is called Clusty.com, an odd name meant to suggest its method of returning search results in topic clusters. Combining search results into groups of similar materials can be an extremely useful feature. Clusty takes it a step further and provides a list on the left side of the results page that details the topics of the clusters and the number of hits within each cluster. By clicking on the three tabs ("clusters," "sources," and "sites"), you can choose whether the results list displays in topic clusters, by the web sources searched for the results (Ask.com, Gigablast, msn.com, WiseNut, Wikipedia, Open Directory Project, and others), or by the domain type (for instance, how many results are from .edu sites or .gov sites or .com sites). These statistics can be a quick way to evaluate the usefulness and integrity of the information on the website result.

Clusty also allows you to preview the actual web page of each result on the list by clicking on the icon of a magnifying glass next to the result. That brings up a portion of the

Mastering Online Research

web page, displayed beneath the result. If it looks promising, click on the link to the site. You can also choose to have the full web page display in a new window by clicking on the multiple window icon. You can click on the cluster icon to display the cluster in which that particular search result is included, which will appear on the left column.

The clustering of search results also permits searching by a specific term within the cluster of sites, and the term is highlighted in the results (unless you choose to turn that function off). For example, if you do a simple search in Clusty for "tsunami," the approximately two hundred top results will be returned in subject clusters, such as "Indian Ocean (27)," "tsunami warning (11)," and "relief (18)." Each cluster has sub-clusters beneath it that can be accessed by clicking on the plus sign next to it. The twenty-seven results for "Indian Ocean" can be further divided into smaller clusters of sites pertaining to "death (3)," "generate tsunami (3)," and "history, deadliest (3)," among others. In many ways, this search is similar to the method you would use to browse in an online subject directory. You can also search within clusters for another term to refine your search results, using the "find in clusters" search box at the bottom of the results summary in the left column. Enter the word "Indonesia" and the results list will display the thirteen results for your sub-query and highlight the word "Indonesia" in every instance.

To give you a hint of the search engine's capabilities, the "tsunami" search results page led off with three links to top news stories in a box at the top of the page. Clusty is a relatively new resource, incorporating the award-winning search

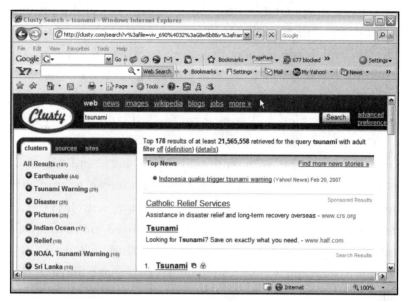

Clusty.com results box for "tsunami"

technology from another search software company called Vivisimo, founded in 2000 by three scientists from Carnegie Mellon University. It's impressive and fun to use—you can even adjust the size of the display font on the results page if you accidentally left your eyeglasses at home. And check out the "Clusty Labs" link at the top of the results page for some new features in the testing stage (if "labs" is not displayed as one of the links, click on the "more" double arrow to reveal more of the links). One of the new features called "Shakespeare Searched" will allow you to search Shakespeare's works clustered by topic, work, and character, and another is "Clusty Ben," devoted to resources about Benjamin Franklin. As the website's "About" page says, "With a name like Clusty, it's gotta be good!"

Mastering Online Research

MAMMA.COM

The search engine Mamma.com has been around since 1996, created initially as a graduate student's thesis. Its registered slogan, not surprisingly, is "the Mother of All Search Engines," and it is a powerful tool for research. Mamma.com distinguishes itself as a "smart metasearch" engine, explaining on its "About" page that "every time you type in a query Mamma simultaneously searches a variety of engines, directories, and deep content sites, properly formats the words and syntax for each, compiles their results in a virtual database, eliminates duplicates, and displays them in a uniform manner according to relevance. It's like using multiple search engines, all at the same time."

How does Mamma differ from the other metasearch engines? By its ability to search "deep content sites." Deep content refers to data that is not easily found on the Web, because it is buried within webpages that are not accessible to typical surface webcrawlers or it is generated on the fly by queries to searchable databases only found by deep web search engines. We will look at techniques to access the information on the Deep Web, which is also called the invisible Web or the hidden Web, in chapter eight. At present, Mamma is the only search engine promising to include deep content in its search. Others may soon follow.

One feature of the Mamma website that deserves special notice is its Deep Web Health Search, which allows you to obtain results from a query run specifically on the major health websites and online databases, not on the entire Web. It is perhaps the best resource you can use for accurate, timely information on health topics, including diseases, symptoms, treatments, and medicines. Mamma's specialty search engine presents its results in a format that is most useful, with a definition of the search term and brief text extracts from web pages retrieved from WebMD.com, Mayo-Clinic.com, eMedicine.com, and other handpicked sites.

Another feature Mamma offers is a free downloadable Desktop Search, which will find all types of files stored on your own computer. You can instantly access e-mails, attachments, documents, images, audio and video files, and other types of data by using an easy search screen. Busy researchers might welcome this new access tool.

WEBCRAWLER.COM AND METACRAWLER.COM

These metasearch engines are part of the InfoSpace team of search engines and draw on the same research sources as Dogpile.com. The same features for advanced searches and Preferences are available, too. Webcrawler's mascot is a graphic spider who changed his name from "Spidey" to "Hunter" and his color from brown to blue. If you prefer low-key graphics and you are not a dog lover, Webcrawler will give you the same level of functionality as Dogpile. If you like your web pages clean and simple, MetaCrawler might appeal more. No dogs are fetching results or spiders spinning webs to catch the information for you.

The variety of search engines and options for conducting advanced searches offer the online researcher an unprecedented opportunity to access information of all kinds and qualities. How to evaluate those search results and the websites from which they are mined is the next skill that you need to master. Chapter four will start you on your way.

CHAPTER 4

EVALUATING WEBSITES

The internet is as rich a source of information as anyone could ever imagine. All manner of people have contributed to its treasure—and to its trash. How can you distinguish between the two and make your research expeditions enjoyable and satisfying?

One of the most important ways to evaluate a website is to look closely at the information *about* the site. You want to determine (1) who sponsors the website, whether an organization or an individual; (2) the expressed viewpoint or possible underlying motivation for the information offered; (3) whether the website is a current one, with updated resources; and (4) the reliability of the information. It's important to know whether the information comes from a national institution, a politically or religiously motivated group, an enthusiastic hobbyist, a professional service looking for clients, a product salesperson, or students at a middle school. Much of this can be found on the website home page itself, if you know what to look for. The URL (Universal Resource Locator) can also be mined for information.

DOMAIN NAMES

Even before clicking on the link on your search results page, you can find out one important piece of information about the website: the type of organization that hosts it. All website addresses contain a top-level domain name, such as ".com" or ".org," which describes the general category of the entity that is hosting the website. When a new website is created, its particular domain name is registered with the appropriate suffix to indicate its web category (for example, "smithtownmoving .com" for a commercial website, a hypothetical moving and storage firm in Smithtown on Long Island).

Websites with ".com" as their domain can be registered by any individual or business or other entity—it's the most common domain and identifies the site as a commercial or general site. The domain designation of ".edu" indicates that the website has an educational affiliation; schools, colleges, universities, and some research institutions use this domain. It's usually a good indicator of a website with educational value and reliable data.

The domain suffix of ".org" is used primarily by non-commercial organizations or groups, large or small. Institutions such as hospitals or various kinds of nongovernmental agencies also use ".org." The domain is not a guarantee of the high quality of the posted resources, however.

Government websites at the local, state, and federal levels are designated ".gov" to indicate their top-level domain. This includes websites ranging from the Library of Congress to the smallest sub-agency in the U.S. Department of Agriculture. From most of the government sites you can expect accuracy, although you should always check the timeliness of the information. Anyone who already doesn't believe what the government tells us is true won't be convinced by the ".gov" in the website address, but as taxpayers who ultimately pay for all the costs of government websites, we certainly ought to avail ourselves of the resources.

As the Web expands, new domain designations are being created to handle the enormous volume of websites. Among them are the suffixes ".info" for informational sites; ".net" for internet service providers and other related businesses; ".mil" for military sites; ".tv" for websites of television networks and stations; and ".biz" for sites clearly doing business on the Web. More suffixes will be added in the future.

The domain name suffix helps to keep order on the internet, where billions of domain names mingle; also, specifying the type of website allows the same name to be used for multiple websites. The hypothetical website www.businessleadership.com might offer fee-based seminars and workshops on business leadership training, whereas the website www.businessleadership.org might be a service organization of top executives who annually sponsor a scholarship for students in business management schools.

Some companies and individuals register their names in all available domains so that searchers can find them by name without knowing the exact domain type. All these hypothetical domain names would point to the same website, by automatically redirecting the search URL to the main page: AmandaPools.com, AmandaPools.org, and AmandaPools.biz. However, AmandaPools.edu and AmandaPools.gov would not be allowed. There is also a flourishing online business in reselling domain names that are popular or valuable for some particular reason. You occasionally might encounter the sellers of original domain names when you try to acccss a website by entering its URL directly into your web browser; if the address you've asked for doesn't exist, some browsers display a domain-registration site instead.

THE HOME PAGE

The first step in evaluating a website begins when you scan the results list of your basic keyword search or advanced search query. Select the most promising one—the link that seems closest in topic and most specific to your search query—and click on it. Your search terms may be highlighted on the page, which makes it easier to scan the text and graphics to see if the page contains useful and relevant information. If the information seems of potential value to you, then the next step is to visit the website's home page to get a sense of the reliability of the source.

Focus on the primary questions you need to answer about a website:

- Who sponsors the website?
- What's the purpose of the website?
- How many visitors does the website draw?
- How recently was the information updated?
- How objective is the information likely to be?

- Can the reliability of the information be verified by other sources?

When you click a link from your search results list or a hyperlink from another website or an online subject directory, often you will bring up the home page of the website. That's not always the case, since some links go directly to the page of most relevance to the link, but usually there is a clickable button or navigational icon on the page to bring you back to the home page. A visual scan of the page can provide helpful information about the site's likely reliability and usefulness in your research.

Websites are produced using various design programs to create visual interest. Some are highly sophisticated (for example, large multinational corporations and computer software companies), while others are plain and functional (libraries, research databases, student essays). Still others are idiosyncratic, displaying their owners' particular taste, whether delightful or dreadful. The graphics, photographs, buttons, and icons exist only on the surface layer of the website, sometimes referred to as the website's "skin." Even on a plain, no-frills website, you may find wonderful resource material. On the other hand, if a site offends or repels you on its home page by its graphics or language, it's not worth a second click. You risk encouraging malicious contact if you proceed further past the home page into the website—the website can place cookies (small files that collect information about you) on your hard drive or you could unknowingly download spyware that tracks your online activity. Always keep your virus and spyware protection up-to-date and routinely run the programs to eliminate cookies and spyware. When a home page doesn't feel right to you, don't click on any icons. There are plenty of other sites to visit.

WEBSITE SPONSORS

At the foot of the home page, many websites list their "brick-and-mortar" address (that is, their street address in the real world), as well as contact information including telephone numbers and fax numbers. This is useful if you are looking for information on a specific geographic area: A site might be a perfect resource for you except that the local focus is Alaska rather than Alabama. Sometimes e-mail addresses also appear here, but often there is a "contact us" page link that provides automatically directed e-mail through the website itself.

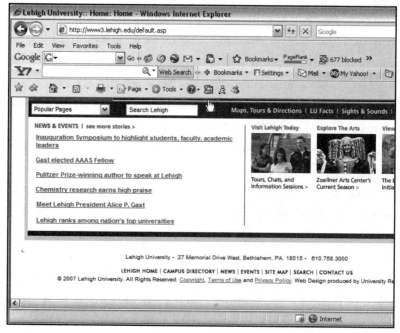

Foot of home page

Many websites, especially those sponsored by large corporations, have a hyperlink from the home page to an "About" page, which lists the company history, products, and services, and often information about its governing structure, organization, and personnel. The "About" pages can be extremely useful in determining the sponsor of the site and the company's affiliations, whether parent companies or subsidiaries. This information will give you some inkling of the probable slant of the data provided on the website—if the website is maintained by a subsidiary of a huge agricultural conglomerate, it might have a tendency to promote the benefits of biogenetically altered grains, even if the website's name is something like HealthyWholeGrains.com.

Many smaller organizations use either the home page or an "About" page to explain their reason for existence. Frequently you'll see a separate link to a "Statement of Purpose" or a page titled something along the lines of "Our Goals and Commitments." Read those, too, if you're seriously considering basing your research on materials posted on this site. What people and organizations write about themselves on these pages can be revealing.

OTHER CLUES ON THE HOME PAGE

Individuals' websites that come up in your search results list require evaluation in order to make sure they contain accurate information. As a writer myself, I am fascinated by these opportunities to peer into the minds of the people who host personal websites. As a scholarly editor, I am trained to look for discrepancies, fuzzy thinking, outright errors, and other weaknesses in the material I read. Few people who post information on personal pages have the opportunity of professional editing, and even the best grammar-and-spelling-check program can't spot a factual mistake. Often you can get a good idea whether their material is reliable and well researched by browsing through a few pages.

As you try to get a sense of the person behind the information, ask yourself the following questions about the site:

- Is it logically organized? Or is it rambling and scattered?
- Are the links to other pages and other websites operational? Are they sensible?
- Does the website give source citations for quotations of others' texts and mention other resources that have been used to compile the site?
- Is there a biography or résumé of the site host, to help you judge his expertise and credibility?
- Are there obvious errors in dates, or misspellings of names and terms?
- What is the overall feeling you get from the site? Does the person genuinely want to share information? Is there an agenda she is pushing? Is there a balance of enthusiasm and concrete information about the topic of the site?

The answers to these questions will help you decide to what degree you can rely on this site as a research source. Much of what is posted on the Web by individuals is of value and interest to others—it really is a community out there, with the variations of capabilities and personalities typical of any community.

If the topic that you're researching is of a controversial nature, it's a good idea to investigate the links to other websites that often appear on the home page. You wouldn't want to quote from material posted on a website that also linked to the website of a hate group, for instance, without knowing it. If I sound overly suspicious, I apologize—but it is with good reason. The internet offers the best and the worst of humanity's efforts to communicate our opinions and beliefs, and there are wolves who post in sheep's clothing. No entity monitors the World Wide Web, which is why you should evaluate the sites you use to support your own opinions and conclusions.

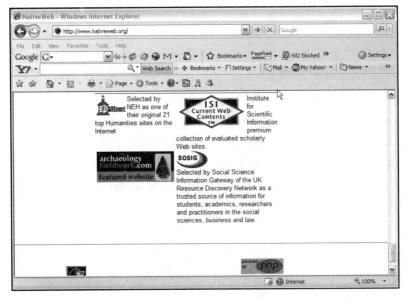

Internet awards at foot of home page

At the foot of the home page (or in a link to another page), you may find displays of the internet awards the website has received. Some respected awards instantly confirm a site's credibility. For example, the appearance of the logos for the

Magellan Four-Star Award and the Top 5% Best of the Web Award indicates that the site has been evaluated and judged to be of value to the internet community. Websites may also display awards and recommendations from specific organizations that monitor web content, including the National Endowment for the Humanities and the Institute for Scientific Information. The absence of awards, however, is not a contrary indication: Not every website owner has the inclination to pursue competitive recognition.

Some website home pages have counters that display the number of visitors to a site over a given period. Even these can tell you a bit about the information's credibility. Counters were much more common when the internet first entered general usage, before the hits on a popular site had to be recorded in the millions or billions. (Rest assured that those clicks are being recorded somewhere in cyberspace, though, even if they're not displayed.) Some of the sites for organizations and individuals still use counters, which can help you to gain a sense of how many people are interested enough in the topic to visit the site.

However, if a site is hosted by an individual who focuses on a narrow subject area, a tally of visitors to the site over the past year might be sadly small—you can build a website but you can't make people come to it. (How to draw visitors to your site is the topic of a number of hefty books.) Of course that website might contain the nugget of information that makes all the difference to you in your search! And it might be hosted by an individual who would delight in sharing more material with you if you contact the person through the e-mail address on the site or telephone with your query.

TIMELINESS OF THE INFORMATION

Somewhere on a website's home page you can usually find a notification of when the site was last updated. Often it's at the foot of the page, near the contact information for the webmaster (the person who maintains the technical aspects of the site) and the copyright line. If the date shown is several years earlier and this would affect the information that you need, don't give up instantly. You might want to scan a few of the pages to determine whether the updates have actually been made but are not reflected in the date on the home page. It happens sometimes.

If the content posted on the website is mainly historical, literary, or artistic, it can still be perfectly valid even though not recently updated. The fact that most information posted on the Web dates back no earlier than the 1990s doesn't make much difference if you're researching an ancient philosopher or a piece of music composed in 1783. What the sources said in 1995 is probably still true a dozen years later. If you know your research subject well, though, you presumably also know whether new scholarship or a dramatic new development has thrown previous opinion into doubt. At least you would pick up signs of the new interpretations of data in your searches on the Web, enough to determine whether the information on a site is so outdated as to be useless.

Timeliness of updating is crucial when your research interests center on politics, international issues, science, technology, and current events. If you need up-to-the-minute information, your best bet is to subscribe to RSS feeds and news alerts, which deliver real-time updates to your computer in a constant stream. These tools are discussed further in chapter eight.

Earlier in chapter three we looked at advanced search techniques that incorporated the "cached" web pages available on Google and Yahoo! results lists. Don't confuse the date that a page on a website has been cached (visited by a webcrawler) with the date on which it was last updated. The webcrawler can document visits to the same web page every month but the data will not have been changed.

When you do locate a website that hasn't been touched in a while, it can be fun to travel back in time. Like space debris, the content is preserved forever on the Web, or at least until the host removes the website from active status. Graduate students apparently are among the most likely to abandon their sites and move on, and it seems universities continue to host these sub-pages of a departmental website for quite a while before purging them (those sites are called orphans, by the way). That's one reason it's important to check the dates on the site. Political websites, especially grass-roots ones, also can be interesting to read when they linger online long after the races have been decided—and they can provide a time capsule, suitable for the views of a character in a novel or a flavor of the period for a nonfiction piece. As technology advances, there will probably be fewer pieces of abandoned flotsam on the World Wide Web, but it's kind of neat to stumble upon.

Mastering Online Research

GAUGING OBJECTIVITY

Evaluating the objectivity of online resources is especially critical if you're researching a topic that polarizes opinion. You need to look very carefully at who is sponsoring the website, their purpose, and the likely objectivity of their information. Mastering the skill requires intuition and thoughtful analysis.

One example of a controversial topic that requires good judgment in assessing sources is the death penalty. People usually have a strong opinion on the use of capital punishment in the United States. Those who want to abolish the death penalty are just as firm in their beliefs as those who see capital punishment as the deterrent to, and ultimate consequence of, heinous crime. Very few folks take a middle-ground position on this issue. If you search for the keywords "death penalty" or "capital punishment," your results will include websites of all different persuasions. Your task in mastering the art of online research is to learn how to differentiate among them.

For instance, the website called Pro-Death Penalty (www.prodeathpenalty.com) offers a very definite slant on the issue, evident from the first quote posted on the home page. On this site you will find emotional descriptions of murder cases and links to various other sites and statistics that promote capital punishment, often through personal testimony from murder victims' families.

The website hosted by the American Civil Liberties Union (www.aclu.org/capital/index.html) takes the opposite position, as you can surmise from the brief description appearing in the search results list: "The death penalty is the ultimate denial of civil liberties." This site offers a comprehensive view of the legal aspects of capital punishment and clearly represents its advocacy for a moratorium on the death penalty, including a counter that monitors the number of executions carried out in the United States.

Giving equal time to both views is the website titled Death Penalty Information, High School Curriculum (www.deathpenaltyinfo.msu.edu). Sponsored by Michigan State University, this site presents a balanced view of all sides of the capital punishment issue, intended to help high school students and teachers in their study of this topic.

The website of Capital Punishment, the Death Penalty (www.religioustolerance.org/execute.htm) is produced by a small organization called Ontario Consultants on Religious Tolerance. This website is an example of one that claims objectivity in its reporting ("all points of view on the death penalty" appears on the home page) but gives immediate signals of an agenda being promoted by its authors, including a comment about receiving death threats via e-mail. (Most organizational websites do not attract death threats, which should alert you.) Unlike many sites, however, these folks are open about their agenda of promoting religious tolerance and attempt to put aside their personal biases and faith traditions, offering an essay on a web page entitled "Your First Visit?" that clearly defines who is writing the content and the criteria they are using. This seems both admirably honest and helpful to a researcher.

You might tend to overlook a search result titled Death Penalty Links, at www.clarkprosecutor.org/html/links/dplinks.htm, because it seems so narrow in scope. Actually, the website is a

Mastering Online Research

surprising treasure trove of links to over a thousand websites pertaining to capital punishment. The stated purpose is to help Clark County, Indiana, residents understand and make decisions about the death penalty, whether they are law enforcement personnel or ordinary citizens. In fact, it offers a "one-stop" research source that is both deep and broad in its coverage, certainly useful to researchers from around the world—which you might not suspect from its county prosecutor website address. However, this is an instance of relevance ranking based on the number and quality of the hyperlinks to and from that website, which brought it to the top ten search results.

Individuals often host websites to express their personal opinions to the virtual world, and this is particularly true on controversial issues. A website hosted by an individual in support of capital punishment, for instance, opens to a dramatic color photograph of a wooden electric chair. Similar websites are hosted by individuals expressing the opposite point of view. Such sites might offer some first-person opinion quotes, which can be used in your own work with proper attribution of the source and permission from the website owner, if necessary (see chapter eleven). However, it would be a mistake to take these individuals' information as seriously as, say, a website from an organization that has been recognized as contributing to this field over a number of years. You have no definitive way of judging the individuals' skill in research or their ability to differentiate between facts and propaganda—from either side. For color and flavor, though, the impassioned words on an individual's website might be just what you need.

VERIFYING THE RELIABILITY OF SOURCES

As delighted as I am by all the information available through searching on the Web, I also take the job of verifying the reliability of my sources seriously. Misinformation can be transmitted either intentionally or inadvertently, and I wouldn't want to be part of that.

Especially when a certain fact, interpretation, or other piece of information is critical to the research project on which you are working, take the time to verify it with at least two or three sources. Don't assume that the first source has conveyed it correctly. You may be publishing or distributing the results of your own research work, and a factual error can destroy your credibility in no time at all. Not every error can be prevented, because we're all human, but practicing due diligence is a good thing for everyone.

And as mentioned in chapter one, keep a complete record of where you have found online materials that you may use in your work. Bookmark the site and also note down the source on paper or in a "sources" document file. Websites are time-sensitive and the page may not be available when you go back to retrieve the information at a later time.

Errors on the World Wide Web can arise from simple mistakes in transcribing information. When print documents are scanned electronically to create digital files, the resulting product requires careful proofreading against the original to pick up any errors that the scanning might have introduced by misreading characters. Because the scanning processes are becoming more sophisticated all the time, fewer of these problems arise. But do watch for typographical errors when

Mastering Online Research

using online documents that were digitalized in the earlier years of the internet—you can usually find another version of the document (especially books and poems) against which to check it. You wouldn't want to propagate the error.

Even when the information is correct, it may be rendered inaccurate by simple line spacing or punctuation. I often see quotations of poetry that have been obtained from websites where the lines were not displayed as in the poet's original version. Poets can be very picky about their line breaks—after all, it affects the cadence of the language and thus the reader's perception of the poem—so usually I check poems in several different sources, locating a version of the original poem as first published, if possible.

Because the content of sites on the internet is not monitored, for the most part, there's no guarantee that what you read is true; therefore, I try to stay with established sites sponsored by institutions and corporations. If I'm looking at an individual's website and quickly find errors, then I don't trust any of the work on that site; I'll look somewhere else. I find the same thing to be the case with attitudes. When someone is slanting content in a way that raises my suspicions, I take the information on that website with a grain of salt. (This advice doesn't apply to political and activist sites—they're often biased in favor of their own arguments. I just attempt to determine the direction of the slant and go from there.)

Finally, when it comes time to publish or distribute your research project, make the effort to recheck any links to websites that you've included. It's annoying to readers when they get an error message that the source is not able to be found.

Some websites will automatically redirect you to the new URL address if the site has moved, in which case you will want to update the URL in your research. Other sites and pages apparently disappear entirely. If citing the website was important to your work, you can try searching for it by title, or by using an "exact phrase" search on an advanced search engine for a string of words that would likely be unique to the website. Sometimes research collections merge, just as corporations do, and the data remains the same even though the organization's name has changed.

WEBSITES THAT REQUIRE REGISTRATION

Occasionally the websites that appear in your search results list will require you to register in order to access the pages on the website. These are called *proprietary websites*. Some charge a fee for usage; others are free. Many people feel uncomfortable providing personal information in exchange for the ability to browse or search a website. And unless you are a big spender, you probably don't want to pay for information on the World Wide Web. Let's explore the pros and cons of registered-only sites so you can make informed decisions.

Newspapers and other periodicals were among the first websites to ask visitors to register their names and e-mail addresses in order to access the content—motivated, of course, by commercial ambitions to make money by selling internet subscriptions to their publications. Once the internet community figured out how to exchange money (or its equivalent) through the use of secure internet transmission of credit card data and fund transfer services such as PayPal, magazines began to offer online access by paid subscription, which in turn opened the door to internet-only magazines and newsletters. Newspapers began to charge small fees to researchers who wanted to access articles in their archives and later added premium services (access to read the most popular columnists online, for example) that were available by paying monthly fees. Marketing services figured out how to capture information about potential customers by asking them to register at the commercial websites they visited, and the race for data took off.

How does the requirement for registration affect you as a serious internet researcher? It's an individual choice. Certainly you could avoid accessing any websites that require a login and password. You'll miss out on some material, but that might be more acceptable to you than providing your e-mail address. If you're reluctant to give out any personal information at all, then you wouldn't even consider registering for a site that required online payment to access its databases or searches.

In an informal survey, I asked some people who do quite a lot of research and other business on the internet whether they registered to use websites and what they thought about the practice. Most replied that if the website was sponsored by a professional organization or by a company from which they might want to buy something, they would register. They understood that the organizations might be attempting to increase their mailing lists and the companies trying to better define their markets. But there were a handful of tips that they offered:

Read carefully. Read the privacy policy posted on the website to determine whether your information will be kept confidential or shared with or sold to others.

Decide how you want to be contacted. Consider whether you want to receive e-mails or postal mail from the website sponsor. Companies and organizations are required by law to give you the opportunity to refuse continuing e-mail contacts even if you furnish your e-mail address. If you don't want to receive any e-mails from the website, be sure to check the box on the registration page to disallow them. It's called opting-out.

Consider an extra e-mail account. If you're interested in receiving e-mail updates or newsletters from a company website, consider setting up and using a different e-mail address for those kinds of messages. You can get free e-mail accounts from a variety of providers, including Yahoo!, Google, Hotmail, and others. Use this e-mail account for commercial webmail only and keep your primary e-mail address private.

Think before you click. If you register to download a free software program or an image, make sure you read the terms of the license agreement. This document spells out in detail your restrictions and permissions for using the material, and the legal remedies for any problems that may occur. As with any legal agreement, don't just automatically click the "I Accept" button.

Exercise caution. Be very cautious about registering on commercial websites that sponsor online gambling, entertainment, pornography, and the like. Those sites are more likely to make you vulnerable to e-mail solicitation, spam, and even viruses.

When they were just idly browsing the internet, most people agreed, they didn't bother to register on a website but moved on to the next one that looked interesting. When they were searching for some specific piece of information, they spent the time to register. But it took a lot to get them to spend real money for data on the Web.

As an example, the websites for which I have registered are mostly online editions of newspapers such as the *New York Times* and the *Houston Chronicle*, a few craft and fiber sites that offer free patterns, and fewer than a dozen online stores from which I order occasionally. I'm also registered with several professional associations and discussion groups online, and of course my local library.

What are some advantages to registering on websites? The most significant is that registering with sites that send you e-mail updates of important news in your field or subject area saves you a lot of personal research time and effort. The expansion of RSS feeds directly to your computer and news alerts from major news media are a boon to serious researchers, especially those whose work focuses on current events. You can read about how to use these features in chapter eight, and you might find them perfect for your needs.

Another advantage of registering is the ability to save information that you've selected as useful on a site and to store information you've entered. Many health and weight management websites create a personal profile for you when you register, in which you can track your progress. Similarly, websites such as CollegeBoard (www.collegeboard.com) allow parents and students to register for free accounts to save profiles of financial information, test scores, evaluations, and so on to help in the college admissions process.

Registering to access professional or institutional websites also may allow you to participate in research studies, obtain access to articles and reports not available to the general public, and search databases and archives. A website at the University of Pennsylvania's Positive Psychology Center run by Dr. Martin Seligman, for instance, has more than 400,000 registered users around the world who access its wide-ranging resources for free and fill out online questionnaires as part of a research study on "authentic happiness" (the name of the site).

A number of print publications also have online formats, which allow registered members to benefit from special dis-

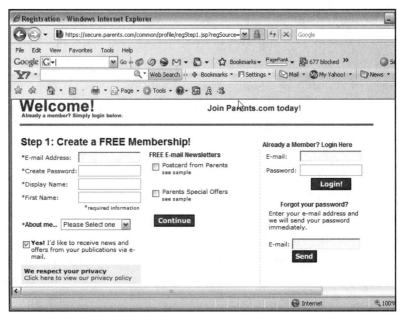

Member registration page

counts, search the magazine's archives, read some of the articles in the current and past issues, and post to online discussion groups and blogs. Registration is usually free, but not always. The more expensive academic journals and trade publications often include a free online subscription with a paid print subscription, and offer an online-only subscription option too.

LOGGING IN TO A SITE

Once you have registered for access to a website, you'll be asked to log in with your username and password each time you want to access the site. Logins provide security for the site, which is important if the website stores any personal information about you, such as your credit card data and street address. Logins allow the website to track your visits to the site as well. Some, such as Amazon.com, compile histories of your purchases and the pages you've browsed to better target your individual interests and their marketing strategies.

Logins also serve to screen out the people who have not paid for access to a site, if the site is fee-based. Many websites offer the option on their login pages of enabling your browser to go directly to the site without typing in your user identification and password. This saves time, but a cookie or marker is placed on your computer's hard drive to permit this speedy registration. If your browser is set to reject all cookies (the highest level of security), the feature won't work. Most security software programs such as McAfee and Norton allow you to specify whether you accept cookies or not, and to allow particular cookies from favorite sites to remain when others are deleted.

SECURE AND NONSECURE SITES

When you log in to a website such as an online store or a bank or credit union that offers online transactions, you will be automatically diverted to a secure website connection that will protect your sensitive financial information from outsiders. Similarly, when you register with a website for the first time and need to enter your personal information (e-mail address, name, password, etc.), you should be able to transmit this data over a secure connection (sites that don't require passwords to enter may not use secure connections, however). A secure website shields your data from being copied by unauthorized internet users as it travels through cyberspace. Many reputable websites display the logo of the security software that protects your data on their website. When you proceed to the "checkout" of an online store, you also will be transferred to a secure connection. Sometimes you'll see a tiny gold padlock in the status bar at the foot of your screen, indicating that you are on a secure site.

If you look closely at the URL of the website before you enter your new member information or after you hit the "checkout" button, you should see that the usual "http://" at the beginning of the URL has changed to "https://." The addition of the "s" indicates that you are accessing the internet on a secure connection. Don't ever transmit sensitive information without checking for that little "s."

Occasionally when visiting a website, you may see a pop-up security warning window with the message, "This page contains both secure and nonsecure items." It's intended to alert you that some of the components making up the web page may be brought in from nonsecure sites, which theoretically leaves you vulnerable to data thieves. You may see this message if you open your e-mail using a web-based browser rather than the e-mail program on your own computer. Take the warning seriously and decide whether you want to proceed to open the page. More often than not, the error message is sent because one or more of the files called to display on the page (perhaps a graphic or a logo) is not stored in the correct "https://" location but is stored elsewhere on a nonsecure "http://" location. That won't do any harm. If it's a website that you trust, go ahead and open the page.

Every researcher learns to recognize the potential pitfalls, whether in accuracy of data or security of access, as she becomes more experienced in navigating the Web. Use common sense on the internet and always—always—back up your important data regularly. If your virus protection software is outdated, buy a new program. If you're concerned about security when browsing so many websites, install an anti-spyware program and run it frequently. But don't let these standard safety precautions make you timid about surfing the net. There's a world out there waiting for you.

CHAPTER 5

THE WORLD OF HYPERLINKS

In addition to using keyword searches and advanced searches supported by search engines and their indexed databases, you can search the World Wide Web through another method—browsing. Hyperlinks allow you to jump from page to page within a particular website and to follow a trail of information by visiting multiple websites. Browsing, also called "drilling down," may not be as speedy as searching by keywords and queries, but it has its own rewards. Once in a while, you'll stumble upon a nugget of information you would never have found otherwise.

SUBJECT DIRECTORIES

Online subject directories are the best source for drilling down through hyperlinks. Subject directories are websites comprising collections of hyperlinks to websites organized by categories that cover a wide range of topics. The websites to which the hyperlinks direct your search have been selected and evaluated by human editors. This is very different from a basic keyword search, in which the term or phrase is queried to a search engine's database of web pages that have been indexed by robotic webcrawlers. In an online subject directory, the collection of website hyperlinks are organized and maintained by human beings—real people who are usually experts in the subject for which they are assembling links. These people may be paid editors, but often they are volunteers who possess expertise and the desire to share their knowledge with the online community.

The subject directories are organized as descending levels of categories and subcategories, similar to a library's Dewey Decimal Classification number system or the Library of Congress subject classifications. In the early years of internet researching, subject directories were more common, before the exponential growth of websites made it increasingly challenging to evaluate and include worthwhile pages. But several directories are still strong resources, and the technology of hierarchical subject organization supports the popular web access points called *portals* or *gateways*.

Online subject directories in general can be classified into two categories—academic and commercial. For the writer, teacher, or serious researcher, the academic subject directories will be more useful, for the most part. But commercial websites whose listings are determined primarily by the companies or individuals willing to pay a fee to be included can still be intriguing sources of information. Some of the subject directories also offer keyword and advanced search capabilities.

To introduce you to a basic form of subject directory, let's look at Yahoo!'s categorized guide to the Web. You can access it by clicking on the "Directory" link at the top of the Yahoo! search page. If the link does not appear along with other links such as "Images" and "Video," click the "More" link to display "Directory" as one of the additional options. Yahoo!'s "Directory" search page offers features and editors' picks, but our research interest lies in the browsable categorized guide. By clicking on the links to various subject categories, you can go directly to websites that match your research goals, or you can keep drilling down through subcategories until you find the results you're searching for. Categories also often provide hyperlinks to other subject directories. For example, selecting the category "Social Science" on the Yahoo! "Directory" page will show you the next category level, where you can select "History" as your next link. On the "History" category page you will find a link to "Web Directories," all pertaining to the topic of history. If you're just beginning to get comfortable on the World Wide Web, this general subject directory is a good place to practice.

COMMERCIAL SUBJECT DIRECTORIES

You are probably familiar with some of the commercial subject directories, which organize shopping websites, city guides, portal home pages, and other websites that allow you to click through different levels to pinpoint exactly what you're looking for. Think of them as similar to online yellow pages of a telephone book. In fact, if you visit the www.yellowpages.com website, you'll see exactly how the hyperlinks are organized by subject category.

The browse lists of hyperlinks for the Yellow Pages website descend like the branches of a tree, from broad limbs to smaller branches to specific twigs. The technology itself is sometimes referred to as a "tree."

The visual design of the Yellow Pages site is straightforward, displaying the links in ordinary fonts without graphics. The Browse by Topic A-Z page of the search directory About.com is also very user-friendly. The format is simple to use and it's easy to see the subject organization. Other subject directories may appear much more graphically diverse, but the organizing structure underlying the clickable photos and logos is similar.

The home page for msn.com (produced by Microsoft) is an excellent example of a visually rich subject directory website.

About.com directory page

This style of website is called a portal, because it opens the door to so many other websites and online resources. You may already be using msn.com as your home page on your computer—it's a popular choice because it offers so many services. You can get breaking news, sports, travel tips, weather reports, horoscopes, career information, financial news and articles, entertainment news, video, and much more. The eye-catching graphics and clickable photos are the visual layers that mask the hyperlinked subject categories in the directory. If you click on one of the text-only hyperlinks at the top of the home page, you'll be able to see the directory more clearly. Choosing "Careers and Jobs" will bring you to a results page that contains hyperlinks to CareerBuilder.com, another online company, which in turn contains links to a job search, employer listings, helpful articles, salary calculators, résumé posting, and other services. All these "Career and Jobs" hyperlinks at msn.com are managed by CareerBuilder, which operates on the business principle of "vertical organization." All of the links point to services and content supplied by this one website, rather than directing the user outward to other websites.

The Best of the Web subject directory is all about linking to other websites rather than linking within one website. This online subject directory is a little unusual. Founded in 1994 to encourage users to vote on the best sites on the World Wide Web, the site has continued to evolve along with the online community. According to its home page (www .botw.com), "To rank among the Best of the Web, a site must adhere to the strict criteria of editors who ensure that it contains substantive unique content, navigates in a user-friendly manner, contains no broken links or pictures, is up and running 24/7, and conforms to universally accepted web standards." It's a good site on which to practice your skill at drilling down through websites, because the editors are vigilant about keeping a spam-free search environment, and new links are added daily.

The "tree" of a subject directory offers choices at every level. Let's take a look at just one Best of the Web category, the Arts, one of fifteen top-level categories in the directory that range from Business to Science to Sports to Reference. If you browsed the directory with an interest in learning more about the modern mystery novel, for instance, you might drill down through the following links in descending order, each level more specific than the previous one:

- Arts (selected from among 15 categories)
  - Literature (selected from 38 categories and 1 website)
    - Genres (selected from 19 categories and 4 websites)
      - Mystery (selected from 5 categories and 1 website)
        - Magazines and e-zines (selected from 2 categories and 10 websites)
          - *Crime Time* magazine selected from 10 websites)

Crime Time, a magazine published in hardcopy in the United Kingdom and online, offers reviews of the latest mysteries on both sides of the Atlantic, as well as articles by and interviews with professionals in the mystery publishing field. I am an avid mystery reader myself but never knew this resource was available, so I couldn't have found it by name on a basic search. A keyword search on "mystery magazine" did not find it within the first fifty results. Drilling down through the subject directory eliminated the need to wade through dozens of irrelevant results that might contaminate a keyword search, too; every website displayed in the subject directory was in some legitimate way related to the search topic. That's brought to you by human intelligence. Of course, a linked website may change its content after the editor has screened it, but for the most part the results of your browsing will be relevant to your search.

HYPERLINK IDENTIFICATION SHORTCUT

Websites are organized by a hierarchy of pages, each with its own URL that extends onward from the top-level domain name. As we discussed earlier, some web pages are composed of standard HTML text, some are PDFs (static images of documents), and some web pages are created "on the fly," dynamically generated by software programming that retrieves and displays information. Drilling deeper within a site permits you to search for increasingly specific information as you move through the pages. You can do this by clicking on the hyperlinks in the text (usually appearing in blue or another color with underlining) or by clicking on the site's navigational tools for moving from page to page. Navigational tools and menus appear at the sides, top, and bottom of the screens, depending on the design of the graphic user interface.

Rather than actually going to each hyperlink or web page, you can save time by taking a peek at the URL of the hyperlink before clicking on it. Using your skills at decoding and evaluating URLs, you can display the URL address and determine what kind of page it is, and sometimes who maintains it, if the hyperlink takes you outside the website itself. This is a very useful shortcut when you're looking at a page that has lots of links as well as drop-down menu choices.

How do you see the URL for the link without clicking on it? It's easy. Even though the link is a part of the normal text (for example, "Visit the museum's <u>online bookstore</u> for a catalog of the <u>current show</u>"), when you roll your cursor over the text link, the actual URL for the link appears in the plain gray footer bar at the bottom of the web page. (This gray bar is called the status bar, and if you don't have it showing on your browser, go to the "View" menu on your browser toolbar and check "Status Bar.")

For instance, in this hypothetical example, rolling the cursor over the hyperlink "<u>online bookstore</u>" will display the URL www.museum.org/bookstore.html in the gray status bar. If you click on it you will go to the HTML web page for the bookstore. The "<u>current show</u>" will display the URL www.museum .org/shows/images/current/0407/picasso, from which you can surmise that the museum has online images of the works in the Picasso show, which is the special exhibit for April 2007. Looking at a hyperlink's URL is one of my favorite online research shortcuts.

ACADEMIC SUBJECT DIRECTORIES

Subject directories were part of the web environment long before the first "spider" started crawling the websites, and they continue to offer wonderful accessibility to information resources. The commercial directories overlap the academic directories to some extent, but you can usually drill deeper within the academic subject directories.

First, let's get over the intimidation caused by the word "academic." That simply serves to distinguish a site built and maintained by a university, organization, research institution, government department, public service sector company, volunteer group, or some other entity not supported primarily by advertising revenue. You could also call them "noncommercial." The academic directories are set up to be used easily and successfully by anyone, degreed or not.

The largest, most comprehensive human-edited directory on the World Wide Web is called the Open Directory Project (ODP), constructed and maintained by a worldwide volunteer staff of nearly 75,000 editors. Since its inception in 1998, it has built a database of over four million websites in approximately 590,000 subject categories. Because the folks who keep up with this directory are committed to keeping the internet a free resource for every "net-citizen," there is no advertising or paid placement on the website. All the data is available for free, and there is no cost to have a website listed in the subject categories. The Open Directory powers the core directory services for the Web's largest and most popular search engines and portals, including AOL, Google, Yahoo!, AltaVista, Ask .com, Clusty, msn.com, WiseNut, and hundreds of others.

The Open Directory is available in many languages and has a search feature as well as the browsable subject categories. If drilling down is your preferred style of researching, you'll probably want to bookmark the URL of the main page (www.dmoz.org) and start your searches there.

Mastering Online Research

The Open Directory Project page offers sixteen main subject categories, similar to the main page of the directory Best of the Web. The top-level categories are:

- Arts
- Games
- Kids and Teens
- Reference
- Shopping
- Business
- Health
- News
- Regional
- Society
- Computers
- Home
- Recreation
- Science
- Sports
- World (directory listings in other languages)

The main category of "Society" contains nearly 266,000 links to web pages. If you click on the "Society" hyperlink, the category is subdivided into other more specific subcategories, such as "Activism," "Crime," "Genealogy," "Language and Linguistics," "Military," "Paranormal," "Philosophy," "Religion and Spirituality," "Social Science," and about thirty others. Each subcategory provides the cumulative number of the sites it contains—which, incidentally, is helpful in providing an overview of which subjects have the most widespread presence on the web.

The subcategory of "Paranormal" is almost guaranteed to be an exciting browse, with more than 2,200 listings. Clicking on that link opens the next directory subcategory level, a page organized in five sections. The first provides links to general online sources for the subject, including encyclopedias, magazines, news, and media, as well as organizations and chats and forums. The second section offers more specific links, to websites on the Bermuda Triangle, crop circles, divination, ghosts, investigators, near-death experiences, psychics, and so on. The @ symbol next to any entry indicates that you will

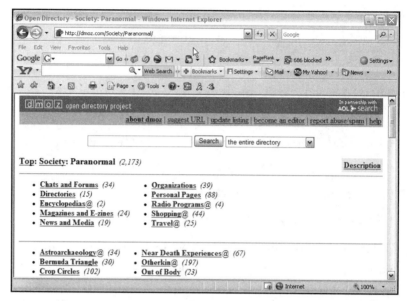

Open Directory second level page

be referred to another "Society" subcategory in which it is primarily listed—for instance, "Reincarnation@" brings you to the "Religion and Spirituality" subcategory (which makes sense, because for many people reincarnation is a spiritual belief, not a paranormal experience—clearly there are real people thinking behind these listings).

The third section of the directory list contains links to other categories in the Open Directory, similar to cross-references. Among the suggested categories and subcategories are "Science": "Science in Society": "Skeptical Inquiry and Society": "Philosophy": "Metaphysics" (the descending levels are separated by colons). The fourth section provides links for the "Paranormal" subcategory in other languages.

The fifth section of the directory page provides one recommended site with a gold star, and twenty or so other web pag-

Mastering Online Research

es that might be of interest. If none of the links look enticing, use the handy shortcut of rolling over the hyperlink title of the website to see the actual URL in the gray status bar at the foot of the screen to determine the sponsor of the site. If you're doing serious research, you don't want to waste time visiting a site with a URL like www.ethansbloodcurdlingscreams.com.

The subcategory "Ghosts," for example, has close to five hundred websites devoted to the subject, indicating its popularity as a search topic. At least one of them might have a photo of a real ghost, right? Now you have a definite target for your search.

The next level of the directory displays only nine subcategories of "Ghosts" (the number narrows substantially as you drill down through the topic), including "Ghost Tours," "Investigators," "Exorcism/clearing," "Stories," "Chats and Forums," "Personal Pages," "Places and Hauntings," "Directories," and "Organizations." If you select "Places and Hauntings," on the next page you can choose where you would like your haunted places to be located—current choices are Australia, Canada, Ireland, the United Kingdom, or the United States. The number of links for Australia is zero, so any supernatural inhabitants must have recently migrated. The United States boasts fifty-one links, so that would be a good subcategory to select.

The next level brings up only two related links—one for "Regional": "Paranormal," with only one link, and the other for "Ghost Investigators" in the United States. The exterior website links (outside the Open Directory Project) at the foot of the page offer a number of targeted sites of varying levels of sensationalism and sincerity (Creepy Cleveland and Ghastly Ohio are among the least tempting), some offering photos of mists and orbs. One stands out as more credible than the rest: Emily's Sunland Page, a personal website collection of photos, stories, and more about the Tallahassee Sunland, a haunted former mental facility in Florida. When you click on Emily's March 23, 2005, update link (the last update, in fact), you'll see a photo of the Sunland house with a little girl's face hovering above the porch. The enlarged section of the photo looks like a genuine ghost image to me.

Because the plan was to drill down to the absolute bottom level of the Open Directory, click on the last "Ghost Investigators" category and then choose a state that has a few of them. New York has nine, and among those websites listed in the directory is one hosted by ghost investigator and author Linda Zimmerman. She's a serious paranormal investigator who uses the latest electronic and computer equipment in her investigations. I've met her in person and I think she's the real thing—but that's only my personal opinion. To end this search with goosebumps, read some of Linda's Ghost Blog at www.ghostinvestigator.blogspot.com.

So, we went through an entire subject directory, top to bottom, and found what we were looking for—one photo of a perhaps-genuine ghost posted on a website. If we had used a search engine, would it have been quicker? Sure. A basic keyword search for "ghost pictures" on the Google search engine turns up scads of good results, including a link to About .com with a few of the most famous ghost photographs ever taken. But then you wouldn't have learned to drill your way through a massive subject directory!

WEBRINGS

In addition to subject directories, there is another research area that might be of use if you would like to access a number of websites on a topic of interest without scrolling through the list of results from a general search engine. Groups of websites band together in what is called a webring. Think of it as a circle around which you can travel forward, backward, and randomly, to access the websites of any member without going outside the ring.

Webrings are formed by people who are interested in the same topic, knowledgeable about the subject matter, and united in their desire to help one another and others interested in their topic. For example, a publisher of romance novels has a webring; many of the authors they publish also belong. The webring helps the authors to keep in touch with what's going on in that publishing company and in the world of romance writing in general.

Quite a number of webrings are hosted by a company called WebRing, whose slogan is "Creating communities, connecting people." When you access one of the webring sites hosted by WebRing.com, you will see a special navigation bar at the top of your browser. On this NavBar are search boxes for WebRing and for the specific ring you have accessed. The History Ring, for instance, makes it easy to search all the member sites on the Web with related content. In order to be accepted as a History Ring member, a website has to contain detailed historical information on events, figures, and fields of study.

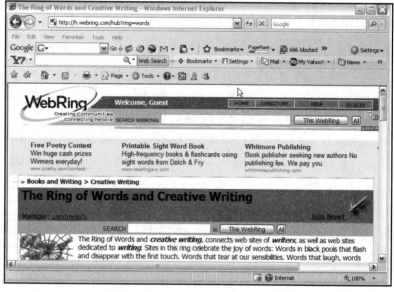

Webring navigation bar

Webrings are good for noncommercial website owners, because members bring traffic to their sites and create more exposure, and they are good for researchers who want to focus on a particular topic. You may need to become a webring member in order to search the ring, but membership is usually free. There are many thousands of webrings on the World Wide Web that can be located by searching on any major search engine for the keyword "webring" and a subject area of your choice.

In the next chapter, we'll survey more databases and directories that can help us search effectively on the Web, so start coming up with some topics you might want to know about!

CHAPTER 6

THE BEST WEB-SITES TO BEGIN YOUR RESEARCH

Now that you've honed your online research skills, it's time to dig in. Perhaps you already have a few ideas of what you'd like to search for. If not, the list of questions on the next page will help to fire up your engines, so to speak. Take the time for a practice session devoted to one topic. Plan to spend an hour or so searching on the internet, really digging deep into your subject. Follow any hyperlink that speaks to you. Set yourself a goal of discovering some new fact or connection that relates to your life in some way.

Notice the word *life*. This exercise is about expanding your life knowledge, not your work knowledge. (You can do that another time.) It's supposed to be fun. If you are a teacher, don't go right to the education websites—go to knitting or quilting websites, or check out what's new in the golfing world. If you're an accountant, take a trip through some history or genealogy sites, or research your favorite breed of dog or cat. This is really a window-shopping trip to enjoy browsing and searching on the internet. You can tackle more challenging searches later in the chapter, where all those lists of websites appear. Feel free to start with any of the suggested resources in the lists, if you like—or simply jump into a search engine or subject directory and engage!

So, ask yourself some of these questions and when one resonates with you, start searching. When you've found enough information to satisfy you, choose another question if you have the time.

- What country did your grandfather or other ancestors emigrate from? Can you find the town or city?
- If you could live anywhere, where would you choose? How much would a house cost there?
- How did your favorite author or actor get started in his or her career?
- Where can you find the finest brewed beers in the world?
- Whatever happened to [fill in the blank with a person or an object]?
- When did NASCAR start up? What do those drivers and their crews eat on the road, anyway?
- Where was your first apartment or house located? Has the neighborhood changed?
- What's the connection between quantum physics and spirituality?
- Remember that traditional dessert that your grand-mother used to make on the holidays? Does anybody have a recipe for it?

Mastering Online Research

- What would your name mean in Chinese? What are the characteristics of the Chinese year in which you were born?
- Why are ferrets prohibited as pets in New York City?
- How does someone become a Navy SEAL?
- How are a tulip tree and a tulip similar? How are they different?

Serious research on the web will draw upon all the skills you have learned in defining clear search queries, browsing through subject directories and hyperlinks efficiently, and evaluating the search results. Eventually you will discover a group of favorite web resources that you go to over and over again, because they fit your style of thinking and of organizing information. They'll become familiar and your search speed will increase.

As technology advances, websites will upgrade their own search systems to deliver your results with greater relevance. For example, the Google Custom Search Engine is a new product that allows webmasters to choose which pages they want to include in their index and to determine their own relevance ranking. Yahoo! also offers a similar product. Microsoft's Windows Live incorporates much more than the usual search features, and a website called ProgrammableWeb.com is being developed for users who want to search for "mashups"—web applications (programs) that combine data from different sources into a new type of result (for instance, combining a map of the city of Dublin with a database of crimes and violent incidents). Searching will continue to become easier and faster and better targeted.

The marketing field has used and sometimes exploited search engine optimization (known as SEO) since the days when commerce first appeared on the World Wide Web, but the academic study of SEO is in its beginning stages. Because the development of technology travels so quickly from the research labs to the marketplace, the new advances sure to spring from those brainy computer science students will be accessible to all of us in record time. But for now you have an impressive toolbox of skills to use every day. And like any other pursuit, the more you practice, the more expert you become.

A NOTE ABOUT LIBRARIES

Each public library system makes subscription searchable databases and publications available to patrons, according to what its budget has allowed the library to license. Visit your local library's website to find out if any of these resources are available to you (the library's website will often list the available databases by subject category). Many will be accessible from your home computer.

Some of the services offered without charge to the patrons of many libraries are the Thomson Gale databases (literary and other) and the Gale Virtual Reference Library; Twayne's Authors Series; Wilson Biographies Plus; the EBSCO full text magazines, academic journals, and nonfiction books; business, financial, and economic information; medicine, health, and science; the ERIC education resources; ProQuest's genealogical database of searchable census records; full-text newspapers and archives; and directories of all kinds.

        Mastering Online Research

THE LIBRARY OF CONGRESS

The Library of Congress is the stellar source to search for a collection of any author's works, so we'll spend a little time exploring how to do that. You can use similar techniques in searching other large databases for authors, artists, scientists, political and historical figures, and the like. The Library of Congress website is most easily accessed at its main URL address, www.catalog.loc.gov. You will see two search options, one for a basic search and one for a guided search that allows you to specify Boolean operators, among other features. I have found that in searching for information on a book or an author, the basic search is the easiest and fastest.

If you open the basic search screen, you can enter a search term and choose from a drop-down menu of various search parameters. The "Basic Search Tips" box on the page offers clear explanations of the different kinds of searches available. Because it's the national library and a resource for librarians and archivists, the search options include searching by LOC catalog numbers and by call numbers, but you can also search by author name or title. The Library of Congress indexes its author names by surname. For example, you could enter "Cooper, James Fenimore" in the search box. The results page displays all entries matching that name, in order of relevance: first all exact matches; then entries for James Cooper (no middle name); then for James Cooper with various middle initials. Birth and death dates are given for most entries, but sometimes there is a note that it is data from the "old catalog"—printed before the holdings of the library were entered into a database.

Occasionally that information is all you can access, particularly for old and obscure works.

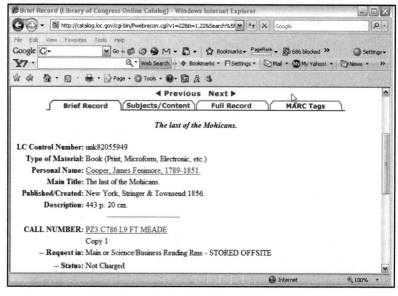

Library of Congress brief entry

The LOC listing provides clickable links to the author, book title, date of publication, and even whether the item is available in electronic format. Scanning through the entries, we can see that there have been many editions of James Fenimore Cooper's works from the nineteenth century continuing into the twenty-first. Selecting the 1856 listing for *The Last of the Mohicans* brings up the brief entry for this edition. From that screen you can access the full bibliographic record. If you were in Washington, D.C., you could request to see the book itself in the reading room.

The Library of Congress basic search also allows users to search by subject browse and by keyword. For deeper re-

Mastering Online Research

search, follow the helpful tips online for using the guided search feature.

SUGGESTED ONLINE RESOURCES

The websites on the following pages are by no means a comprehensive list of what's available on the World Wide Web. You won't find any sports websites here, or popular culture, or shopping sites, because links to those kinds of sites are readily available on any large commercial search engine or subject directory. This list is probably a bit idiosyncratic, since I've compiled it from sites I personally like and use. However, you might find them useful as starting points for your searches, because they offer a wide variety of indexes, hyperlinks, searchable databases, and authoritative data. These sites have been around for a while, which lends credibility; many are the products of university and government research institutions. Any one of them can lead you forward to a dozen—or a hundred, or a thousand—other great web resources, although it rarely takes that many web pages to find what you're after.

A few of the sites listed here require paid subscriptions, but most can be used freely, or at least with a free registration (see chapter four for information on registering for website access). Try a few, and see for yourself if you find them helpful. Use your browser feature to bookmark or save as favorites the sites you want to revisit.

SEARCHABLE DATABASES

The World Wide Web started with databases, so it's no wonder that databases are the most common searchable sources online. Those I have listed here have a long history, some since the early 1990s, which is as far back as anyone can go. These particular websites make it easy to find primary source documents as well as other secondary sources of information about them.

Project Gutenberg

www.gutenberg.org/wiki/Main_Page

The first and largest single collection of free electronic books, presently containing over 19,000 downloadable books in its searchable database. Founded by Michael Hart, the inventor of ebooks.

Bartleby

www.bartleby.com

A public-domain text archive of literature, reference works, and verse with searchable databases, developed from Columbia University's Bartleby Project. Their slogan is "Great books online." An easily navigated site of enormous value.

EDSITEment

www.edsitement.neh.gov

"The best of the humanities on the Web," sponsored by the National Endowment for the Humanities. Subject areas include art and culture, literature and language arts, foreign language, and history and social studies.

Intute

www.intute.ac.uk/

Excellent site incorporating the EEVL Internet Guide to Engineering, Mathematics, and Computing website formerly hosted at the Heriot-Watt University in Edinburgh. Resources for science and technology, arts and humanities, health and life sciences, and social sciences. Created by a network of United Kingdom universities and partners. Subject specialists select and evaluate the websites in the database, which contains nearly 115,000 records.

On-Line Books Page
www.digital.library.upenn.edu/books
Great website offering a database of over 25,000 online books with browse and search capabilities. Founded by online research specialist John Mark Ockerbloom at the University of Pennsylvania.

University of Virginia Hypertext Collection
http://etext.lib.virginia.edu
The Electronic Text Center at the University of Virginia Library has 90,000 documents organized by librarians into subject collections. The database is browsable and searchable. Online texts of many authors are available, including illustrations and images.

Virtualology
www.virtualology.com
A virtual education project whose stated mission is "to foster an understanding of humanity's great moments, exceptional minds, remarkable talents, infamous actions, great events, natural history, scientific discoveries, and the celebration of individuals." This virtual museum of art, history, library, science, natural history, and war is an extraordinarily rich source for research, suitable for all ages.

ENCYCLOPEDIAS

Okay, I'll admit that I am an encyclopedia junkie, having learned to spell the word from Jiminy Cricket singing a jingle on the *Mickey Mouse Club* TV show. My career has included a number of years as a senior editor for the *Encyclopedia Americana*, working on both the print and online editions, so I'm picky about how articles are updated and organized. Ideally you can read a good encyclopedia article and come away with an accurate overview of a topic or of the life and works of an individual, whether contemporary or historical. It's nice if there is a bibliography or reference list, too, and lots of hyperlinks to other connected resources. Encyclopedias are great starting points for research—try these out on your next idea.

HighBeam Encyclopedia.com

www.encyclopedia.com

Offers free access to more than 57,000 searchable or browsable articles from the *Columbia Encyclopedia*. More than 35 million searchable articles and images from 3,000-plus reference sources are also available through links from HighBeam Research, for a modest membership fee.

Encyclopedia Americana Online

More than 25 million words plus web resource links for every article, but only available through subscriptions by institutions, libraries, and schools. Check with your local or state library to find out if they have a subscription for patrons to access online. To access *Encyclopedia Americana* online, go to Grolier Online (http://go-passport.grolier.com/splash). This is my favorite encyclopedia.

Encarta

http://encarta.msn.com

Microsoft's online encyclopedia of 45,000 articles for "students of all ages." A premium version is available online for an inexpensive annual subscription fee.

Wikipedia

www.wikipedia.org

Free encyclopedia that anyone can add to or edit, with 1.5 million articles in English as well as articles in many other languages. Wikipedia links often appear near the top of the results list on basic and advanced search results pages because of the site's popularity and volume of information. Some of the articles are frivolous (who really wants to know all the product lines of Herbal Essences shampoo?), but some are extremely helpful. Not all the content is written by experts or reviewed before posting online—an interesting concept, but it makes me nervous when I've read a "fact" in a Wikipedia article that I personally know to be incorrect. Double-check information from Wikipedia with another online source, just to be sure. Students should be aware that some university and college departments do not accept references to Wikipedia articles as legitimate research.

LIBRARIES AND ARCHIVES

Librarians and archivists quickly embraced the new technologies of the internet when the online tools first appeared (once they got over the idea that the printed book was supposedly fated to disappear from existence, that is). Because the online systems of information storage and retrieval are similar to those used in libraries, websites developed by libraries and archives tend to be excellent, easy-to-use resources.

Librarians' Index to the Internet

www.lii.org

"Websites you can trust" from a publicly funded website. Search and browse over 20,000 entries maintained by librarians and organized into fourteen main topics and nearly three hundred related topics. Well worth a visit.

Library of Congress Gateway to Library Catalogs

www.lcweb.loc.gov/z3950/gateway.html

Search more than five hundred library catalogs around the United States and the world, including the Library of Congress. Extremely useful gateway for searching multiple libraries. As mentioned in the "Note about Libraries" (on page 136), the online catalog search site for the Library of Congress database itself is more easily accessed at its direct URL, www.loc.gov/index.html.

The WWW Virtual Library

www.vlib.org

Oldest catalog of the Web, started in 1991 by Tim Berners-Lee, who is the creator of HTML and of the Web itself. Run by expert volunteers. Subject categories cover just about anything you might want to know.

Perry-Castañeda Library Map Collection

www.lib.utexas.edu/maps

Up-to-date, comprehensive collection of online maps at the University of Texas at Austin. The collection has historical maps as well as contemporary maps from all over the world.

BUBL Link

www.bubl.ac.uk/link

Selected internet resources covering all academic subject areas, produced by the Strathclyde University in Glasgow. More than 12,000 websites organized under the Dewey Decimal Classification System of subject areas. It's a beautiful thing.

Internet Public Library Reference Ready Reference

www.ipl.org/ref/RR

Annotated collection of internet resources in numerous subject areas, sponsored by the School of Information at the University of Michigan.

The National Archives (United Kingdom)

www.nationalarchives.gov.uk

Online access to one of the largest collections of catalogs and databases in the world, with 900 years of history and fascinating documents and other resources.

TVlink Film and Television Website Archive

www.timelapse.com/tvlink.html

Enormous archive of web links related to the movie industry and television. It has replaced www.imdb.com as my search resource, since the Internet Movie Database now charges a subscription fee for services.

REFERENCE SOURCES

There are so many reference sources on the internet that it's difficult to limit suggestions to only a few. Some are very nearly search engines themselves, and others are online versions of respected print reference volumes. The best have well-thought-out hyperlinks and serious search capabilities.

Refdesk.com

www.refdesk.com

A free and family-friendly website, one of the most crowded portals on the internet; contains links to more information than you ever knew you wanted. Calls itself "the single best source for facts on the net," and it may well be true.

Reference.com
www.reference.com
Online service provided by Lexico Publishing Group. Includes tabs for a dictionary, thesaurus, almanacs, encyclopedias, and other web reference tools.

LexisNexis
www.lexisnexis.com
Superior research database that is available only to subscribers. Initially developed as a premier resource for legal research (Lexis) and news and business information (Nexis) for corporate customers and libraries, the company now also offers a service designed for independent professionals and smaller business, called LexisNexis AlaCarte! This service is free to search the database and charges a fee for only the documents you retrieve. Be sure to check with your local library to see if they already subscribe to LexisNexis for their patrons' use.

Infoplease
www.infoplease.com
Sponsored by Pearson Education, this website contains "all the knowledge you need." An excellent source, including 30,000 biographies, an encyclopedia, almanac, sports facts, atlas, thesaurus, and much more.

Answers.com
www.answers.com
Calls itself "the world's greatest encyclodictionalmanacapedia." Provides free access to over four million topics from over one hundred

dictionaries, encyclopedias, almanacs, and other reference works. It's quite a remarkable mix of popular culture and serious information.

Whatis.com

http://whatis.techtarget.com

Leading internet technology encyclopedia and learning center, providing definitions, computer terms, tech glossaries, and more. When you don't know exactly what an internet term means, go to whatis.com first.

Dictionary of the History of Ideas

http://etext.lib.virginia.edu/DicHist/dict.html

Online edition of *The Dictionary of the History of Ideas: Studies of Selected Pivotal Ideas* published by Scribner in 1973–1974, searchable and browsable alphabetically or by subject (nature, humanity, art, history, politics, religion and philosophy, and mathematics and logic).

Quotations Page

www.quotationspage.com

Oldest quotations site on the Web, with more than 25,000 quotations from over 3,000 authors, added to daily. Browse by subject, author, or keyword. My quibble is that the source of the quote is not always provided, only the author and quotation.

Yahoo! Babel Fish

http://babelfish.yahoo.com/

Now part of the Yahoo! website, Babel Fish will translate up to a 150-word block of text from one language into another. You can also enter a URL and get a translation of the web page. Features include searching the Web for the translated words and comparing the original language version with the translated version. The service supports simple Chinese, English, Dutch, French, German, Greek, Italian, Japanese, Korean, Russian, Portuguese, and Spanish. The translations may be a little rough, but the web service has been popular for a long time, since it was first developed by Alta-Vista in the late 1990s.

World Gazetteer

www.world-gazetteer.com

Current population figures and other statistics for countries and regions around the world. Easy to use.

Population Reference Bureau

www.prb.org

Provides reliable information on U.S. and world population trends and related social topics, including aging, education, health, poverty, marriage, ethnicity, and family planning.

Tourism Offices Worldwide Directory

www.towd.com

Guide to official government tourism offices, convention and visitors bureaus, and similar official agencies in countries around the world, searchable by country. U.S. state tourism agencies can be searched by state.

The Chicago Manual of Style Online

www.chicagomanualofstyle.org

Essential guide for writers, editors, and publishers, published by the University of Chicago Press. This online version contains all the information in the big orange hardcover book (now in its fifteenth edition), plus it's searchable and browsable. The annual subscription fee is very modest, and you can sign up for a thirty-day free trial.

GOVERNMENT WEBSITES

Your tax dollars pay for a lot of the services and resources on the U.S. government websites, so feel free to use them whenever you're searching online. Depending upon which department has issued the content, government documents and reports are in the public domain and can be used without copyright restrictions. The government tries to make its web presence welcoming and simple for even inexperienced searchers to use.

The last three resources in this list will help you research governments other than that of the United States.

U.S. Copyright Office

www.copyright.gov

Complete site for all information about copyrights, including searching for registrations and recording copyrights for all works. It's definitely worth a visit.

USAGov

www.usa.gov

The U.S. Government's official web portal. Search for organizations, agencies, state and local governments, and online services.

GPO Access

www.gpoaccess.gov

The U.S. Government Print Office offers access to resources of the federal government.

Library of Congress State and Local Governments

http://www.loc.gov/rr/news/stategov/stategov.html

Research center of the Library of Congress relating to state governments, with excellent links to individual states.

U.S. Federal Government Agencies

www.lib.lsu.edu/gov/fedgov.html

Louisiana State University's comprehensive directory of links to federal agencies.

Federal Citizen Information Center

www.pueblo.gsa.gov

Searchable collection of guides available from the U.S. General Services Administration. Consumer-oriented, multilingual, and rich with links.

Directgov (United Kingdom)

www.direct.gov.uk/en/index.htm

Public services all in one place from the government of the United Kingdom. Excellent site to research UK information.

THOMAS (Library of Congress)

http://thomas.loc.gov

In the spirit of Thomas Jefferson, legislative information from the Library of Congress. Abundant coverage of legislation, current and historic.

National Center for Education Statistics

http://nces.ed.gov

This portal sponsored by the Institute of Education Sciences, U.S. Department of Education, offers a variety of data related to all forms and levels of education in the United States, including statistical tables.

Foreign Government Resources on the Web

www.lib.umich.edu/govdocs/foreign.html
Up-to-date resource on foreign governments and related information, searchable by country or subject. A helpful resource from the University of Michigan Library.

CIA World Factbook

www.cia.gov/cia/publications/factbook/index.html
Comprehensive data from the Central Intelligence Agency, including maps, historical background, and current information on the world's nations.

BUSINESS

Many commercial web portals offer constantly updated business information, sometimes for a subscription fee. The sites below are those that I have found most consistently useful, and most are free to access.

New York Times Cybertimes

www.nytimes.com/ref/business/business-navigator.html
Selective guide to internet websites on business, financial markets, and investing resources, with hyperlinks.

CNNMoney.com

http://money.cnn.com
An active portal for the latest financial news and much more from CNN.com.

ThomasNet

www.thomasnet.com

Formerly the Thomas Register, this site provides a directory and search for industrial information, products, and services.

globalEDGE

http://globaledge.msu.edu

Directory of annotated links to global business resources, maintained by the Center for International Business Education and Research at Michigan State University.

GENEALOGY

The pursuit of genealogy as a leisure pastime has exploded on the internet, where information is so much easier to find than hunting about in musty record rooms and cramped historical societies. Genealogical research also has great rewards for historians, writers, and researchers tracing individuals who are not their ancestors. These websites listed here are the best I've discovered. (See also FindaGrave.com on page 173.)

Cyndi's List of Genealogy Sites on the Internet

www.cyndislist.com

A well organized subject directory and index to sources for genealogical research. A great starting point for new researchers.

The Statue of Liberty-Ellis Island Foundation

www.ellisisland.org

Information on the Ellis Island Immigration Museum and the American Family Immigration History Center. Searchable Ellis Island/Port of New York records, including ship manifests. Note that you need to register in order to search this site, but registration is simple and free. To access all areas of the site, a paid membership in the Foundation is required.

FamilySearch Internet Genealogy Service

www.familysearch.org

The largest collection of searchable, free family history, family tree, and genealogical information in the world. Sponsored by the Church of Jesus Christ of Latter-day Saints, and a truly excellent resource.

The USGenWeb Project

www.usgenweb.com

Official site of the USGenWeb Project, a volunteer organization providing free online genealogy research tools. Formed ten years ago as a group of volunteers posting family history information on-line, this site is now one of the largest free collections of genea-logical data and has over one million visitors each day.

HEALTH AND MEDICINE

So many websites offer healthcare, healthy living advice and medical information that it's hard to know which to trust. Especially in researching any information on medicine, disease, or healthcare, you need to be able to rely on the source. Here I've narrowed the list of recommended web-sites to those sponsored by major accredited institutions or responsible organizations.

Mamma Deep Web Health Search Engine

www.mammahealth.com

The Mamma.com metasearch engine offers a specialized feature that searches a dozen or so hand-picked health and medicine websites (including those listed below). The search results page is grouped by website source.

Mayo Clinic

www.mayoclinic.com

The Mayo Clinic website is full of excellent information for consumers, including searchable databases of diseases, symptoms, and healthy living tips. It is sponsored by the Mayo Foundation for Medical Education and Research.

National Institutes of Health

www.nih.gov

The U.S. Department of Health and Human Services' National Institutes of Health website is a portal to news, research, health information and available resources, and much more. Provides browsable categories and health topics.

Healthfinder

www.healthfinder.gov

Sponsored by the U.S. Department of Health and Human Services, this website offers reliable, searchable information on diseases, conditions, and injuries and an excellent database on prescription and over-the-counter drugs.

WebMD

www.webmd.com

A brightly designed, searchable, user-friendly website with an excellent system of hyperlinks between documents. The slogan for WebMD is "Better Information. Better Health." Articles are written for the general reader and the medical literature reference sources are provided for each article.

HISTORY

The World Wide Web is a wonderland for history buffs. You can search for anything about anybody in any period—and probably find it. Not only are there millions of web pages detailing the history of specific times, places, and people, there are also websites on which you can see the history in primary source documents. My choices of the best starting points are listed here.

Chronology of U.S. Historical Documents

www.law.ou.edu/hist

Texts of historical documents (most organized by twenty-five-year increments) beginning with a letter of Columbus to the king and queen of Spain in the 1490s and continuing to the present. Compiled by the University of Oklahoma.

EyeWitness to History

www.eyewitnesstohistory.com

Described as "history through the eyes of those who lived it," this site offers first-person accounts of historical events categorized by period. A fun portal for history researchers of any age.

EuroDocs

http://eudocs.lib.byu.edu/index.php/Main_Page

Created by Richard Hacken at Brigham Young University, this list of links connects to Western European primary source documents, organized by country and region.

LAW

One online resource stands out above all others for information on U.S. law and legal matters (there used to be a couple other good ones but they've been subsumed into the website listed here). If you don't find what you're looking for in this source, try searching the government resources listed above. You might also be able to access the LexisNexis database mentioned on page 146 if your library has a subscription for patrons' use.

FindLaw

www.findlaw.com

A robust subject directory for legal information and a comprehensive set of legal resources on the internet. FindLaw.com is searchable and browsable by categories.

POLITICS

Online sources for political news and analysis are found all over the web. The two websites listed here contain broader-based information than the average site.

CountryWatch

www.countrywatch.com

Well-regarded website providing demographic, political, economic, business, cultural, and environmental information on each of the recognized countries of the world. The CountryWire provides daily news coverage for every country in the world and a significant news archive. Unfortunately it is accessible only by paid subscription. Check to see whether your library or business organization has a subscription. If you often write about the global scene, you might want to purchase an annual individual subscription.

Political Database of the Americas

http://pdba.georgetown.edu

Political database for North, Central, and South America and the Caribbean, providing reference materials, primary documents, and statistical data. Sorted by category and also searchable by keyword or by country/region. A collaborative effort by the Center for Latin American Studies at Georgetown University and the Secretariat for Political Affairs of the Organization of American States.

NEWS SOURCES

Sources for online news are common. I've limited the list below to directories or portals that allow easy access to online news media and online newspapers all over the world, as well as websites for individual news sites that I prefer. A comprehensive list of newspaper websites is not included here, because it's more efficient for you to click on a hyperlink in one of the subject directories below.

As you research the Web more frequently, you probably will want to add a list of online sources to your bookmarks or favorites that you check every day for news and updates. If you want to advance a little further technologically, it's easy to add RSS or XML feeds directly from news sources to the home page of your browser, which will automatically deliver continuous news updates to your computer. Most browsers now support RSS and XML feeds and include the feed readers as part of their service. See chapter eight for detailed information on researching current events and using this technology.

Kidon Media-Link

www.kidon.com/media-link

This website in the Netherlands contains links to 18,340 newspapers and other news sources from every country and territory in the world. Every country (arranged by continent) has its own integrated page of links to newspapers, magazines, television, radio, and news agencies. The United States is subdivided into individual states—even my hometown *Poughkeepsie Journal* has a hyperlink.

NewsLink

www.newslink.org

Well-organized directory website with 9,000 national and international newspaper, magazine, radio, television, and news service links, including a section of major U.S. city blogs.

BBC

www.bbc.co.uk

The British Broadcasting Corporation's home page, available online in either the international version or the United Kingdom version. It's got plenty of links to news in thirty-three languages, it's searchable and browsable, and you can access BBC radio and television, too.

CNN

www.cnn.com

The Cable News Network online provides a rich source of up-to-the-minute news and features, both searchable and browsable. Writers, check out the Offbeat News section for story ideas.

MSNBC

www.msnbc.msn.com

Major cable television news network MSNBC, online with popular broadcast show material, breaking news, entertainment, and much more.

National Public Radio

www.npr.org

Feature stories, news, interviews, archives of past programming, and all the things that make National Public Radio so many people's choice of radio listening, available online.

Reuters

www.reuters.com

The world's largest international multimedia news agency is a global information source with strengths in financial, technological, business, corporate, and entertainment news. There's also a tempting link to Reuters Oddly Enough news, which reports on news of the most unlikely occurrences around the world, both humorous and horrible—the stories are a great source of inspiration for writers. The Reuters Oddly Enough news is also available through the Yahoo! News web page.

RELIGION AND SPIRITUALITY

A large number of websites fall into the category of Religion and Spirituality, ranging from the personal prayer blogs of a faith-based youth group to broad historical surveys of the world's religions. Nearly every major religion has an official website. Religious and sacred texts are also easily available to research online in websites both large and small. I've listed several web resource directories that will lead you to hundreds more.

Virtual Religion Index

www.virtualreligion.net/vri/

Searchable and browsable directory site analyzing and highlighting important content on religion-related websites. Editor Mahlon H. Smith provides links to materials on most of the world's religions, in many obscure websites that might go otherwise unnoticed. Formerly hosted at Rutgers University.

Academic Info: Religion Gateway

www.academicinfo.net/religindex.html

Rich collection of links to world religions, religious studies, and comparative religions. Primary and secondary sources; excellent annotations of links.

Internet Sacred Text Archive

www.sacred-texts.com/index.htm

Largest freely available archive of full-text books about religion, mythology, folklore, and the esoteric on the internet. Constantly adding new works, many translated into English.

Beliefnet

www.beliefnet.com

The largest spiritual website, unaffiliated with any religion but full of great information on all the world's major religions and belief systems. Contemporary, with content from spiritual teachers and leaders, book reviews, groups, and so forth.

Interfaith Calendar

www.interfaithcalendar.org

Calendar of "primary sacred times" for major and minor world religions for the current year and several years into the future. Includes a glossary of religious holidays.

SCIENCES

If you want to research in-depth information on the sciences, the World Wide Web has riches beyond imagining. Listed here are several respected web sources to start you in the right direction. If you are only looking for general overviews of science and technology, an online encyclopedia or reference source might be your best choice.

Biology Links
http://golgi.harvard.edu/BioLinks.html
Harvard University's Department of Molecular and Cellular Biology offers a page of biology links to resources within the biosciences, including genetics, immunology, evolution, biochemistry, molecular biology, and zoology.

ChemDex
www.chemdex.org
Based at the Department of Chemistry at the University of Sheffield, England, this subject directory of over 7,000 links has been a web resource since 1993. You can drill down through thirteen top-level categories.

Mathematics WWW Virtual Library
www.math.fsu.edu/Virtual/
Comprehensive collection of mathematics-related sources, from the department of mathematics at Florida State University. Part of the World Wide Web Virtual Library system.

Echo: Exploring and Collecting History Online: Science, Technology, and Industry
www.echo.gmu.edu/index.php
Sponsored by the Center for History and New Media at George Mason University, this site presents the recent history in science,

technology, and industry with impressive thoroughness. Searchable and browsable collection of resources, including links to online collections, bibliographies, organizations, and journals.

The Net Advance of Physics
http:// web.mit.edu/redingtn/www/netadv/
Directory to the field of physics on the Web, browsable by subject or alphabetically, with a special page of links on the history of physics. Maintained by the Massachusetts Institute of Technology.

STATISTICS

Sometimes you just need to know the stats. The websites listed here are excellent resources and can lead you far beyond the world of number-crunching.

Statistical Resources on the Web
www.lib.umich.edu/govdocs/stcomp.html
The University of Michigan Library's Documents Center provides this extremely comprehensive directory of links to online statistical resources, mostly in the social sciences. Global coverage, links to major institutional and government databases and archives, plus much more.

Statistical Abstract of the United States
www.census.gov/compendia/statab/brief.html
The U.S. Census Bureau's Statistical Abstract, published since 1878, is also called the National Data Book. Provides most recent statistics on the social, political, and economic organization of the United States, browsable by subject. Data is available in Microsoft Excel spreadsheets.

FedStats

www.fedstats.gov

A gateway to statistics from more than a hundred U.S. federal agencies, in subject directory format. Browsable and searchable, it even has a section with links to government web pages for kids.

Don't fret if your topic of research interest is not listed here. Conducting a search on any of the search engines will quickly give you relevant subject directories, portals, university department websites, online reference sites, and individual web pages, so you can begin reviewing them for content and quality of information.

RESEARCHING PRIMARY SOURCES

The techniques used to find text documents and digital images are covered elsewhere in this book, so we won't repeat them here. Instead we'll briefly look at how to find specialized historical documents, such as maps, diaries, and other primary source material.

The general term that we can use to describe historical documents such as journals, letters, diaries, lists, drawings, and publications is "primary sources." Any books or articles written about these materials would be called "secondary sources." Depending on the needs of your project, you might want to look only at primary sources or draw on a combination of both.

Entering "primary sources" in a Google basic search brings up a list of results that combines major research institutions with sites helpful for classroom teachers. One great resource is the Primary Sources on the Web collection at www.eduplace

.com/ss/hmss/primary.html, which offers a wonderful directory listing of primary source collections suitable for classroom use, both for U.S. history and world history.

A more specific search for a primary source also can net useful results. You can use an advanced search to specify "letters" or "diary" or "journal," for instance, and add either a time period or a name to the query. Even a basic search for the keywords "letters Abigail Adams" brings up many results, because she and her husband John Adams exchanged correspondence for nearly forty years, much of which was preserved and published. If you visit the website www.masshist.org/digitaladams/aea/letter/ you can access over 1,100 letters. Not only is the text of each letter transcribed for easy reading, but an image of the original handwritten document appears as well. When doing primary research, it's always exciting to see the real thing.

Similar collections can be found for other historical figures. The journals of the Lewis and Clark expedition, for instance, are available online accompanied by images, maps, and other resources at http://lewisandclarkjournals.unl.edu. This primary source is easily located by entering "journals of lewis and clark" as a basic keyword search on any major search engine.

If you want to find the diaries, journals, and letters left for posterity by the ordinary people of the world, you may have a bit more difficulty. Funding for online documentary projects influences what collections are available. However, searching for "historical diaries" brings up a creditable list of internet-accessible materials you can poke around in until you find something fascinating.

Mastering Online Research

HISTORICAL MAPS

Most major search engines have a specific "Maps" search available on the main search page. Those searches are great for contemporary maps and driving directions, but what happens if you want to find a map of Boston in 1812? Entering "Boston 1812" in the search box brings up a modern map and a list of all the businesses in the area whose telephone numbers end in 1812.

Even an advanced search isn't conducive to finding historical maps of a specific place and time. A basic keyword search on Yahoo! for "historical map" returns much more relevant results of collections and archives of maps. Notice that the singular "map" is preferable for a search like this, because many collections use that form of the word in their titles. Searching for only the plural form reduces your results by half. "Map" will add "maps," but not vice versa, in all search engines.

My preference in searching for maps of specific places and time periods is to use the browsable links on one of the major subject directory websites described in chapter five. For example, switching to the Yahoo! Directory Search page to look for historical maps provides a browsable list that is easy to review for relevance. You can access the "Directory" page by clicking on "More" on the main Yahoo! search page, until you see the link to Directory appear at the right. Click on that link, and the Yahoo! "Directory" categories will be displayed. Select the hyperlink for "Arts" and then click on the "Humanities" category in the "Top Categories" list. Select "History," then select "Maps." (It takes much longer to describe this process than to do it.)

The results list will give you about forty hyperlinked collections of maps from all over the world and from many time periods, an indescribably rich resource. Many of them are primary source documents. Use the technique of drilling down through relevant online collections until you find the exact maps that you need.

Take a close look at a handful of what you can find with this simple directory search.

David Rumsey Map Collection

www.davidrumsey.com

Focuses on eighteenth- and nineteenth-century North and South American cartographic materials. Includes maps, atlases, globes, school geographies, and maritime charts.

Historical Atlas of Europe

www.euratlas.com

Online historical atlas showing the states of Europe and the Mediterranean basin at the end of each century from A.D. 1 to A.D. 2000. In English and French.

Panoramic Maps 1847–1929

http://memory.loc.gov/ammem/pmhtml/panhome.html

Non-photographic representations of cities portrayed as if viewed from above at an oblique angle from the late nineteenth and early twentieth centuries.

Historical Maps of Africa

www.lib.utexas.edu/maps/historical/history_africa.html

Includes maps of pre-colonial Africa as well as individual colonies and expedition maps.

Historic Cities
http://historic-cities.huji.ac.il

Maps, literature, documents, books, and other materials concerning historic cities around the world.

Once you enter the world of primary source research, you may not want to leave it. Whether you're reading the original diary of a Civil War soldier online or holding a pair of Sitting Bull's beaded moccasins in your hand at a library archive, the thrill of reaching back into history is indescribable. And addictive.

CHAPTER 7

SEARCHING FOR PEOPLE AND PLACES

The World Wide Web connects people all over the globe. Billions of web pages, databases, government documents, public records, search firms, and even blogs contain personal information in accessible form—whether you like it or not. All the major search engines and portals offer search capabilities for finding people on the internet. Everyone has heard the stories of high school sweethearts reunited, some happy, some not; but you can also use these searches to hunt for your heroes and role models, experts you might like to interview, possible team members for projects, and so on. You can also hunt for yourself, if you're prepared to see the results.

In this chapter, we'll discuss how to use the resources of the Web for reliable, legally obtainable information about real people, and look at the best ways to find experts and authorities on various subjects. We'll explore techniques for researching places online that will make you feel as if you've

Mastering Online Research

been there. And we'll look at the technology on the Web that is most revealing of people—blogs and file-sharing networks.

SEARCHING FOR PEOPLE

If you have conducted many of the activities of modern life—bought a house, installed a telephone line, bought or sold stuff on the internet, exhibited work in art galleries or craft shows, written a book or article, committed a crime, performed or spoken publicly, or subscribed to a magazine, to list a few—your name, and possibly your address, phone number, and e-mail, are posted on the Web. Therefore, the first place to start your search for a person is usually by entering his or her name in a basic keyword search in a major search engine.

Most of the search engines have a People Search or People Finder on their main home page. In Yahoo! you can search for someone's telephone and e-mail address on the "People Search" page, which is found by clicking on the "More" link above the search box on the Yahoo! home page and then selecting "All Search Services."

On the main Google search page, you can search for telephone numbers as well as for personal names. To find a residential phone number for an individual, enter "rphonebook:" followed by the name and city/town ("rphonebook: arthur smith Detroit"). To find a business phone number, enter "bphonebook:" followed by the business name and location. You also can search for reverse listings of phone numbers that will give you the name of the person to whom the number is registered. This can be useful if you have a

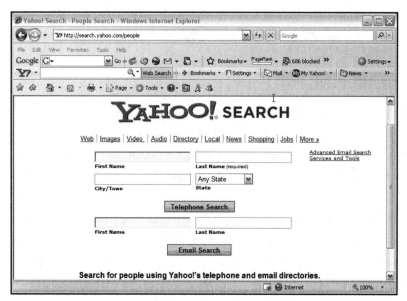

Yahoo! People Search page

phone number but no name or location (say, from a telephone bill or a caller ID system on your telephone—or a mysterious scrap of paper). Enter "phonebook:" in the search box, followed by the telephone number beginning with the area code, without spaces or punctuation (phonebook:8025551234). The results will give you the name and location of the residence or business.

You may find different information by searching on multiple sites—an e-mail from one source, a street address from another. Most web search sites are ethical and draw their information from public access databases, such as telephone directories, property records, court records, and the like. More in-depth results may be found by using the pay-for-search websites, which we'll examine later in this chapter.

Mastering Online Research

You might find a basic Yahoo! or Google keyword search for a person's name to be just as effective as a phone or e-mail search. Smart search engines have made it a little easier to search for names by including common variants of many first names in the results list: if you enter "Joe" in a search box, often the results will include "Joseph" automatically. ("Pat" also brings up "Patricia" but, curiously, not "Patrick.") As with other keyword searches, be sure to search for variant spellings of both first names and last names. You might want to try searching for nicknames, too.

The websites listed are free to use. Some are more effective than others—and some people are easier to find than others.

Yahoo! People Search

www.people.yahoo.com

An easy search page to find individuals by name. You can request a free search for address and phone number, e-mail address, and reverse search of a phone number to determine who is at the receiving end. (You can also search for unlisted phone numbers and cell phone numbers by using one of the paid services advertising on this page.)

Lycos People Search

www.lycos.com

Lycos is a portal search engine with an emphasis on commercial sites (for example, shopping and entertainment), so it's no surprise that its "People Search" links to a results page requiring you to pay a fee to access the information. However, you can use it to find out the city or town of residence for the person you're seeking—and even several past addresses, if they're accessible on the internet. Using that information you can then search in the specific city where the person lives, or track his or her history backwards.

Google Directory

www.google.com/Top/Reference/Directories/Address_and_ Phone_Numbers

Subject directory that provides a complete hyperlinked list of other search sites to look for people, such as residential and business listings, consumer guides, and city pages.

AnyWho

www.anywho.com

Sponsored by AT&T; provides searching through public information White Pages and Yellow Pages for published phone numbers only. Data is updated every three months.

Military.com Buddy Finder

www.military.com

From the home page you can search over 20 million records of military personnel, by selecting "Buddy Finder." The records have been compiled from the Department of Defense records and from the membership of Military.com, an organization connecting military personnel and families in all branches of service. In order to access more than the person's name and service, you'll need to register for a free membership.

ZabaSearch

www.zabasearch.com

Search by name, age, and location in any or all of the United States. The free search results also link to YouTube.com, if you want to find posted images of the person. For more detailed information, there are premium services that require a fee.

ZoomInfo

www.zoominfo.com

A great site that searches public information and presents summary results ranked by the number of references to the person found on the internet. You can register for free and update your own profile, if you like. ZoomInfo can also be used to search for businesses, and it serves as an employer resource as well.

SPECIALTY SEARCHES

Find a Grave

www.findagrave.com

If you're interested in locating someone's grave, famous or not, try here. The data is searchable by name, date of birth, date of death, yearly necrologies (all notable people who died in a particular year, going back to 1900), and other categories. You can add submissions to the website, too, if you register for a free membership. Presently there are about 13 million grave records in the database, and the site is updated continuously for new residents. The updates for famous people are done by the website's staff, and other records can be added by interested members. This site draws more than 25,000 visitors a day.

Dead or Alive

www.deadoraliveinfo.com

Not all the people listed on this site are dead. If you're looking for a famous person and can't recall whether he is dead or alive, this will give you the answer. It's also useful for birth and death dates of famous individuals, causes of death, most recent deaths, and other categories that are searchable. Links to Wikipedia articles are provided when available.

Chamber of Commerce Locator
www.chamberofcommerce.com
City and regional chambers of commerce can be an excellent resource for searching for people and businesses. This website has a searchable database of chambers, with the names of the directors and all contact information. You can request information on a city or town by e-mailing or phoning the chamber office, and if you are searching for a particular individual, you might find a helpful local person who can give you some information or directions to pursue.

PAID-SEARCH WEBSITES

Information is a commodity that can be bought and sold. When you are searching for a person on the Web, you will immediately be presented with numerous paid search services clamoring for your business: Many are legitimate, but some are scams—the sites that take your money and then deliver only the most basic results that you could find yourself in five minutes of searching.

Before you pay a fee for research, check to see if the site has sample results for each level of search—for instance, criminal records checks, employment histories, education verification—and whether the depth of information will be sufficiently helpful to you. You can also search on Google or Yahoo! for the search company's name and add the keyword "complaints" to your search string. That will bring up any disgruntled customers who have posted complaints on the Web. Some complaints are caused by unrealistic customer expectations—for instance, there is no complete national crime database that can be searched by one of these services. Reports from law enforcement vary from state to state in availability, and they don't always share.

The websites listed here are reputable, to the best of my knowledge. I've used some of them and have been satisfied with the results. Many folks use these services to find an out-of-touch friend, a former classmate, a deadbeat ex, or a missing family member. The sites are also helpful in adoption searches. Professionals such as reporters, writers, human resource staff, and employers also consider the modest fees worth the information returned on a background search. The ability to check criminal records is useful, too.

There are also websites accessible only to bonafide, licensed investigators who can prove that they legally are permitted access to the information in the course of their professional work. Privacy laws are in place for every citizen's protection, and some websites have increased their security since the 9/11 terrorist attacks. Don't try to fake a private investigator license number for access. It only works in the movies.

Intelius

www.intelius.com

A very professional website whose search results are helpful even if you don't pay the fees for detailed searches. Searching by name, you can retrieve information on the person's past and present locations and possible related people, with their ages included. That might be enough information to narrow your search; if it isn't, Intelius offers levels of fees depending on how much research you need and the length of time you want to use the service.

PeopleFinders
www.peoplefinders.com
One of the most popular search services. It's easy to use and you can choose your level of access by paying for a twenty-four-hour period, a one-time search, or a thirty-day membership. The fees are reasonable, and the sample search results are informative about what you can expect to find.

USA People Search
www.usa-people-search.com
The site provides background checks, criminal records, property checks, marriage records, and much more. The databases can be searched for free to determine whether the person you're looking for is available there; you can then pay a fee for detailed reports, if you like. The sample search I conducted turned up multiple names and addresses over the past twenty years for the person, and all the information was accurate.

SEARCHING PUBLIC RECORDS

Public records are another source for locating information on individuals and businesses. Some of the websites described previously search public records to provide the data they deliver, but it's also possible to search public information available online yourself.

The U.S. government has an enormous collection of public information, of course. However, much of the data is not made available online, and certain restrictions apply to accessing information. For example, even though you may file your income tax return online, no other person has the right to access it because it is not considered a public document. Recent concerns with privacy have limited the information government agencies post, such as motor vehicle records and other personal data.

Under the Freedom of Information Act (FOIA), U.S. citizens have the right to request access, in writing, to public materials not covered by certain exclusions and exemptions. The FOIA regulations apply only to federal documents; state and local government agencies have their own applicable public access laws. You can find information on how to request information under FOIA and hyperlinks to various agencies on the Department of Justice website (www.usdoj. gov/oip/index.html).

Access to public records and information online has become more restricted in the past few years because the internet has become a source of information that can be used in harmful ways by predators, terrorists, and other criminal elements. As a researcher, you also have the option of going offline to follow up on records and documents not available on the Web. State archives, county courthouses, municipal licensing bureaus, and the like are usually open to the public. Searching first on the Web will allow you to be more efficient in using your resources.

The following websites combine free searches with fee-based ones. Your skills at drilling down through the online hyperlinks will help you to get the most information for the least investment. Searching on several sites may offer bits of information that you can piece together into a whole.

BRB's Free Resource Center

www.brbpub.com

BRB Publications is the parent company of Facts on Demand Press and operates a website for legal and investigative professionals. However, a section of the site offers an excellent free resource center with a comprehensive and searchable list of free public record sites along with additional tools to locate sources for civil records, criminal records, driving records, real estate records, public record vendors, record retrievers, legislation, and more.

USAGov

www.usa.gov

The U.S. Government's official web portal is a good resource for public records. Search for organizations, agencies, state and local governments, and online services.

Pretrieve

www.pretrieve.com

This free search engine specifically searches only public records. You can enter a name and a location for a person or a business, and the resulting page will permit you to search on property, criminal, financial, professional, and local information for that person or business. It provides a street address and phone number as well. Within each category you can search for specifics on databases such as state-wide sex offender registries, donations to political campaigns, state and federal prison inmates, patent records, aviation licenses, and much more.

Vitalrec.com

www.vitalrec.com

Perhaps the most comprehensive site on the internet for locating U.S. vital records information, this website allows you to search by state or territory. You can search the Social Security Death Index, and you can order vital records such as birth certificates, death records, marriage licenses, and divorce decrees, available for a fee.

SearchSystems

www.searchsystems.net

Public records directory contains over 38,000 individual databases and offers both basic and advanced search capabilities. Its scope is international. The recommendations on its website are impressive. Browse to get an idea of the resources it offers, but in order to use it you must register and pay a small monthly or yearly fee.

FINDING EXPERTS

When I worked as an acquisitions editor for a book publisher, I searched for people teaching and writing about the topics on which I wanted to publish new books. Coming up with book ideas and locating the perfect authors to write them was challenging but enjoyable, and it was satisfying when the pairing worked out. Although you may not be looking for other people to write books, you might be on a committee to arrange programs and speakers for an organization, for instance. Or you might have one fact in your research you haven't been able to verify. An author who has written a book on that subject might know the answer and be willing to help you out in a quick e-mail or phone call. (Make sure your question is succinct—you wouldn't want to impose on her time for more than a few minutes.)

The world has become a smaller place since the evolution of the World Wide Web. With a few thoughtful search queries you can find an expert in a particular field and usually a way to contact the individual by e-mail or by phone. How do you locate these experts? By searching online for who is teaching, writing, and giving workshops or speaking on what topics.

If you know which individual expert you wish to contact, you can simply conduct a basic name or keyword search on Yahoo! or Google or any other search engine. Often that is sufficient. But if you don't know who the experts are, how can you search for them by name? Searching college and university websites can be a successful way to identify and contact experts; people with acknowledged expertise in their field can also be found through general searches for the topic on the internet. And the websites for national and international speakers bureaus are great starting points for identifying experts within particular categories.

When I start to look for an expert or an authority in any field, I begin by searching on Amazon.com to see what books have been published in that field within the past dozen or so years. If you go back much further in publication dates, you're liable to find experts who have retired or died or moved on to other topics of interest to them but not to you. On the other hand, you could ignore that time constraint and find splendid individuals who are still working avidly in their fields at advanced ages—every rule has exceptions.

The Amazon.com page for each book offers information on when the book was published and by whom, as well as editorial reviews, reader star ratings, and reader comments that I scrutinize carefully. Often the author's hometown or employer will be mentioned (in the reviews, or in the author biography that appears in either the book description or on the back cover using the "Look Inside this book" feature)— helpful contact information if I select that author as my expert. After I've identified three or four people writing well-reviewed books in the category I'm researching, I then run a basic search on Google or Yahoo! to see what else they have been doing. Online biographies and more contact information are often available at their academic institutions or companies. If the experts are in academia, I can search the university or college website for their course offerings and look at the course descriptions and reading lists. For experts or consultants outside of academia, I can search for names and then for the firms or organizations for which they work, or for hosts of the seminars and workshops they present. These techniques allow me to get to know an expert very well before ever contacting him or her.

Another good way to find experts is to visit the websites of a few speakers bureaus—organizations that arrange speaking engagements for high-profile clients. All the websites listed here are similar. You can scroll through an alphabetical list of their clients and read their biographies online, and search for speakers by category, even by cost. Unless you're actually hiring a speaker, though, you won't be able to access contact information. That's where you go back to the people searches described earlier in this chapter. At the least you'll have a wish list of experts to sift through.

- www.leadingauthorities.com/
- www.allamericanspeakers.com/
- www.nationwidespeakers.com/
- www.internationalspeakers.com/

In addition to speakers bureaus, there are websites that specialize in connecting experts with people who are interested in contacting them for seminars, interviews, media opportunities, and so on. Most require membership for users, usually at no cost. Websites such as Experts.com and Profnet.com allow users to search for experts in various predetermined categories; this may be a speedier way to find experts than to do the research and analysis of qualifications yourself. However, I would not rely solely on these types of websites where experts self-select themselves and pay a fee to register in their fields of expertise. Many of the websites that result from a Google search for "find expert" are used primarily for locating expert witnesses to testify in legal matters, such as ExpertPages.com; some of these companies verify the experts' credentials or else note that they have not done so.

SEARCHING BLOGS

You might want to visit the blogs (short for web logs) to get a taste of what occupies the thinking of actual people in any demographic group. Bloggers, online open forums, and discussion groups post to the Web on just about every subject in the world.

Mastering Online Research

Just a word of caution here—the legal protections of privacy and copyright and against libel and defamation apply to the World Wide Web and the blogosphere as well as to real life. You can't reproduce large sections of someone's blog because it's a personal journal automatically covered by copyright law. Use good sense when drawing verbal pictures from real life. And if you're writing about a living, breathing person, double that advice.

Blogging has been around in one form or another for years, but it was in 1999 that blogging really exploded as a popular form of communication unique to the internet. Since then blogging in all its forms (online journals, diaries, commentary, photographs, videos, music, and more) has created a network of "social media" that is enormous in scope. According to the Wikipedia.org article on "blogs," at the end of 2006 more than 60 million blogs were being tracked by the blog search engine Technorati.com. That's a lot of opinions and observations being expressed out there. Blogs are also used commercially to influence consumer and political opinion, and they are used by groups and individuals to promote agendas of all kinds.

The Google Blogger is a free service that allows anyone to quickly and easily create a blog, name it, and post thoughts, photos, and messages online. There are a number of other websites that specialize in hosting blogs. A popular early blogging website, Blogger.com, was acquired by Google in 2002, which means that you can search for blogs posted on that site going back to January 2000. The Google Blog Search can be accessed from the main Google search page by clicking on the "More" and "Even More" search selections above the search entry box. It can also be accessed from the Blogger.com home page, which at the time of this writing still has retained its web presence. The Blogger.com features are the foundation of the Google search, so searches done on either site will return similar results. Only the graphic displays are slightly different.

Let's see what kinds of information you can find by conducting a search on Google Blog Search. If you wanted to research what young Asian American people are saying about the culture in which they were raised, for example, reading the thoughts expressed in their own words in blog posts might be very helpful.

If you run a simple keyword search from the main search page on "Asian American culture," you'll get over 45,000 results, sorted by relevance. "Relevance," as judged by the Google algorithm, is more important in a blog search than in other kinds of searches. Remember, the default uses the Boolean logical operator AND, which looks for all three keywords in no particular order. If you sort the results by the date posted, the results could devolve into bloggers writing about a visit to an **Asian** restaurant that served **American** style cuisine and ignored the owners' **culture** altogether. The above sentence contains all three search terms but not in a way relevant to your query.

At the top of the Google Blog Search results page are suggestions for the top blogs (thematic collections, not individual posts) matching your keyword search. In this search the related blogs were "About Race Relations" and "MANJA: News about Asian American Arts, Artists, and Culture," both potentially worth exploring.

On the left side of the results page are links that allow you to select from blog entries posted anywhere from within the last hour to within the past month. You can also fill in specific dates in a search box. If you'll be researching this particular topic for a while, you might want to subscribe to the Blog Alerts, which will notify you when blogs meeting your search criteria are posted. You can also set up RSS feeds to receive blog content automatically. (Chapter eight explains how to do this.)

The customary Google advanced search options are also available from the blog results screen, although in this case they may prove too limiting. For example, running an advanced search on the exact phrase "Asian American culture" doesn't give you any more refined results; rather, it makes the search term too narrow, and only a couple hundred blog posts are returned. When people are writing spontaneously, as they do in many blogs, they tend to use a looser, more colloquial style and quite a bit of jargon. The sentence "I grew up in SF in an **Asian** neighborhood where my parents wanted me to do well in the **American** world but still expected me to do the traditional stuff from their **culture**" would not be found in the "exact phrase" search, although it would in the "all of these words" search.

You can go to the advanced search page to specify the usual Boolean operators for search strings, the number of results per page, the language in which the posts are written, and the date range of the search. Specific to the blog search feature, you can enter words to search for in the blog title, a particular URL to search within, and an author name to find blogs and posts written by a certain person. Many bloggers use screen names to protect their identity; others use their own names. Once you've found a blogger with valuable information to impart, you can search for blogs posted by that screen name. If you search for any blog author, be sure to click on the "more results from" link below each search result.

As you become acclimated to the blogging world (a.k.a. the blogosphere), you might want to branch out in your online searching to other blogging sites. Try these:

Feedster
www.feedster.com
An established blogging site that offers content channels of many types, including one called Life Experiences "from people around the world to give you a glimpse inside their lives."

Technorati
www.technorati.com
Another well-known site that provides up-to-the-minute blogs about news, music, internet videos, and popular culture, as well as the top tags (topics) bloggers are posting on.

SearchEngineWatch.com
http://serachenginewatch.com
If you really get into blogging, check out this site for news on advances in searching blogs and RSS feeds.

RESEARCHING PLACES

The internet contains scads of information on the inhabited and uninhabited areas of our planet. You can search for the tiniest spot in the least populated area of a small country and you'll probably find a web link or two. You can tour big cities, college campuses, historic sites, national parks, and real estate for sale or rent—sometimes using 360-degree visual tours to give you a real sense of being there. You can fly through the streets and all over the world using Google Earth and aerial photos to map your way. You can find online images of small town fairs and big city nightlife. You can check out the typical weather and research unusual weather events. And you can find statistics on area, population, government, major industry, education, and so on for most places in the world. The online research skills that you've already mastered in the earlier chapters can be put to good use in searching the reference websites listed in chapter six. Other tips for researching places will be described in the following pages, using a specific example of one American city that is interesting for both its historical past and its modern development. Bear in mind that nearly all of these techniques can be applied to any place, anywhere—and you can easily do your own research by following a strategy similar to the one described here.

There are many different aspects to places—the physical layout, attractions, demographics, events, even the cultural feel. The purpose of searching for details of locales is to make you feel as if you've actually visited the place. That's important whether you're writing an article or novel or looking for real estate to buy. There are many ways to approach this kind of research, and I'll share here the ones that I use. As you do your own searches, you might come up with different methods, too.

MAPS AS RESEARCH

You're probably familiar with using the maps on Mapquest .com, Yahoo! Travel, Google Maps, Ask.com, and other search engines. Many of the sites allow you to search specifically for maps by category, similar to image searches. Researching a locale requires more creative searching than looking for driving directions, and the depth of information you want to find will determine how intense your map search is. Maps contain much more information than you might expect. You can find maps of modern cities anywhere in the world that show the major traffic patterns, bus routes, cultural attractions, even areas of highest crime or major ethnic populations. You can find detailed geological survey maps that clue you in to the terrain of a specific area. You can track the development of a particular place by comparing historical maps created in different time periods.

San Antonio, Texas—home of the Alamo and the world-famous Riverwalk dining and entertainment area—is a great place to visit. I selected it for our "model city" because it has so many historical and contemporary materials available on the Web. If you want useful, accurate details of any city, where do you start? How about with a few good maps?

A basic Google search for "maps" turns up the Perry-Castañeda map collection at the University of Texas (an excellent resource for maps of all kinds). The website www.lib.utexas .edu/maps is a directory that is searchable and browsable by region, country, city, special topics, and other categories. The home page directory lists maps of current interest, such as worldwide avian influenza maps and the Alaska Iditarod route map. There are also online maps of general interest from areas around the world, and topical maps such as tsunami maps, oil and gas maps, and September 11, 2001, maps. If you click on the links, the search results are not restricted to the maps in the Perry-Castañeda collection but link to outside web resources as well.

The directory allows you to search for maps in any of the states' online map collections, both historical and current, and in metropolitan areas and by several census categories such as race. You can search historical maps of the world, atlases, and narrow topic maps such as the distribution of the principal European languages in 1911.

Clicking on the directory link for the state of Texas (a distinct category of Perry-Castañeda maps) and then on cities beginning with "S" brings you to this list of hyperlinks for San Antonio:

- **San Antonio** (from Google Maps)
- **San Antonio** (from Lonely Planet)
- **San Antonio** (from Yahoo Travel)
- **San Antonio - Clickable Map** (from Johnnyroadtrip.com)
- **San Antonio (aeronautical)** 1:500,000 D.M.A. 1989 (174k) Not for navigational use (from University of Texas Map Collection)
- **San Antonio - Bus Route Map - Interactive** (from VIA)
- **San Antonio - Crime Maps** (from San Antonio Police Department)
- **San Antonio - Freeway Maps** (from Texas HighwayMan)
- **San Antonio - GIS Mapping Application** (from City of San Antonio)

- **San Antonio (planimetric)** 1:100,000 U.S.G.S. 1985 (888k) (from University of Texas Map Collection)
- **San Antonio - Tourist Sites** (from Texas Outside)
- **San Antonio - Superfund Sites Map** (from TNRCC)
- **San Antonio - Traffic Map** (from TransGuide)

The first several maps are linked from popular searchable websites—you can search those sites directly for any city or place that you wish. The specific maps from San Antonio and Texas sources are brought together here for you. Other states have similar resources in this online directory.

From the San Antonio Police Department Crime Maps you can access a list of the crimes committed in the city with a searchable database for crime statistics and interactive map locations. (So now you know where *not* to go.) From this page you can also drill down to the SAPD home page, which offers a menu of police department organizational information, community and volunteer policing guidelines, victim assistance, databases, and searchable files of old homicide cases, both solved and unsolved. Whether you're researching for a relocation or a crime novel, the police department site might give you a different perspective on the place than, say, the Chamber of Commerce or Tourism websites. Most U.S. cities and towns large enough to maintain a police department will have similar resources on their websites. You can find them by searching for keywords "police department [city name]."

You can click on the other hyperlinks in the list for San Antonio and find a variety of detailed maps of the downtown area, the city, the traffic flow (updated every five minutes), the locations of bars and restaurants, the tourist sites, the bus

Mastering Online Research

routes—even the Superfund toxic waste cleanup sites. You can download GIS (geographic information system) mapping software if you truly want to explore the terrain. The map collection contains links to similar maps in other locations.

You can also "fly" to San Antonio (or anywhere else) through the new broadband 3-D feature at Google Earth. Presently still in beta stage, the service will allow you to select locations anywhere in the world and see them from an aerial view. Using the trial version to go to the Alamo in San Antonio feels like flying in a helicopter over the city. It's breathtaking, and it gives you an up-close view of whatever location you're researching. The service will improve even further as it completes beta testing. Check it out on Google.com—registration is easy and free.

Other good sources for maps of cities, regions, countries, and specialized areas are subject directories like those discussed in chapter five and basic searches plus a location keyword on large search engines. There are websites that are aggregators of map searches as well. One of those is www.maps .langenberg.com. Similar to a metasearch engine for maps and census date, Langenberg.com allows you to search for maps by location on the large search engines but also to search by type (street, city, country, aerial, topographic, earthquake/fire/storm hazards, and U.S. geological survey maps). Links to the U.S. Census Bureau and the FedStats website make it a cinch to find statistics.

Not all maps are of contemporary areas, of course. Sometimes we need to know how a place looked in a different century. We'll explore those kinds of historical sources in chapter ten (see page 278).

TRAVEL SITES

If you're looking for information about a city for background, the websites sponsored by online travel booking agencies can be a good resource. But for a major city, a great place to start is the Yahoo! Travel page at http://travel.yahoo.com. This is basically a subject directory you can search by hyperlinks to more specific categories. The search page offers commercial ads and direct links to hotels, flights, and so on, but there's also a feature called "Destination and Hotel Guides," which has a drop-down menu where you can select a major city in the United States or elsewhere. You also can click on the hyperlinks displayed for a variety of cities. (Another hyperlinked section offers "Vacations by Interest," where you can find out the best places for a ski trip, a safari, and the like.)

To continue with the San Antonio example, clicking on the Yahoo! Travel link for San Antonio brings up maps, a slide/photo show, sample plans for trips of three to five days, guide to sites of local interest, and Yahoo! Answers, a browsable section of questions and answers about San Antonio—real questions with real answers, not a marketing ploy. User reviews also are a great resource for comments and photos about the city and its nightlife, festivals, and other attractions, with a hyperlink to the VirtualTourist.com site mentioned on page 194.

Don't forget to check out the travel guide publishers' websites, such as Fodor's (www.fodors.com) and Frommer's (www.frommers.com). You can search by destination and purchase a copy of the pertinent guide online if you wish.

VIRTUAL TOURS

Another research source only available online is the virtual tour, popular on tourist destinations and real estate websites. You can use them to plan a trip or to research locales in which you're interested. Let's continue to look at San Antonio, and find a virtual tour of the Riverwalk.

A basic Google search for "San Antonio riverwalk" brings up pages of relevant results. On the first page appears a result that offers a virtual tour "with QTVR scenes." Even if you don't know what QTVR means, you can guess that it might be a multimedia tour by the word "scenes." Clicking on the link brings you to a website called Virtual San Antonio, which welcomes you to take a riverboat ride in virtual format. That sounds like fun, especially because you can stop along the way to visit the virtual sites. The QTVR tour is in a downloadable browser plug-in called Apple Quick-Time and also requires JavaScript capability if you want to hear the music. The tour is also offered in a normal version that uses JPEG images. The information in the captions could be useful, too.

You can also search on Google or Yahoo! to find places that have virtual tours online. For instance, a keyword search for "virtual Chicago" and "virtual Boston" delivers excellent results for both cities, because both are technology centers as well as major U.S. cities. A search for "virtual Poughkeepsie," alas, is fruitless. "Virtual San Antonio," our example, brings up only the Riverwalk tour above and a related site hosted by heartofsanantonio.com, offering several more small virtual tours. Presumably other cities and towns will develop more of a virtual presence on the Web as time goes on.

Check out the website www.virtualtourist.com for insider views on travel destinations and a searchable database of photos that members have posted for anyone to view. You can specify among many topic categories and combine the search with a keyword and destination. Many of the photos posted are of family groups and friends posing at tourist attractions, but they still can be useful in bringing touches of authenticity to your research. You'll really feel as if you've been to the place.

OTHER SOURCES

The official website of the city of San Antonio (www.sananto nio.gov/) provides plenty of information about what it's like to live and work in the city. Most cities have such websites, and many also have tourist-oriented websites. You can find them with a Google or Yahoo! search. If nothing turns up for an official city or town website, try the Chamber of Commerce research source listed in chapter six.

If you're interested in a certain city or region, you might want to search the online encyclopedias and reference sources for a general overview of the locale (see chapter six). Encyclopedia articles are updated for populations and other statistical data on a schedule determined by the availability of new census reports—the text of the article on any particular city or location may lag behind somewhat. You can also check the Wikipedia.com article for the place you are researching—volunteers who have an interest in that place may have provided more current information (again, you might want to double-check any specific facts on Wikipedia with another source).

Expanding your research on people and places to encompass events delivered in real time is the topic of the next chapter.

CHAPTER 8
ACCESSING SPECIAL SEARCH AREAS

Beyond the capabilities of advanced searches, keyword searches, subject directories, and the general resources of the major search engines, the tenacious web researcher can access special areas of interest. In this chapter we will begin to open up the areas of researching current events online, accessing continuous feeds of updated information through RSS technology, mining information from user groups and online newsletters, searching specifically for scholarly materials, and finding information below the surface of the generally accessible Web. Because all of these search areas are more fluid and individually driven than standard web searches, we can only describe what's out there and how to begin to find it.

RESEARCHING CURRENT EVENTS

One of the most incredible advances made possible by the World Wide Web is the ability to access news of a current event anywhere in the world within seconds of its occurring. Journalists' reports are filed by satellite phone from precarious locations, audio and video images are transmitted directly from an event as it occurs, and breaking news stories can be followed from your internet browser at your desk or on your cellular phone or media player. Even Wikinews.org has a "breaking news" page on which volunteers report the news as it happens.

In this section, we will explore the capabilities of online news websites and the aggregators that deliver the combined results from a number of different news sources to a single web page, and the opportunities for directly feeding updated information to your personal computer or mobile device. We'll look at the why, how, what, and where of RSS feeds—the acronym, in its current use, stands for Really Simple Syndication, which is exactly the benefit of the technology—that can increase your online reach and simplify the assimilation of what you bring back. We've mentioned these continuous feeds of news sources and data throughout the book, but now we'll figure out how the technology can help you most directly. We will also look at news alerts through e-mail and the usefulness of online groups and newsletters.

The great minds at the research development centers for software companies are working constantly to bring more and more targeted content to an increasing population of online users. Limitations on what data can be accessed and how it can be individually conformed to the specifications of any particular user will be solved with new technology, and the new capabilities will become commonplace search tools. Microsoft's Live

Search research teams claim that the new technology now in development stages will completely change the way searches are conducted on the Web—today's search engine technology will be obsolete in ten years. Google is no slouch in the development of new technology and internet tools, either.

What does this mean for the serious researcher? First, if you are interested in researching current events, it means you will have the opportunity to access ever-expanding resources. Second, you could spend your entire day just trying to keep up with the breaking news and the background stories on multiple newspaper and media sites and not get any work done at all. Third, you might want to be brave and learn to embrace the new technology that can help you handle the abundance.

NEWS RESOURCES

Remember when you were in fifth or sixth grade and you had to bring in newspaper clippings of current events, or watch the evening news on television for homework? I don't know whether those media are still part of the curriculum, but if so, I'm sure they're joined by homework assignments to research current events on the Web.

A dozen or more years ago, the news media began to reshape itself to fit the world of cyberspace. Though initially reluctant to sponsor an online presence allowing free access to the news and not much advertising revenue compared to the print revenues, newspapers have now tapped into the potential. These days, there's plenty of advertising displayed on their websites, and some of the major newspapers such as the *New York Times* allow access to their most popular columns and archives only for fee-paying members. Even small weekly newspapers have websites, most of which are both browsable and searchable, deliver frequently updated content and contain hyperlinks to additional related web resources.

Online News

You can access the major national and international newspapers online efficiently by searching through newspaper directory websites such as the two listed in chapter six (www.kidon.com/media-link and www.newslink.org). Each of those sites offer hyperlinks to the newspapers' websites. These directories also include links to radio and television broadcast media, which can deliver audio and video files to your personal computer or mobile device such as your cellular phone or iPod or other media player. This is called *podcasting* (derived from the Apple iPod, the first of the mobile devices to use this delivery system).

Accessing streaming audio and video files from radio, online music providers, and other media through mobile devices is great for its entertainment value. If you're researching entertainment or popular culture, perhaps the podcasting technology will be part of your daily work. For most serious researchers, however, podcasts are of secondary value—you can usually read a transcript of a radio interview online instead of listening to it. One website that might be of use to researchers and trackers of current events is the video-sharing website YouTube.com—you can watch videos of breaking news stories posted by members all over the world. You can also add this site to your RSS feeds for continuous automatic updating.

Major web search engines such as Google and Yahoo! have their own customizable news pages where you can read about current events in syndicated content from the Associated Press, Reuters, and other wire news services. Before the advent of individual RSS feeds, this technology was the best available. If your research does not require up-to-the-minute current events content, these online news sources will probably be adequate. A fifteen-minute cycle of updating news from the financial world won't make much difference to you—unless you are using that information for active trading on the stock market. In that instance an RSS feed would be invaluable.

Google also provides news alerts to members. You can go to www.google.com/alerts and create a news alert that will tell you whenever a certain keyword search term appears in a new posting online. You can specify the search to include news, blogs, web, groups, or comprehensive, individually or all together. The alerts can be delivered to you once a day, as the search results come in, or once a week, depending on how closely you want to track the information. Yahoo! Alerts are similar, and the results can be delivered to your e-mail or mobile device. Many other online news providers are launching desktop news alerts, such as BBC.co.uk and FoxNews. com, in addition to the RSS feeds discussed in this chapter.

Open Content News

Wiki technology is also part of the Web's delivery of on-line news. The term *wiki* derives from a Hawai'ian language word meaning "fast," and wiki technology developed as an open content, collaborative software effort, which is now sponsored by the Wikimedia Foundation. In addition to the well known Wikipedia.org volunteer-compiled encyclopedia, there are other wiki projects under development. One is Wikinews.org, a news source written by volunteers. You might find it interesting to read, especially because you can look behind the currently posted articles to see the history of their updating as news stories continue.

RSS Feeds

When you access a major online newspaper you can browse through the news and the other sections of the paper available online (not all content of the print editions is posted) or use the search feature to find what you're after. If you're only looking at one or two newspapers every day, that can be accomplished in half an hour or so. But if your research needs require that you monitor a dozen news sites every day, you're going to want to sign on to an RSS news aggregator. For a small monthly or annual fee (most offer a free trial period so you can check out the service), online news aggregators will gather many sources together and display summaries for you.

This can be handy, especially if you are researching an area of current interest or fast-changing fields such as finance or politics. The world of online research is benefiting from an enormous upgrade in web technology within the past few years—the RSS feeds deliver continuously updated information directly to your browser.

You can receive RSS feeds from news sites and blog sites—the technology is available to any site that publishes content on the Web—and also other kinds of digital content, such as images, photographs, and audio and video files. Websites use XML (Extensible Markup Language) as their standard coding language to deliver updated content to your computer. The

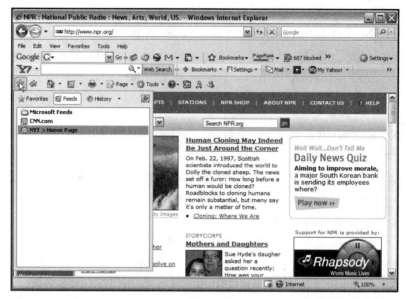

RSS feed from National Public Radio website

software that translates the content into readable text and images that can be viewed on your computer's internet browser or e-mail program, your cell phone, and other media devices is called a *feed reader* (more on that topic on the next page).

Depending on your research interests, you can subscribe to a single feed from an online source such as a newspaper, or you can subscribe to a news aggregator site that will display as many feeds as you can handle. News aggregators are synchronized with your browser's feed reader, allowing you to access the updated content easily.

On Internet Explorer, you can view and manage your RSS feeds by clicking on the yellow star icon for "Favorites" on your toolbar, the same way you access your "Favorite" sites or "Bookmarks." The window that displays the Favorites has a tab at the top for "Feeds." Clicking on that tab will bring up a list of the RSS feeds to which you currently subscribe; any new feeds you add will appear there. Clicking on a feed name will bring the contents of the feed (headlines and brief summaries of the articles) into the right side of the window. If you click on a headline, the full text of the article will be displayed.

You can choose the amount of time between updated feeds and the order in which they are displayed—by date or by title. You can also choose to mark the ones you've read, which won't be displayed again.

Feed Readers

In order to receive an RSS feed from a website, you must have a reader that will construct the XML data into human-readable content. Because this technology is still fairly recent, the feed readers described here may change or be superseded. Not to worry. The website offering the feed will provide a list of compatible feed readers for you to download as part of your subscription process.

Google offers a feed reader online to members at no cost, where you can manage your subscriptions and access the content. Learn about the reader at www.google.com/reader. My Yahoo! also has a feed reader for members. (Registering as a member of Google and Yahoo! is easy and free.) Mozilla Firefox and Internet Explorer browsers have feed readers built in to their newer versions of the software. You can also use Bloglines and NewsGator (more on that one on page 208). If you want to add a feed reader to your own computer, you can download software (or buy it in the box). FeedDemon and Awasu are currently the most popular for Windows operating systems, and NetNewsWire is the reader of choice for Macs. Cellphones and other mobile devices require other feed readers (for example, Newsclip).

Subscribing to Individual RSS Feeds

The most common symbol to indicate the availability of RSS feeds is a small icon of a bright orange square with white radio waves appearing on your browser toolbar and on the website pages. Some websites use a bright orange rectangle with the letters RSS or XML to indicate the availability of feeds.

RSS Favorites list

Microsoft Internet Explorer, Opera, and Mozilla Firefox browsers automatically detect feed capability when you access a website. If the website has feeds available, the toolbar icon turns from gray to orange. Clicking on the orange icon

Mastering Online Research

will display the available feed or multiple feeds from which to choose on that site. If you see a feed that you want, you can subscribe to it. Generally feeds are free of charge—although given the speed of change on the World Wide Web, it may not always be the case.

If your browser supports RSS feeds (which you will know because there is an RSS icon on your toolbar), you can easily subscribe to any newspaper or content delivering website by following a few simple steps. If your browser hasn't been updated recently and doesn't include an RSS feed reader, you can download a newer version of the browser (they're usually free) by searching for the browser name online to locate available updates.

Websites that offer RSS feeds also have the technology to allow you to subscribe. Look for the orange icon on the site, or a menu item on the home page called "RSS." If you don't see either, enter the keywords "RSS feed" into the site's search box. This should bring you to the page on which all the available categories of feeds are listed.

For example, if you want to subscribe to the feeds from the ChicagoTribune.com, you can select the categories you want from a list of news sections (latest news, nation/world, local news, travel, leisure, opinion, business, sports, entertainment, and technology), and a long list of blogs including letters to the editor, popular culture, and sports blogs. Each of these categories has its own feed, so you can customize what you want to receive. When you click on the icon to subscribe to one of these feeds, you must specify the feed reader to which you want the data delivered.

You can subscribe to RSS feeds by following the "How to Subscribe" instructions on the website of interest to you. (Internet Explorer's browser "Help" utility has clear instructions, too.) You can also subscribe by using your own feed reader to search or browse for websites to which you want to subscribe. If you are logged in to Google Reader, for instance, you can click on the yellow "Favorites" star icon and then click on "Add Subscription." A small window will appear with a search box, in which you can type a search term or copy the URL from the website that you're looking at in another browser screen. I entered "beliefnet.com" in the search box and Google instantly returned results for several different sections of that site that were available for RSS feed. When I clicked on my selection, the feed was added immediately to my reader.

Subject Directory Feeds

You can personalize your RSS feeds more specifically to your research interests by using content from a subject directory such as Yahoo's Categorized Guide to the Internet, described in chapter five. Subject directories are created by human editors who organize and evaluate the content of the websites linked in each subject category. Yahoo! Directory offers RSS feeds in several categories that might be helpful to you, and more categories are continually added to the feeds. Among those presently available are "Arts," "Business and Economy," "Computers and Internet," "Education," "Entertainment," "Government," "Health," "News and Media," "Recreation and Sports," "Regional," "Science," "Social Science," and "Society and Culture."

The advantage to subscribing to RSS feeds in a subject directory is that any new content will be noted for you auto-

matically, at whatever update interval you select. That saves
you time that you might spend scanning the directories for
new links.

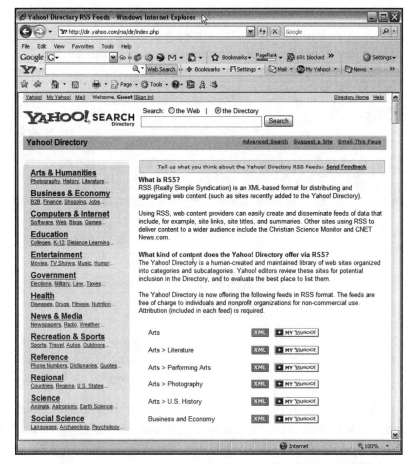

Yahoo! Directory RSS feeds

News Aggregator RSS Feeds

A news aggregator compiles headlines from hundreds of online
sources and displays them as headlines with short text extracts.
The news sources are organized by category folders, and you

can customize the feeds and folders to suit your own research interests. When you subscribe to an aggregator service, you can immediately access their standard feeds, which include categories in just about every area of interest. You can add your selection of newspapers, blogs, and other websites, and manage the folders just as you would in any other software application.

Newsgator RSS aggregator

NewsGator Online (www.newsgator.com) is deservedly one of the most recommended aggregators. It's easy to use, and it pulls from a wide variety of news sources and bloggers, including CNN, the *New York Times*, the *San Francisco Chronicle*, *Wired News*, *USA Today*, and many more. You can also read headlines from specialized categories such as health, science, technology, entertainment, opinion, videos, podcasters, software development, and business.

Mastering Online Research

NewsGator Online requires a web-based feed reader, and the one I chose (FeedDemon) has the ability to synchronize the delivery of the RSS feeds and allows me to set up a "watch" for certain keywords that pertain to my research interests. Both FeedDemon and NewsGator can be downloaded for a free trial period, so you can try out the technology for yourself. NewsGator also markets off-the-shelf software packages that include feed readers for Windows mobile technology and e-mail applications, if you would like to receive your news on a cellular phone or in a Microsoft Outlook e-mail inbox. Similar software (NetNewsWire) is available for Mac users to access NewsGator.

The news aggregators use the same methods as the individual website feeds. To add feeds, you can browse by category or enter a search term in a search box to find feeds that match your interests. There are obviously timesaving advantages to being able to view all the headlines in a category in one screen. You can also set up a folder into which a keyword search can deliver all the headlines that match your search term.

NewsGator Online can deliver the feeds to your computer, your e-mail, and a variety of mobile devices. You can choose to have certain feeds directed to any one of these locations—for example, delivering only podcasts to your cell phone but all feeds to your personal computer.

Even if this technology seems a little overwhelming at first, it's a revolution in online research capability. Give it a try on your favorite news site and also search for keywords on your favorite place or topic of interest. You might find it speeds your research and allows more time for other pursuits.

ONLINE NEWSLETTERS AND EZINES

Probably not the first stop on any research trip, the world of online newsletters and magazines (ezines) can still yield valuable information. Many of the newsletters and ezines are niche publications addressed to fairly small groups of subscribers. Some are funded by subscriptions fees, some by voluntary donations, and some support themselves by revenue from advertising and website links posted on the site.

The content published in these newsletters and ezines varies, because not all have the advantages of professional editing and design services. You might want to try a few websites just to see what they're like. Be especially aware of opinion-based content and check out any facts before including them in your research.

Searching Google or Yahoo! for "current events ezines" will bring up results for a number of individual website publications. However, it's more efficient to use a web subject directory (any of those described in chapter five) and drill down through the "News" category until you find a link that looks promising. You can search or browse among newsletters and ezines in many subject areas.

ONLINE GROUPS

Internet groups are usually devoted to a particular topic and allow members (and sometimes the general public) to communicate messages and receive news on the topic from other members. Groups are hosted by many large internet sites, such as msn.com, Google, Yahoo!, and MySpace.com, and commonly offer message boards, chat rooms, and photo albums. The Google search engine includes the complete archive of USENET, an early internet group of communicators that operated like a virtual bulletin board. Its one billion postings can be searched back to 1981.

Today's groups often have site search capabilities within the groups and allow you to send messages or ask questions of an entire group of users. If you can match your research interests to a corresponding group or two, you might be able to get quick answers to specific research questions. Be sure to read the FAQs (frequently asked questions, with answers) for the group before venturing new questions. Your answer may already be posted.

THE FUTURE OF CURRENT EVENTS

As the technology for continuous delivery of current news and data advances, it will become progressively simpler to use and even more discriminating in what you have delivered for your perusal. You can choose to have updates delivered to your computer according to your specifications, and you can go out to the Web and search newspapers and other online sources for what you need to keep current. But even now it's pretty awesome—at least that's this news junkie's opinion.

ACCESSING ACADEMIC SCHOLARSHIP

Academic and scholarly papers, research articles, full texts of books, scholarly monographs, and other similar noncommercial publications used to be pretty much unavailable for searching on the Web. Unless a research paper was converted to HTML and posted on the academic's own web page or a library website, it was inaccessible to anyone who had not attended the conference at which it was presented and distributed. Newer technology has liberated those resources. Google Book Search and Google Scholar, two of the advanced features at Google that are still in beta development, and Windows Live Academic allow access to all manner of publications and books of scholarly interest.

When you enter a search term on Google Scholar, you will obtain a results list of books and journal articles that all relate in some way to research on that topic (you can also search by author name). You can sort the list by the most recent items, or you can also search by the primary authors connected to the search term. These results will be different from those you would get from a basic keyword search on the main Google search engine, because those keyword results are based on the relevance ranking algorithm that returns the most popular and most often accessed web pages on the Web. Google Scholar is restricted to only academic and scholarly materials.

Clicking on an item in the Google Scholar results list will frequently link you to a commercial archive of scholarly publications, where you will have to register and/or pay a fee to read the article or thesis. If it's an important article for your research, you might want to pay the fee (usually ranging from ten to twenty-five dollars). But first you could search for that article on one of the research databases to which your public library may subscribe (such as Gale Research or ProQuest—see chapter six), and on the Web generally, in case it has been posted on another website.

Other links will lead you to websites that require a membership in an organization or subscription to a journal for access to the article. Some offer short-term registration to access articles, whether a single article or over a thirty-day period.

Some of the scholarly articles on a results list will be available as HTML documents that can be displayed as a web page. Some will be PDF files that require the Adobe Reader in order to display on your screen (it's free from Adobe—you can search for Adobe Reader on Google and find many sites from which to download it). Other documents, usually older ones, may exist only in PostScript format (.ps files), which most browsers no longer support. If you want to be able to read the PostScript files, you can download software that will allow you to read them from a website called Ghostscript at the computer science department of the University of Wisconsin–Madison (www.cs.wisc .edu/~ghost). If the article or dissertation in a PostScript file looks as if it will be valuable to your research, you could also contact the library at the university or institution where the author wrote it—sometimes it might be easier to obtain a photocopy from the library's archive.

ACCESSING THE DEEP WEB

Anyone who has been engaged in conducting research on the World Wide Web for more than the past several years is familiar with the idea of the Deep Web. Sometimes referred to as the Invisible Web, the Hidden Web, or the Dark Web, the Deep Web is made up of the websites and database content that is not able to be accessed by search engines. It's information that lies underneath the surface of the Web or behind gateways that are impassable to webcrawlers.

According to Marcus P. Zillman, a noted authority on internet resources, in an article published in the online journal LLRX.com (*Law Library Resource Xchange*) at the end of 2006, the Deep Web covers "somewhere in the vicinity of 900 billion pages of information located through the world wide web in various files and formats that the current search engines on the Internet either cannot find or have difficulty accessing." Zillman estimates that only (only!) about twenty billion web pages are currently found by search engines.

Should that alarm online researchers like you and me? Not at all.

Of those 880 billion pages that we can't easily access, very few would be of use to the ordinary researcher, writer, teacher, or student. Some exist only as dynamically generated pages, created on a proprietary website from internal databases into a page for a temporary use (for instance, a shopping cart page at an online store). Some are pages buried deep within company websites, which have no value outside that company's purview. Some are protected by passwords or other restrictions. And some are personal web pages that have never been indexed by a search engine because no links lead into them and no links lead out. Webcrawlers depend on links to find web pages. If you happen to know the URL of a personal page, of course you can access it directly. It's not really invisible, merely unvisited.

Although the number of web pages of information in the deep Web is increasing exponentially, the Deep Web's usefulness as a resource for the general researcher is being over-taken by the development of ever more sophisticated search technology, known as search engine optimization.

Prior to about 2002, search engines were unable to re-trieve non-textual files such as multimedia files, graphics files, image files, audio and video files, and documents posted on-line in other formats such as PDFs (static images of pages cre-ated in Portable Document Format). Using more complex al-gorithms and new search and retrieval technology developed by Google and other search engines to find them, those files are now able to be included in search results lists. Formerly "hidden" file types such as Excel files (.xls), PowerPoint files (.ppt), and PostScript files (.ps) are now searchable. As re-cently as 2005, it was not always possible to search PDF doc-uments by keyword, but now it is. Improvements to search capabilities are being made every day.

Even the retrieval of real-time availability of airline flights and hotel rooms used to be considered as part of the Deep Web because that information was held within the proprie-tary databases of the various airlines and hotels. Now, if you search on Google for flight status, the Google algorithms are able to show you real-time status of departing and arriving flights, by airline and flight number. The search is even quicker if you add the airline to the keyword search ("united flight status"). Yahoo! Travel offers the same feature, as do some other specialized websites.

Some of what used to be considered "invisible" is merely a misinterpretation of the meaning of the Deep Web. Librar-ies and archives that have their own search engines on their websites to access the documents in their databases had their web pages termed "invisible" because a webcrawler couldn't access the documents directly. However, human users have no difficulty in using a search engine on the Library of Congress website. The data is not invisible to us, although it may reside on sites that are impossible for webcrawlers to search.

WHAT MAKES UP THE DEEP WEB

The existence of the Deep Web is in large part determined by the ability of search engines to retrieve information in response to a user's queries. Databases contain information records (or fields) that are stored in tables of related information, using software programs such as Access, Oracle, SQL Server, DB2, and others. In order to bring the information in the databases into a format that will be readable and valuable for humans (or computers), software programs and human programmers write queries to the databases. Much more complicated than online search engine queries, these queries direct a sequence of information retrieval and analysis in the databases that eventually results in content that can be displayed on a web page or printed in a report. That's the quick, nontechnical explanation.

Search engines cannot go inside those databases to search for your keyword or advanced search query, because the databases only respond to the method of querying described above. If the end product is a web page of fixed HTML or XML content that can be displayed on a website visited by search engine webcrawlers, only then will that content become available to you. Otherwise the web page remains part of the Deep Web.

Dynamically Generated Content

Billions of web pages are created "on the fly," assembled in response to a specific query. For example, online encyclopedias have many different elements that display on the web page of an article, including images, text, maps, statistics, and so on. You can go directly to Wikipedia.org and enter "Wichita Kansas" into their search box and the full article will display on the screen. That encyclopedia is *not* part of the Deep Web—it is a fixed web page that can be indexed by the webcrawlers. All of its components already are in place in the coded language of the page—you can even see the code if you click on the "Edit this page" tab at the top of any article.

On the other hand, the Encyclopedia Americana Online article on "Wichita, Kansas" technically would be part of the Deep Web, for two reasons: (1) the pages of the article on Wichita are dynamically generated by the encyclopedia's programming scripts, bringing together files from a variety of databases (images, text, bibliographies, hyperlinks to other related articles and websites, etc.) to display on the page as the user requests it; and (2) the webcrawlers cannot penetrate the password-restricted barrier to the web pages, because this is a paid subscription site.

Deliberately Excluded Web Pages

Other kinds of Deep Web content intentionally are made difficult to access. As we know, webcrawlers regularly visit pages in order to retrieve updated content for the search engine indexes. Some websites do not wish their content to be searched by webcrawlers, for one reason or another—perhaps the information is sensitive or proprietary, or they simply don't want to encourage uninvited visitors. In those cases, the websites contain in their HTML or XML code a "robotic exclusion," which is a file that tells the robot webcrawler to move on. Those websites deliberately remain dark. Ordinary researchers cannot access the web pages, either, unless they have authorization. Often these types of websites contain proprietary materials that only employees of a particular company can use; the internet is used as the data transmission method but the intention is not to make the website a part of the public Web. One example might be a website that tracks sales information for a national auto parts dealer; the website would be password-protected and the data it contained would not be appropriate for outside access. Another example might be a staging or test site for new software under development that entails high security.

Continuously Updated Web Pages

An additional type of website that is blocked to a webcrawler is a continuously updated web page, such as a weather or news site. The information presented on the site would not be suitable for monthly, weekly, or even daily webcrawler visits, because it changes so rapidly that an index would be inaccurate within minutes. The home pages and other static pages of such websites, though, are indexed, so you can find them easily through searching—the robotic exclusion only marks off the continually generated information sections.

Unnoticed Web Pages

Another group of web pages that are part of the Deep Web are those sites that simply go unnoticed by the general internet user.

In order to have a site searched by webcrawlers, it has to contain enough substantive content to attract other websites to link to it. In my observation, the personal websites that are visited only by the website author's family and friends are being replaced by the use of popular blogging and file-sharing sites, many of which are indexed by webcrawlers and appear in search results.

The staff members at search engine websites used to spend a lot of time reviewing URLs from applicants who wanted their websites added to the search engine. There were even companies who would guarantee getting your website listed with the major players for a fee. That's no longer commonly done because the sheer volume of new web pages makes it practically impossible. The thinking now is that if a site is worthy of being listed, it will be found.

How to Use the Deep Web

Locating websites to search on the Deep Web is the real challenge. There are no actual designated "Deep Web sites" to target. The search engine optimization technology is advancing so rapidly that a lot of what used to be hidden on the Deep Web is now able to be found through normal search channels on the "surface" Web. Internal searches at organization and company websites, university websites, and government and public records websites can be considered as Deep Web searches. But today it's increasingly uncommon that you will find a site with information that is not accessible in any other way, unless it is behind a security firewall, which prevents unauthorized users from accessing it.

Large corporations such as BrightPlanet offer "information harvesting" services that will provide search results incorporating both surface and Deep Web data to clients for fees that the ordinary researcher couldn't support. Even those information brokers legally must restrict themselves to public information, though.

Internet expert Marcus Zillman, mentioned on page 214, hosts a useful website at www.deepwebresearch.com, which is a resource he created to bring together the latest sources on an ongoing basis for research on the Deep Web. He maintains a Subject Tracer Information Blog to help users access different kinds of Deep Web information, including articles, papers, forums, audios, and videos. One good source for finding databases on the Deep Web to search is Zillman's research paper entitled "Academic and Scholar Search Engines and Sources," first published in 2004 and updated in 2007. This research paper is available as a PDF (http://whitepapers.virtualprivateli brary.net/Scholar.pdf) and is licensed under a Creative Commons License, which means it's available for anyone to use, with some clearly stated restrictions.

Zillman's Awareness Watch free monthly newsletter is also a good resource for researchers looking to penetrate below the surface of the Web. The January 2007 issue is a special report on Deep Web research, containing hundreds of reliable sources to assist you in identifying best practices, strategies, websites and new technology applications that can be leveraged to mine the content of the Deep Web. The report is accessible as a downloadable PDF at www.awarenesswatch.com.

Because the earlier chapters in this book discussed the techniques of online research in so many areas, there aren't really any new secrets as to how to search the Deep Web. You use the same developed techniques of drilling down through sub-ject directories, from general categories to narrower categories.

What is different in searching the Deep Web is that you look for information databases that are not included in the general group of websites that are searched by major search engines. You need to be highly immersed in the details of your research topic to find such databases and websites; sometimes they are seemingly obscure links from general subject directories or other web pages in your search cat-egory; more often they are mentions of helpful sources in online forums or discussion groups that someone on the inside happens to know about. People researching informa-tion technology and hardware/software development per-haps most easily can find Deep Web content to search; ordi-nary researchers rarely have a need for this level of granu-larity in searching.

If you locate a database that you want to search, and you can gain access to it, pay close attention to the search query protocols for that search engine. Deep Web databases use their own search engines; when you enter a keyword or search string, focus on structuring the query in the clearest terms to return the results you want. Remember to read the FAQs or search tips on any new website before launching your search query. Some searches will support Boolean and logical operators, some will use modifiers (such as "define:") in their search boxes, and some will use site-specific abbrevi-ations or terms for searching. This is especially the case with "legacy" sites whose archives have been around since the be-ginning of the internet. Because these sites are not indexed by the major search engines or accessed by the general web community, there is no need to update the search technology.

In browsing for a website that might be considered part of the Deep Web, I found a website called FreePint.com that specializes in providing the latest information to people who work as information searchers. FreePint is based in the United Kingdom and bills itself as "a global network of people who find, use, manage, and share work-related information." The organization publishes a free twice-monthly online newsletter, which is accessible to any site visitor in its current issue and in the archives. The 2005 newsletter, hidden in the website's archive, seemed as if it might qualify as a Deep Web source, so I thought I'd have trouble finding any of the articles in an ordinary search. Not so. An excellent article on teaching information and search skills from the 2005 issue popped up in the first ten results of a Google search for "information search skills," even without the author's name. I think the Deep Web is surfacing. You might want to check out the FreePint website for in-depth material on information searches, though.

If you are thoroughly engrossed in the field of deep online research, there is a weekly newsletter that you might want to monitor for organized summaries of the most valuable and authoritative web resources available. Called the Internet Scout Project, it is part of the computer science and library science departments at the University of Wisconsin–Madison and has been publishing since 1994. It provides a full-text search of over 6,000 summaries of websites that were evaluated as being of the highest overall quality, compiled by a staff of librarians and information specialists. The subscription is free and it's easy to register at www.scout.cs.wisc.edu.

The next chapter will explore searching for online images and video and audio files, categories of data that until recently were unable to be retrieved by search engines. Not only are these files easy to find now, but reviewing the search results is a lot of fun.

CHAPTER 9

SEARCHING FOR IMAGE, AUDIO, AND VIDEO FILES

In addition to the other kinds of information already mentioned, the Web can be searched for images, audio files, and videos. Image files can be photographs (current and historic), illustrations, works of art, maps, documents, and other static images; audio files include spoken text such as famous speeches and news audio clips, as well as varieties of music and sound compositions; and video files include film archives, news archives, video clips, and animations. The techniques for searching websites and databases for images are the same as those for visual and audio files, so in this chapter we will focus most closely on image searches, with specific recommendations for audio and video file searches following later.

Some of the major search engines such as Google and Yahoo! offer separate search windows for images and for video, with slightly differing advanced search options. As search technology advances, the functions available for retrieving these distinct types of files will be more targeted and specific.

Image search is the fastest growing vertical—or niche—search category today, according Nielsen/NetRatings, a leader in internet media and market research. All the techniques for online research—basic keyword searches, advanced searches with Boolean operators and other filters, subject directories, and using hyperlinks—are exactly what will help you in searching for images on the Web. We'll look at how those techniques can be adapted for the visual internet world, and we'll explore the kinds of images and other graphic materials that are available and how you can use them. There's a lot of jargon associated with image files. But even if you don't know a bpp from a ppi, you might like to venture into a few of the resources that we'll explore.

INTRODUCTION TO ONLINE IMAGES

If your dinner table conversation often revolves around rasterizing, vectors, and image compressions, please don't expect to learn anything new in this section explaining the basic types of images that are found on the Web. But if you just want to know enough about the topic to recognize types of files and know what they're suited for, stick with me. Remember, too, that new formats are being invented all the time, so if you encounter an unfamiliar one, look it up on Wikipedia .org. Their computer-related articles seem up-to-date and authoritative, and the hyperlinks from those articles are good.

IMAGE CLARITY: PPI AND BPP

The images you see on the Web are digital images, most of which are constructed of grids of tiny squares or dots called pixels. The word "pixel" is derived from "picture element," and it takes a lot of pixels to make a photograph appear clear and colorful. Many home computer monitors are set to display 1024 x 768 pixels on a screen (some display at 1280 x 1024), at 72 or 96 pixels per inch (ppi). A photograph described as 300 x 450 pixels measures roughly four inches high by six inches wide at 72ppi. Each pixel contains a certain number of bits that determine how much color can be displayed in the digital image. The number of bits per pixel (bpp) indicates the number of colors each pixel can take for display. (An 8-bit pixel uses one byte of data storage.) Common bpp values are 8bpp, which allows display of 256 colors; 16bpp (highcolor), which allows "thousands" of colors; 24bpp (truecolor), which allows "millions" of colors; 32bpp, which allows highest color; and 48bpp, which is a total saturation of color mainly used by professionals. If you look at the display settings for your own monitor, you can see how many colors are available for display.

The more pixels per inch, the sharper the image, of course, because the pixels carry the detail. This is called the resolution of an image, and it applies to just about all digital media, including video files and DVDs. Digital camera owners will be familiar with this term, because cameras record and store photographs in files made up of pixels, measured in size by bytes (actually, kilobytes) of memory—more on that on page 227. The size of the file depends on the resolution of the image. A low-resolution image has fewer pixels per inch, and a high resolution image captures much more visual information in many pixels per inch—even more than the human eye can see.

High-resolution image files can be very large and therefore difficult to store and transmit. There are image compression tools that can reduce the number of pixels in an image, but the data detail is permanently lost. Depending on the planned use of the image, the loss may be perfectly acceptable.

FILE SIZE: KB AND MB

The amount of data stored in a digital image file is also important information to have when you're thinking about using an image either in print or online. To understand file sizes, you must first know what kilobytes and megabytes are (and if you are familiar with the metric system, the prefixes will tip you off to their meanings). A kilobyte (K, or Kb) equals a thousand bytes, while a megabyte (MB) is equivalent to a thousand kilobytes, or a million bytes. An image file that is 33 kilobytes in size is much easier to transmit via e-mail or to post online than an image file that is 2 megabytes in size. High-resolution images in raw, unprocessed form can easily reach 3MB in size. Image-editing software such as Adobe PhotoShop or PhotoShop Elements can help you to make photographs more manageable. These programs are widely available, along with several similar programs. You may already have one that was included with your digital camera or scanner.

In order for everyone to view and distribute images on the World Wide Web, a system of standards was set up to define certain types of files with specific characteristics. There are several primary image file formats, as file extensions appended to the image filename, you'll see when exploring the Web.

GIF. This stands for Graphics Interchange Format and has a limit of 256 colors, which makes it suitable for illustrations, animations, and graphics but not for color photographs (you can use GIFs for black-and-white photos).

JPEG. The .jpg or .jpeg extension stands for Joint Photographic Experts Group format and is the format most often used for photographs and by digital cameras. A JPEG can be compressed successfully to smaller sizes without great loss of detail and is recognized by many operating systems.

PNG. The .png, or Portable Network Graphics, format is the successor to the .gif file format because it supports true color (16 million colors) and can be edited as a PNG and then made into a JPEG for the final form of the image. This is a fairly new file format but increasing in use.

BMP. The .bmp extension stands for Bitmapped Image. This file format is used in the Microsoft Windows operating system for graphics images, but since it is rarely compressed, it's not used often on the Web.

PDF. The PDF (Portable Documents Format) is another common image file format, as mentioned earlier. This format was created by Adobe and preserves the exact image of a document in a fixed format that can be displayed identically on any display device. Adobe offers free downloads of its Adobe Reader software, which allows you to display the PDF on your screen. Many websites that post their documents in PDF format also offer the Adobe Reader download to users.

SEARCHING FOR IMAGES

If you've never searched for images on the Web, you're in for a treat. You can find photographs and other images at the click of a search button and then spend hours at your computer marveling at the talent in the world. That's easy and fun. Learning to refine your search so that you can obtain the results you need is a little more challenging.

The tips and techniques presented here are general instructions that apply to most web search sites that handle images. The images may be displayed in slightly different ways, and some sites may provide more technical details about the images than do others. A list of specific image-search engines follows later in this chapter, with significant points noted about each of them.

The millions of images posted on the Web are not identified in any standard system except by size and file type, as discussed earlier in this chapter. There are no universal naming conventions, and most of the time the search engine will try to search on captions or text attached to the image file. However, as these can range from very descriptive to somewhat idiosyncratic to completely random, the results aren't always what one might expect.

The Google search engine has a volunteer program in which viewers are encouraged to label images, adding detailed identification tags to the Google database, in order to benefit future searchers—a slow process. The search engine optimization projects are developing programs that will be able to recognize and categorize the content of images (by identifying the shape of a tree, for instance), which will be great. But until that day arrives, we'll just have to locate and review the images ourselves.

HOW TO INTERPRET IMAGE SEARCH RESULTS

Shall we start off with a big bang? If you open the main Google search page and enter "fireworks" as the keyword, you can choose to search only images by clicking on the "Images" button in the list of choices above the search entry box. The results list, a brightly colored page bursting with energy and celebration, displays clickable thumbnail images of more than 630,000 photos and of fireworks displays pictures.

Underneath each image is its size in pixels and kilobytes, the descriptor or caption attached to it, and the URL of the website in which it was found. You don't want to spend the time to look at every photo on a results page—it's too time-consuming. Instead, you can use your skills in understanding the URL address and quickly scan the URLs and captions for pertinent information, which will help you preview the images for usefulness and availability. You'll still be clicking on a few possible photo choices from the results list as you narrow your selections, but it will be a lot fewer. When you find an appealing photo, click on the thumbnail image to see the full photo in its original web context with a Google frame header at the top of the page (you can also click "Remove Frame" to view it as a full web page). You can then return to the results list by using the hyperlink at the top right of the frame.

We'll use the image search for the keyword "fireworks" as an example to provide an overview of the results you'll get

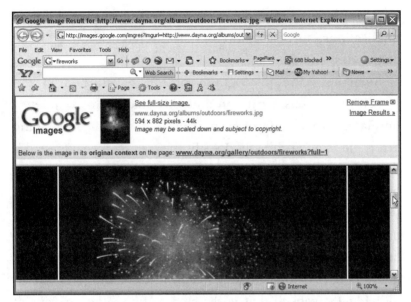

Google Image search result with frame header

from such a broad image search, as well as the pertinent issues of permission and copyright. You can try a search yourself and look for similar qualities in the images in whatever search topic you choose.

On a search results page, the source of a thumbnail image is immediately recognizable from its URL address. If the URL is www.encarta.msn.com, you know the photograph is from the Encarta online encyclopedia. If you click on the thumbnail image, you will see a full-size preview of the photo as it appears in the encyclopedia article. The names of the photographer and the stock house that is licensing the rights appear in a credit below the photo on the website. You would need to contact the stock house (not Encarta) to request permission to use this photo, and the fee could be hefty. The same is true for most photographs that appear in commercial online publications, such as encyclopedias, reference sites, online magazines, and the like.

Sometimes the photograph or image returned in the search results has a caption and URL that seem completely unrelated to your search term. Unless it's an image labeling error, the image probably does fit the criteria for your search. Some search engines capture images by scanning the caption, or even the text surrounding the image, and others will scan the entire URL as well. For example, an image of a fireworks display with the caption "Razorbacks win the games played in ..." does not contain the keyword. However, "fireworks" actually is part of the longer, specific URL of the page on an individual's website that is devoted to fireworks displays at sports events. The search engine grabbed this photo by its URL rather than its caption.

An interesting photo of fireworks at the National Washington Monument turns up as a thumbnail result for a keyword search, with the URL listed as www.homeschoolblogger.com. That would lead you to think that there's an educational article on fireworks attached to it. Clicking on the thumbnail photo reveals some hidden information in the Google frame header—the source for the photo is given as "upload.wikimedia .org/wikipedia/en/thumb/8/86/..." rather than the homeschool blogger's website, which indicates that the photo was borrowed from Wikipedia to illustrate the article on her website. The next step is to wonder if she had permission to do so, right? And if she did, you could probably get permission to use the photo as well.

The most efficient way to find out is to go to Wikipedia .org and search for "fireworks," which brings up an article by that title. Scrolling down the page, you can find the same photograph illustrating the section of the article on fireworks for the U.S. Independence Day. If you click on the photo, you will access a new Wikipedia page that reveals the source of the photo and any other pertinent information. The photo was taken by an Air Force staff sergeant as part of his official duties—and thus, as a work of the federal government the photo is in the public domain. It's free for you to post on your site or include in your article or presentation, giving proper credit to the photographer, of course. Not all works created by federal employees are so easy to access; even though the images or documents may be in the public domain regarding copyright, access may be restricted for other reasons.

The image in a thumbnail captioned "La Rosa Fireworks" is thrilling but gives no indication that this photograph comes from one of the largest fireworks companies in Europe, although its URL www.larosa-fireworks.it, tells you that the site is hosted in Italy. Ordinarily you might not choose to review this photo because you assume the text will be in Italian based on the URL suffix. However, if you take a chance and click through to the La Rosa home page, you'll find videos of magnificent fireworks displays, and if you click on the icon of the British flag at the top right of the screen, all text will appear in English. If you wanted to use photographs or multimedia files from this site, you would need to request permission through the La Rosa company from whoever snapped the photos or created the videos originally. Foreign copyrights are also protected in the United States.

Here's a quick tip to refine your image search using key-words without switching to an advanced search: Add a date as one of your keyword search terms. If you want to search for images of the fireworks displays that marked the millennium celebrations worldwide, for instance, add the year "2000" to the search term "fireworks." Instead of 630,000 results, you'll get about 5,400 results, many depicting the New Year's spec-taculars. You'll also get Fourth of July 2000 fireworks and oth-er artworks or images that are dated to that year. But if you narrow the search by also adding "millennium" to your image search string, the results will be fewer than 150—possibly not enough for a good selection. That's one of the shortcomings of being overly specific in the search string for basic searches.

SAVING ONLINE IMAGES

An online image is simple to save to your computer's hard drive. If you will be saving a number of images or photographs as part of your research, it's a good idea to create a new folder for images named for whatever subject you're researching. If you have several research projects going at once, keep the on-line image research together in a folder with the text research. A jumble of unrelated and poorly identified images is not fun to sort through, especially if you're on a tight deadline.

Photographers who handle thousands of digital photos use commercially available file labeling, storage, and retrieval systems to keep track of their image collections. If you turn into a digital image junkie you might want one of those sys-tems for your own computer—but be aware of the copyright issues (more on that on page 235).

Mastering Online Research

Save Picture As screen

To save an image file on your PC, simply right-click with your mouse over the image on the screen. (If you work on a Mac, click the mouse and the Control key simultaneously.) A pop-up menu will appear, from which you can select "Save Picture As." A small screen will open, in which you can enter the name you choose for the file and the location of the folder in which you wish to save the image file. It's best to save the file in the same format in which you found it—such as ".jpg"—to avoid problems in reopening the file at a later time.

COPYRIGHTS AND FEES

Alas, we have to remember that this banquet of visual goodies on the World Wide Web is not a free, all-you-can-eat buffet. Images and other types of files are covered by the same U.S.

copyright protections that apply to all other types of originally created works. Chapter eleven provides an overview of copyright and permissions to use copyrighted documents, as well as what is considered fair use and how to find works in the public domain that are free to use, but in this chapter we'll limit ourselves to the pertinent points.

From the moment an image is created or a camera clicks, the individual who brought that image or photograph into existence owns the copyright to it. Permission to use that image in another work must be obtained from that individual or from the company to whom he sells or licenses it. Some of the limitations of copyright can be avoided by searching for materials that are deliberately removed from copyright restrictions by their owners (sometimes called "copyleft" materials). You can also search for images on websites that allow use of the images for a modest fee or sometimes at no cost. Many search engines have a feature to specify only copyright-free web pages in the search results, but I haven't found any that specifically search for images that are free of usage restrictions. You can try searching Google or Yahoo! for websites that contain materials that are free to use, share, or modify, and check out whether the websites include images as part of their content. See the following pages for other tips on finding the least costly images to use.

If you know that you want to use image in another publication or in an online post, you might want to restrict your search from the beginning to only those images that are in the public domain and free to use. The easiest way to do so is to enter "public domain" along with your keyword in the basic image search box. The results page will be small—only nineteen images turn up in a Google search for the keyword "fireworks." Of those particular images, only eight are photographs of fireworks and seven of them are found on the same site, called www.pdphoto.org, which offers royalty-free, public domain stock photos and is hosted by a computer programmer who likes to take photos and wants to allow others to use them without charge. (He does offer cautions, however, about using the photos for commercial purposes and reminds users that they may not copyright the photographs in any work either—they are intended to remain in the public domain.) The eighth photo is from a blog, where the author has used a photo accompanied by its public domain license from Creative Commons, a website where individuals can register to share their work with others by deliberately declining copyright ownership.

Professional photographers often sell their images to stock houses, which then control the rights and collect the fees for commercial and non-commercial use of the photos. When a stock house offers a royalty-free image, it doesn't mean "free of charge"; it means they do not pay *royalties* to the photographer—royalties are fees paid to the original copyright holder on a per-use basis, as actors are paid residuals on each re-broadcast of a television show, for instance. The cost of your intended use (single or multiple) is paid as a one-time fee.

The copyright notice on the next page is posted at the foot of a web page containing original artwork and text. Even though the tone is humorous, the message is clear (the name of the website owner has been changed to protect his privacy).

Questions? Comments? Criticism? Contact me.

All works are copyright © 2007 John Smith or by their respective owners, who probably aren't you.

So don't use these images to make money or anything. Or if you do, give me the money.

Model Releases

Professional photographers obtain signed model releases from people who are clearly identifiable in their photographs before selling the photos to stock houses. The releases give permission for the image to be used without restriction. Public gatherings where no one is recognizable do not require releases. When you are planning to use a photograph obtained from a source other than a stock house in a commercial product such as a book or other publication, or for advertising purposes, make sure the proper releases have been signed. Identifiable corporate logos or products may also require permission

SEARCH ENGINES THAT HANDLE IMAGES

You can use any major search engine to conduct an image search using keywords. The results will differ somewhat in how they are displayed and also in the breadth and depth of coverage. Let's look at a few to see the differences.

Yahoo!

Works about the same way as the Google image search, including the advanced search features. If you search for "elephant" in the Yahoo! basic keyword image search, the search results number over 754,000. A Google image search will show 680,000 results—

pretty close. But the search results are displayed a bit differently. Yahoo! offers suggestions at the top of the results page that you might find helpful sometimes. In this case the suggestions are to refine the search to "elephant bar," "elephant man," and "elephant pictures," which doesn't do much. The suggestion of "baby elephant pictures" narrows the results to about 26,000 images (although I had to stop looking after the first twenty—the cuteness level was excessive).

Ask.com

Accessed by selecting "Images" from a right -hand menu of search options on the main website. It's a lovely, clean way to organize a search site, and the search screen offers three samples of search results.

Entering the keyword "tiger" in the search box brings up a results page that is visually thrilling, full of thumbnail photos of big, white sharp teeth and sleek fur. Over 463,000 images of tigers are available to peruse. But in case you weren't looking for the real animal, there are related search links suggested to "Winnie the Pooh," "Tiger Woods," and "Black Panther" (the search engine doesn't distinguish between 1960s radicals and big cats in the photo results). There are also links to expand your search ("Piglet" to "dolphin" to "lion") and narrow your search ("Bengal" to sabertooth" to "tiger tattoos"). Apparently these directed links by category are in lieu of an advanced search feature.

Clicking on a thumbnail image opens a screen with the Ask .com frame header of Image Search Result Details, similar to the Google search, and the image in context on the web page from where it was grabbed. Besides the size and format of the image, you'll see the filename, URL, and online source, along with a copyright reminder and disclaimer. There's also a clickable "Save" link if you want to save the image to your "mystuff" folder on the Ask .com website instead of to your own computer.

If you want to preview the URL of the image and its technical information (size and format), you can roll your cursor over the "Info" link below the thumbnail image to bring up a comment box. That's not as useful as having that information displayed with the thumbnail so you can compare it with other images.

The search engine at Ask.com also powers the image search at Lycos.com (www.multimedia.lycos.com), so the results are virtually the same.

AlltheWeb.com

Now owned by Yahoo!, AlltheWeb.com has similar search features to the Yahoo! search engine. The results page for a keyword search for "bears" mixes images of brown bears, polar bears, Care Bears, and the Chicago Bears, which is a bit disconcerting. The advanced search feature is rudimentary and primarily allows you to select the file extension type (JPEG, BMP, or GIF) and image color scale.

AltaVista.com

Like the Yahoo! and Google image search results pages, a search for "bear" on AltaVista.com allows you to click on the thumbnail and go directly to the full photograph shown in context on its web page. It does not provide a frame header with the information about the image, however. That information is accessed by clicking on the "More Info" link below the thumbnail image, which is a little bit clunky.

AltaVista.com's main image search page offers drop-down menus at the top of the page to specify the size, color, and sources of the images returned in a basic keyword search. If you want to search only on news sites, for instance, that could be quite useful—but apparently the search looks at the text of the image caption, rather than at the filename or URL of the image. A news search for images of "bear" resulted in photos of celebrities and politicians in the news who must "bear criticism" or "bear with a difficult situation." Save this search feature for words that are distinctive in meaning.

Dogpile.com

This metasearch engine screens and combines results from Google, Yahoo!, msn.com, and Ask.com searches. The results are very slim pickings, even for bears.

Mamma.com

Offers a more practical and substantial image search than other metasearch engines. Search for "tiger" and you'll get results pages full of them. Click on a thumbnail image, and the full image will be accompanied by a Mamma frame header giving all pertinent information on the image file, including a copyright reminder and a copyright line under the photo when available. It's nice.

Windows Live

A more recent search engine developed by Microsoft, Windows Live (www.love.com) has an image search on its main search page. The search can be modified by using the options link to specify language, SafeSearch filter level, and grouping of results. Other choices can be made on the results page itself, including the size of the images, a zoom feature, and an easy method to save the image to a scratchpad.

ADVANCED IMAGE SEARCH

Advanced search techniques for images aren't as effective as they are for text documents. At the present time, the searches are limited by the poor labeling of online image files and the lack of meaningful text that can be searched, although those hurdles no doubt will be overcome in the near future. The advanced search features for images on the Google search engine work in the same way as the advanced search for all web content you learned to use in chapter three. Yahoo! also provides a similar advanced search feature for its image search.

As in most image searches, you can broadly specify the size of the image (any size, small, medium, or large) and whether you want color, grayscale, or black-and-white only. (Color photographs can usually be converted to the other formats without much loss of clarity.) You can also specify results returned only in the file format (JPEG, GIF, or PNG). You can specify that the search is to be conducted on a particular domain (for instance, the Yale.edu website or the Pittsburgh.com website).

You can also select which level of SafeSearch filtering you want to use—strict, moderate, or none. If you are searching for a topic that could be construed in several ways, you should pay attention to the filtering level. Searching for photographs with the keywords "sweet sixteen" should be okay without filtering, but not necessarily. A moderate filter will ensure that it is. When I searched an image source for "lion," I was surprised to encounter an "age 18 or over" warning screen—as it turned out, one of the images showed two lions mating. That's okay; it's nature. Still, I'd rather be forewarned than be ambushed by an image I don't want to see.

COMMERCIAL WEBSITES

Many commercial stock houses or image archives offer on-line search capabilities for their databases of available images. In most cases the fee for the use of a photograph or image will be determined by the specific conditions under which the purchaser intends to use the image. For example, a photograph used on a commercial book jacket will cost more than if it were being used in a pamphlet published by a local historical society.

When you purchase rights to use an image, you should have the seller confirm that the proper model releases have been obtained and that you have been informed of any other restrictions on the use of the image. In return, you must adhere to the terms of the licensing agreement. If you license a photograph for an illustration in the text of your book and then the publisher's marketing department wants to use the photo for a big ad in the *New York Times* (you should be so lucky!), then a new license must be negotiated for that particular use. It was not covered by the original agreement.

Commercial stock photo houses (also called agencies) have been around for a long time. In the past decade or so, the smaller houses have been gobbled up by the larger ones, which is great for searching for images but not so great for the freelance photographers who suddenly faced a virtual monopoly on where they could sell their images. Things seem to have settled out with only a few major stock houses handling the majority of images, and a few brave souls who have set up online resources where you can obtain images at minimal cost. That's the community spirit of the World Wide

Web. Let's review a few of the different kinds of commercial sites. Depending on your research, you may only need to view the photos, rather than buy them. It's fun to search for free. Explore and play with these image sites.

Getty Images

http://creative.gettyimages.com/source/home/home.aspx

This corporation is the world's largest provider of imagery, film, and digital services. Its breadth is truly awesome. It furnishes traditional and digital media, although nearly 100 percent of its visual content is delivered digitally. If you have a sum of money available to purchase images for a project, visit the website. You can search for creative photography, illustration, and archival images, and separately conduct an editorial search for news, sports, entertainment, and archival images, too.

The images are simply wonderful in their scope. You can find an 1865 photograph of Dr. Samuel Mudd, for instance, who was vilified for treating the broken leg John Wilkes Booth suffered when he leapt from the theater box after shooting President Lincoln. In the historical photograph Samuel Mudd is misidentified as a member of the assassination plot.

Corbis

http://pro.corbis.com

Corbis is the second largest source for image sales, surpassed only by Getty Images. The company, now owned by Microsoft chairman Bill Gates, has been a mainstay for print images used by newspapers, magazines, book publishers, advertising agencies, and corporations. It continues to grow and acquire new companies and their image resources, adapting its services to the needs of online users.

One of the strengths of Corbis is its ownership of the Bettman Archive. The collection contains millions of images of world significance, some over a hundred years old. Looking for that famous photo of the Hindenburg explosion? It's here. You can search the Bettman Archive under the categories "World Events," "Personalities," "Lifestyles," "Advertising Art," and "Art and Illustrations" by going to their website at www.corbis.com/BettMann100/Archive/BettmannArchive.asp.

Fotosearch

www.footsearch.com

This website offers stock photography and stock video and audio clips from a large number of collections. A search for Abraham Lincoln in the photography section brought up images of the Lincoln Memorial, a U.S. Navy Hornet, a five dollar bill, a log cabin paperweight, and Mount Rushmore.

iStockphoto

www.istockphoto.com

This image service is an example of the best of the online world. It's a collection of well over a million images posted by iStockphoto members, who allow use of their royalty-free photographs, illustrations, and Flash files (digital movies) by users who pay a minimal fee for the one-time right to use the images. "Minimal" on this website means only a couple of dollars for photos that in many instances are as good as those taken by professional photographers. It's a wonderful resource for contemporary photography, especially if you are on a limited budget. You won't find historical or news archives here, just a lot of great pictures.

LOW-COST ONLINE IMAGE SEARCHES

When you are including photographs and images as part of your research, you will want to find resources that offer photographs at no cost or for very modest fees. The following websites can be very helpful in supplying a rich source of images.

Yotophoto

http://yotophoto.com

The Yotophoto website features an internet search engine for finding free-to-use photographs. It indexes over a quarter million Creative Commons, public domain, and other "copyleft" images, and is an offshoot of an image searching program for Wikipedia. Yotophoto indexes various sources of free imagery on the Web including photographs from Flickr, Wikipedia, Stock.XCHNG, Morguefile, PixelPerfect Digital, and OpenPhoto. There are also some public domain historical photographs. Although all the indexed photographs are free to use, Yotophoto requests that proper credit be given to the photographers whose images they index.

Fagan Finder.com

www.faganfinder.com/img

This is an excellent directory to other resources on the Web and one you will want to bookmark. Updated recently by its creator, Michael Fagan, the links are to solid online resources and newer sources for images such as photosharing sites and blogs. You can click on the hyperlinks to NASA, the Fish and Wildlife Service National Image Library, an online edition of Gray's *Anatomy of the Human Body*, Picture Australia, the British Library Images, the British National Portrait Gallery, the National Archives of Canada, and many more resources including Photoblogs.org and a Nature Photo Index.

Victoria and Albert Museum

www.vam.ac.uk

Collections at the Victoria and Albert Museum in London are searchable online, both in text and in images. More than 26,000 images are in the museum, searchable by topic and media type. And the online views of the museum's current and past exhibitions are fascinating—the fashion, jewelry, and textile collections especially so. If you are interested in British culture and society, this website could prove valuable.

Library of Congress Prints and Photographs

www.lcweb2.loc.gov/pp/pphome.html

Not all the photographs and prints indexed in this collection are in the public domain, but it's still worth searching the one million digital images. Each image is accompanied by the detailed information that you would expect from the cataloguers at the Library of Congress, along with clear statements about its copyright and provenance. You can search by keyword, category, or even by individual collection. The group of 2,100 baseball cards from 1887 to 1914 is a treasure.

NASA Image eXchange

http://nix.larc.nasa.gov

The website of the National Aeronautics and Space Administration has a bounty of searchable images from various missions and programs. Go to the website to find the main search window, where you can conduct an advanced search in various media or browse the images in a subject directory. If you want to see a photo of an astronaut taking a hot shower aboard SkyLab 2 in 1973, here's your chance (well, don't you wonder how the water sprays in zero gravity?). Of course the photographs taken of the Earth and other celestial objects from outer space are among the most popular and spectacular. Best of all, the photos on the NASA site are in the public domain.

Artcyclopedia

www.artcyclopedia.com

More than 180,000 works of art are indexed on the Artcyclopedia website—works by 8,500 artists drawn from about 2,300 websites, searchable by artist name, the title of the artwork, and the name or location of the art museum. A subject directory allows you to browse by art movement, medium, subject, and other distinguishing features. The site also has advanced research tools and guidelines for image use. A search for the American Impressionist painter Mary Cassatt, for example, brings up a results page that lists the museums and public art galleries where her works are held (all clickable hyperlinks), as well as galleries and other venues where her works can be purchased in either originals or prints. This site is a good starting point if you are researching a certain artist or art movement.

RESOURCES IN THE ONLINE AUDIO AND VIDEO WORLD

Depending on the subject of your online research, you may or may not find that searching for audio and video files will be of value. If you're interested in history, you can surely find audio files of President Franklin D. Roosevelt's "fireside chats" broadcast on radio in the 1940s. The Library of Congress holdings include early speech recordings of FDR's cousin Teddy Roosevelt at the turn of the twentieth century. Research in video files is obviously limited to the later twentieth century and beyond.

Much of the content of current online audio and video files can be described as "ephemeral"—here today and gone tomorrow. The video file-sharing websites such as YouTube .com rarely contain materials a serious researcher would need. The speeches of politicians and other newsmakers are useful for retrospective finger-pointing, but that can just as easily be done with text transcripts of the speech.

However, if you want to really absorb the flavor of a time period or revisit a significant event, you can do it through audio and video clips. Most operating systems, such as Microsoft Windows, include a media player that will allow you to view and listen to audio and video files quite easily.

The Library of Congress has over 2.5 million audio recordings in its collections, some of which are accessible in digital format. The Sound Online Inventory and Catalog, known by its acronym SONIC, allows online searching of its database, which is organized into categories of recordings. The broad categories include radio broadcasts, news-only radio broadcasts, commercial 78s, 45s, and cassettes, music only, and spoken word only. That's the good news. The bad news is that at the present time you can only search for the bibliographic entries, not the materials themselves. However, that can be useful for deep research background.

The main Library of Congress website (http://catalog.loc. gov) is the easiest place to access the SONIC catalog. Just looking at the list of holdings—from a radio collection of *Meet the Press* broadcasts of 1945–1984 to recordings of the Newport Jazz Festival from the 1950s on—makes me wish I could listen to almost everything in the catalog. Someday in the future, perhaps, this rich cultural and historical material will be digitalized.

So where can you find audio and video files that you *can* access? Happily there are a growing number of websites that archive files in those formats for researchers to use. You can also search for audio and video (and other multimedia) files on the major search engines such as Yahoo!, Google, Alta-Vista, and others, either by keyword search or by using advanced search techniques.

SEARCHING ONLINE ARCHIVES AND COLLECTIONS

One of the best websites for online searches of digital files is the Internet Archive (www.archive.org), which promotes "universal access to human knowledge." The archive is a non-profit internet library founded in 1996 to offer permanent access for researchers, historians, and scholars to historical collections that exist in digital format. The Internet Archive includes texts, audio, moving images, and software as well as archived web pages. As the search tools have advanced, the collection has become more user-friendly for the general public. The potential for finding great research sources is enormous.

On the home page of the Internet Archives is a search box for the Wayback Machine, where you can search by URL and years for versions of web pages that no longer exist on the internet but have been preserved as a cached copy in the archive's databases. Why would you want to do that? Because it's a great way to research the emergence of late twentieth-century culture and technology. You can revisit the sometimes hysterical warnings about Y2K on websites from 1999, or go back and look at your favorite websites in their earlier versions. If you're interested in technology, you can see for yourself how the earliest JavaScripts performed. At present the archive includes about 55 billion web pages. A full-text search feature is planned for the future, but for now the search can only be run on the URL address of a site.

The "Help" file gives excellent information about the archive. The Internet Archive operates basically like a paper research library. You can search and browse through moving images, a live music archive, audio recordings, texts, and software. You can also post questions and comments to a variety of online forums. The drop-down menu in the main search box gives a complete list of the different media and collections in which you can search—there's even one collection devoted solely to the Grateful Dead (well, the archive is located in San Francisco, after all).

Like a scholarly library, the Internet Archive has a set of rules and regulations for using the collections. Much of the material is protected by copyright, and in order to access materials the user must agree to the terms set by the archive. The terms contain a paragraph that sums up all the perils of online research in one fell swoop. It's a thing of beauty—read it slowly.

> Because the content of the Collections comes from around the world and from many different sectors, the Collections may contain information that might be deemed offensive, disturbing, porno-

graphic, racist, sexist, bizarre, misleading, fraudulent, or otherwise objectionable. The Archive does not endorse or sponsor any content in the Collections, nor does it guarantee or warrant that the content available in the Collections is accurate, complete, noninfringing, or legally accessible in your jurisdiction, and you agree that you are solely responsible for abiding by all laws and regulations that may be applicable to the viewing of the content. In addition, the Collections are provided to you on an as-is and as-available basis. You agree that your use of the Site and the Collections is at your sole risk. You understand and agree that the Archive makes no warranty or representation regarding the accuracy, currency, completeness, reliability, or usefulness of the content in the Collections, that the Site or the Collections will meet your requirements, that access to the Collections will be uninterrupted, timely, secure, or error free, or that defects, if any, will be corrected. We make no warranty of any kind, either express or implied.

In chapter five, we looked at a website called Best of the Web (http://botw.org), which provides a hyperlinked subject directory to websites that are reviewed and judged to be of high content and quality to users. Another method to find audio and video files is to browse or search the databases at Best of the Web (and perhaps avoid some of the perils described in the Internet Archive terms above). A quick browse in the BOTW Reference category turns up the British Library Sound Archive, which has a huge collection of 3.5 million recordings, some of which are available in digital files online. A speedy search in the main search window on BOTW for "video files" brings up 1,400 results for related categories, including free software for playing streaming video, websites

Mastering Online Research

with video music clips, and an online tribute to the great runner Jesse Owens, with interactive video.

Most of the photo stock houses mentioned earlier in this chapter also have collections of audio and video files, and even some more advanced multimedia. Visit the sites and search for your topic. Window shopping is free.

USING SEARCH ENGINES TO FIND AUDIO AND VIDEO FILES

Searching for audio and video materials on the major search engines is another one of those "needle in a haystack" challenges. The more closely you can define the target of your research, the better the results. Media files are accumulating online like hangers in a closet, and the vast majority of them will not advance your research one bit. Let's look at how can you use search engines to sift through the haystack.

A simple keyword Google search for "video clips" brings up 82 million hits. That's because the search string lacks definition—there's no particular category or subject of the video clips for the search engine to find. It's only the Google search algorithm that determines the order in which the results are displayed, since no result has any more relevance than another.

If we search again for "corvette video clips" we can narrow the results to less than 700,000. Some of the websites on the results page offer free video clips of Corvettes exploding, crashing, and racing around tracks. If you're writing about vintage automobiles, you might want to go to the advanced search screen and refine your search there by adding the year or model. Or click on the "Video" search option above the Google search window and enter "corvette." Since you're searching in the video database now, the terms "video" and "clips" would be redundant and limit your results.

The video search on the Google search page offers drop down menus for many categories of video files, including the most popular hundred videos of the day, sports, music, animation, and other popular subjects. Entertaining, perhaps, but not much use in doing online research. There's also an advanced search window for "Video" searches, which works similarly to the images advanced search described on page 242, including the Boolean operators.

In the advanced search window, you also can specify the language of the video, the duration (short, medium, or long), and the price (free or "all videos"). If you want to specify the genre, a drop-down list allows you to choose preset categories. You also can sort the results by relevance, rating, title, or date.

A basic keyword Google video search for the name of the former poet laureate and best-selling writer Billy Collins returns sixty-three results. The first pages list a dozen or so animated videos based on Billy Collins's poems. Many of the descriptions list a modest fee for access to the video. One appears to be Collins himself reading one of his poems. By the second page, Billy Collins results have morphed into Billy Joel videos and Shooter Jennings singing at Billy Bob's bar in Texas. It would appear that Billy Collins hasn't produced video files of his poetry readings.

Not necessarily.

When you are researching a topic online, it's always a good idea to use more than one search engine. Switching to

Ask.com for a web search on "Billy Collins video" returns a list of results that include the poet's own website (containing videos) as well as poetry webcasts on the Library of Congress website, news interview clips, and more. Another switch to AltaVista's search engine allows a search for audio files of Billy Collins. The results are hard to distinguish by their titles but the URLs are revealing (www.parisreview.com/media/mp3s is definitely worth a click). The "More Info" link provides the format, size, and contents list of the audio file or MP3. Many of these results are recordings of the poet reading his work at universities and other venues; some are interviews and readings broadcast by National Public Radio or other media.

Another lesson in internet research—perseverance.

In this chapter we have only touched on the issues surrounding copyright of online materials and permission to use them. Suppose some of those Billy Collins audio files were made by fans in the audience, without the poet's permission? Who would own the rights to distribute the file online? Chapter eleven may help you to figure that out—or at least to learn where to ask the question.

If your creative juices are starting to dry up with all this technical stuff, turn your bleary eyes to chapter ten. You'll learn some imaginative techniques and tips for the kind of online research that stimulates writers to do their best work.

CHAPTER 10

RESEARCH SKILLS FOR WRITERS

The World Wide Web is a gathering place for writers. Communicating, sharing ideas and solutions, inspiring and encouraging fellow writers—the online world is the writers group that's open 24/7, no matter where you are. In this chapter, you'll find suggestions for websites that will be helpful to you in developing your writing skills, finding new venues for publishing your work, learning how to present yourself and your work professionally, and stimulating your creativity. As we know by now, the only constant on the Web is change, so be sure to explore new sites and technologies besides your established favorites. You might even end up hosting your own website!

This chapter also takes a closer look at search strategies as they can be used by beginning and experienced writers. You'll learn how to use the Web to help with the market research every writer has to do for a new project. You'll find online resources that can provide the right details to make any kind of writing come alive—whether it's a historical epic, a contemporary novel, a thematic essay, or a newspaper article.

Even when you're writing fiction, it's important to keep your research sources accurate. As an editor I try to save authors from embarrassing oversights, both factual and grammatical—and as an author I try hard to save myself. I once edited a chapter in a book of retold biblical stories in which Mary, the mother of Jesus, sat in a rocking chair on a porch at her cousin Elizabeth's house, wearing an apron and knitting a baby garment. What is wrong with this picture? I asked, and I began my internet searches.

Rocking chairs on porches weren't a common feature of the average home in the hill country of Judea back then. And the debates over whether the Egyptians knew how to knit (maybe those fibers in the tombs were merely knotted yarns) weren't convincing enough for me, much less to assume that a Jewish teenager who had not traveled in Egypt at that time would learn how to make a baby sweater. Okay, it wasn't a sweater. But since sweaters weren't around then, either, I would have checked that out. I was pretty sure that women wore aprons, even if they were merely cloths tucked around the waist to keep their main garments clean. Fortunately the author of the story was in favor of historical accuracy and relinquished the anachronisms. Creatively she had been drawing on her own memories of waiting for her first son to be born—in the Pacific Northwest in the twentieth century.

The research skills that have been explained throughout this book can be applied to any kind of writing you might want to do. In the following sections, we'll look further at how to use background research to establish authentic details and historical settings. Before that, we'll look at some tips on how to present your work in its best light through market research. No matter what your project is, you can locate and gather what you need with online searching. You've already got the skills. Now let's get going.

HOW TO DO MARKET RESEARCH

For writers, one of the best uses of the World Wide Web is to estimate how receptive the market might be for a new book or article, sometimes even before you write it. Writers and editors always wish that pure creativity and talent will turn hardworking writers into best-selling authors, but that is rarely the case. Writers have to become knowledgeable about the genre in which they want to publish, whether fiction or nonfiction. They have to know what types of books are selling, and they have to make a solid argument to a potential publisher about why their particular book or article will appeal to the audience. Writers today usually are required to submit a marketing plan along with the proposal for a book. And when submitting a magazine article query, they must include a paragraph about who the target audience is and why the proposed article fits the publication's needs.

Ultimately, of course, the question of why a particular book sells and others do not is unanswerable—it depends upon the whims of the buying public. There's an apocryphal story about a corporate businessman who, after acquiring a publishing company, went to a high-level editorial meeting to present his great new idea for increasing the company's profits: "Let's only publish best-sellers." But in the actual world of publishing, every author wants to give proposal the best chance of being accepted—and that means doing market research.

MARKET RESEARCH FOR A BOOK PROPOSAL

When you begin to develop a concept for a new book, you need to ask some tough questions to help you analyze the possible market for the book. Many of the questions apply similarly to nonfiction and fiction books (for adults and for children), so we'll look at the questions with respect to both genres and distinguish between them when it's important. Market research can be undertaken for books of poetry, too, although poetry is a more specialized niche in publishing, and information is not so easily found on the Web.

If you have received a positive response from a publisher to whom you sent a query letter about your book, the next step will be to submit a book proposal. Any publisher of non-fiction expects a book proposal to contain specific elements that will help the editors and marketers evaluate whether the book will be a good match for the publisher in terms of content and audience. You will need to supply the following:

- A succinct description of the book, almost like the descriptions found on a book jacket's inside flaps
- A longer, more detailed explanation of what the book will cover and why that topic is important
- A table of contents, often with details for each chapter
- A short biography describing your qualifications for writing this book and your previous publishing credits

- A marketing analysis, in which you will describe the potential audience for the book and support your belief that the book will sell to the target audience
- A sample chapter or two, in order to judge how well you can handle your proposed material (if requested by the publisher)

A publisher of fiction expects the same basic proposal elements, substituting a detailed synopsis of the book's plot and characters for the description of the nonfiction book's topic. Depending on their individual submission guidelines, fiction publishers want to see the first ten pages of the book, a few chapters, or a completed manuscript.

Many writers find that preparing the market analysis is the most difficult part of putting together the book proposal. The World Wide Web offers support in all stages of that process, although some of the market research also benefits from visits to libraries and bookstores (a pleasant chore for a writer). You can apply all of the online research skills you have learned in earlier chapters, and you can benefit from the excellent resources available on the Web specifically for writers.

Your goal is to define what makes this book unique among the tens of thousands of books that will be published—and to convince a publisher that customers will plunk down real money to read it. The more information you assemble to substantiate your claims, the better.

Research: What's the Critical Need Your Book Will Fulfill?

The publisher wants to know why your book matters—and you need to know that, too. Online research can help provide

Mastering Online Research

evidence of the answers to these questions and demonstrate the need for your unique book to be published.

- How critical is the problem or the issue you address in your book?
- How seriously does it affect the members of any particular group? How large is the group?
- Is the book concerned with a short-term problem or does it address an issue that is ongoing and pervasive?
- What significant value will a reader gain from reading your book? Does it offer compelling information, a solution to a problem, authoritative advice to satisfy an established need?
- What makes you the perfect author for this book? What do you bring to the topic that another author would not?

The initial step in answering these questions is to check out what other similar books on your topic may already have been published. That will help you to determine how your proposed book is different from the others. Instead of guessing about the competition and the uniqueness, use the Web to find out.

My first step usually is to visit the online bookseller Amazon. com. In fact it's a good idea to conduct this type of research at the earliest stage of considering a new book idea, when you are preparing your query letter, because you can see whether your idea has already been covered sufficiently, and by which publishers. (Few publishers will publish books very similar in concept to those currently selling well for them—it might cut short sales for the first book, which is called "cannibalizing the market." It's better to look for a competing publisher to query.)

You can browse for books in any category to see where your proposed book would fit best. Amazon has a well developed search engine that will help you to narrow or broaden your searches. Click on a few of the books that appear most similar to your book concept. You can glean information from each one and compile the data into a list of competing books to include in your market analysis.

Product information. Take a look at the product information section. Note how many pages the book has, whether it's published in hardcover or paperback, the date of publication, and the retail price. Is your book comparable?

Competing titles. Who published these competing titles? Are some of them self-published? Do the publishers range from commercial trade houses to university and small presses, or do they group mostly on one side of the scale or the other?

Sales figures. Take a look at the sales ranking figure—but don't take them too seriously. If all the books on your topic are included in the top thousand sellers on Amazon, though, include that fact in your market analysis.

Reader reviews. Read the comments about the books posted by the readers. Is there any consistent thread running through the comments? A wish for a certain treatment of a subject that the other books haven't fulfilled? A complaint about the depth of research in other books, which you could remedy in your own book? If your book does a better job at fulfilling these readers' needs, that's a good sign.

To further substantiate this part of your market research, you might want to run a search on BooksInPrint.com, the publishing industry's largest web-based bibliographic resource. The database contains over 5 million titles (including forthcoming books) and is available for searching at most public libraries. Some libraries make it available for patrons to use from their home computers. You can search by topic, author name, and title. As a publishing resource database, BooksInPrint typically is more current with its list of upcoming books than the online booksellers such as Amazon or Barnes & Noble.

Another method of market research is using basic and advanced keyword searches on the largest search engines to locate websites that support your conviction of the critical need for your book. Refine the search results lists to find the documents, news articles, expert testimonies, and other materials that demonstrate the currency of your book. Drill down through subject directories to find links to the evidence supporting your book's thesis.

Finally, visit university and college websites to take a look at their academic course offerings. For writers in any field, that's a good way to keep up with what the best and brightest teachers and researchers are currently working on. Although you can't base a book of your own on someone's posted course curriculum, you can certainly draw on the concepts to substantiate the interest in your own book's topic.

Research: Who Will Buy This Book?

The next group of questions you need to answer concerns the size of the market for your book and the ability to reach that market. Your research results must convince the publisher that there are enough potential buyers to make the book profitable to sell. There is no reliable formula that can predict how well a particular book will sell, but you can find information online that will help support the existence of the audience. Ask yourself the following questions:

- How large is the group of readers who would be interested in your book? (Authors sometimes answer that question with "Everybody!", but publishers want a more informed and realistic answer.)
- How easy is it to pinpoint the group of potential buyers? Are they in a particular geographic location? A specific age group?
- Are there in fact several different audiences who might benefit from the book? That's called "crossover" marketing and is a desirable position.
- Are there organizations or institutions who might buy quantities of your book for their members or staffs?
- Will your book appeal to people of a certain income level? A particular level of education?

Publishers are very happy when your market analysis furnishes concrete, verifiable numbers of potential buyers for your book—for instance, the membership numbers of trade or service organizations that might be specifically interested in your book's topic. That is not to say that the publisher will pay for a marketing mailing or e-mailing to actually reach those potential customers—but at least there is evidence that the audience exists. How can you locate information on these groups and potential audiences using the Web?

One way is to search or browse the Yahoo! Directory for appropriate organizations. For example, you can easily find listings for various trade organizations, directories of businesses, directories of associations, and so forth. If you want to know how many people are active members of Pet Sitters International, you can find their website on the Yahoo! Directory and get an estimate of membership when you link to the site.

Use keyword searches that relate to the topic of your book, and then brainstorm about what keywords might be used to search for other groups of people who might be interested. Most subject directories on the Web have categories for organizations and interest groups. If you're writing a novel whose main characters interact through a quilting group, find real-life quilters' groups online, search their quilting blogs, find out the circulation of the main quilters' magazines—use whatever you can find to estimate the interest in your book.

You can also search Google Groups, msn.com groups, and Yahoo! groups to find potential audiences. Blogging sites are possible sources for demonstrable audiences of people interested in your topic.

If you are writing a book that will appeal to owners and sailors of yachts in the forty-foot class, for example, you can search the Web for magazines and other publications devoted to that audience (get the circulation numbers), and you can search for geographic locales where that leisure activity is most common. You can cross-search on government websites (regional, state, or local) for those locales to determine the income level and age of residents, and you may even be able to find a statistic about the numbers of yacht owners. Don't forget to check the news sites for yachting events worldwide.

Another piece of information that might be helpful in your market analysis is to define the section of a bookstore in which your proposed book would be shelved. Books normally are only shelved in one place, although major chain stores sometimes put a popular book in two or three shelving categories simultaneously. Looking at the categories of online bookstore sites will help you to narrow down the placement, and a trip to your local bricks-and-mortar store will confirm it. Thoughtful consideration of exactly where a buyer would be able to find your book on a shelf actually helps you to retain your focus on the essential audience for your book.

Analysis: Making Your Case

Once you have completed all the research on the potential market for your book, you'll need to present it in a clear, digestible form for your proposal. A page or two should be sufficient to convey the information. Organize the statistics on your potential market in a bulleted, easy to scan list, and keep your prose tightly focused. An important part of presenting your market research is to demonstrate the compelling significance of your book's topic. In your proposal, this material should be presented in succinct and powerful statements— you can attach supporting documents from the Web or from other sources at the end of the proposal. You may already have done much of this research in the process of defining your book's content for yourself.

In your analysis, explain clearly how your book offers a unique approach to the topic and summarize the main selling point of your book's information on the problem or issue. For example, if you are proposing to write a book about water rights as one of the most pressing global issues of the twenty-first century, provide a brief explanation of the background of water rights, the growing struggle for ownership of water in countries with poor water resources, and the present and future concerns over the sale of the basic necessity of life. Show the publisher how pressing the problem is, and how your book will help people to make decisions about it.

Support your credibility as the perfect author by keeping your presentation of facts current. Scan the headlines of major newspapers every day. If you subscribe to free RSS feeds (see chapter eight) that furnish continuously updated headlines and short extracts of articles, you can speedily go through the major daily newspapers of several cities and the newspapers offering national and international coverage, all in one handy list. Writers of fiction can make a case for the timeliness and relevance of the proposed book by using the suggestions above, too.

MARKET RESEARCH FOR MAGAZINE ARTICLES

When you are doing market research for magazine pieces, the reason and the results are different in some respects from market research for a book. Magazine market research tends to focus on where to submit queries and articles rather than how to reach a buying audience. The audience is already determined by the magazine's paid circulation and point-of-purchase sales. Your task as a writer is to match your interests in writing to the profile of the average reader of the magazine. (If your published article increases per-copy sales, that's terrific, and you can ask for more money the next time around.)

The questions and tips to help define the critical need your book fulfills (discussed previously) are useful to magazine and newspaper writers as well. Even a four-hundred-word filler piece has to grab the reader because it solves a problem or answers a need in that person's life. Especially if you are proposing a lengthy feature article to a magazine or newspaper, you can use the research skills to demonstrate why your piece will appeal to readers and how the information it contains will give them substantial value.

The Web is perfectly suited to doing market research for magazines. Publications large and small have a presence on the Web. Some publish content online only—they are called ezines or webzines. Others publish both print and online editions, and the newest trend in online publishing is making the websites interactive. Readers compete for daily or weekly prizes, chat with one another in discussion groups on topics related to the magazine articles, offer story tips and ideas, and even act as judges for article or story competitions. Editors to whom you submit your article queries are going to evaluate how web-savvy you are as an author—do you furnish a carefully selected group of web pages that augment the information in your article? Do you back up your central thesis with reliable websites that the reader can visit? If appropriate, do you add entertainment or educational value to your readers' experience?

The first step in doing market research to promote your article to a specific magazine involves getting to know the content, style, and tone of the magazine. The best way to do this is to read a few sample copies. Before the easy accessibility of the Web, writers had to buy print copies or request samples from the publisher. Now all you have to do is click.

If you know which magazine you want to research, you can find the website through a Google or Yahoo! search for the title. There are also online sites that offer free access to linked databases of magazines (for example, Wooden Horse Publishing's database at www.woodenhorsepub.com). If you have a subscription to *Writer's Market* online (www.writersmarket .com), you can click on the links to access the magazine's home page. What are you hoping to learn from the magazine's website? Take a close look at the following:

Cover. Examine the cover of the magazine first. Usually the current cover is displayed on the home page; sometimes previous covers are accessible, too. If it's an ezine without a print version, the home page functions as the cover. The magazine's primary focus is emphasized in the article teaser lines on the cover and in the graphic design. Even the most conservative magazines want to grab the attention of readers by the clever use of headlines.

Tables of Contents. Study the table of contents of several issues of the magazine. Discover how the magazine is arranged, what the various sections are, how many features or articles there are, and how they meet the expectations of the readers. Keep in mind that the online version of the magazine may have an abbreviated table of contents, because not all articles, sidebars, fillers, and so on are posted to the Web. If you're serious about writing for a publication, order a print copy—you can usually do that online.

Website. Check out the pages of the website for the information that will help you market to the magazine. A media kit or a web page for advertisers often provides information on circulation and the demographics of the average reader (such as age, income and education level, and geographic location). The "About the Magazine" page gives a "mission statement" of why the magazine publishes for its readers. If the website has a letter from the editor or publisher, read that too.

Online articles. Read the articles posted online to see how your proposed topic and style would fit in. Look at what's been published in the past year, too, if the website has an archive of previous issues. It's highly unlikely that a magazine will publish another article on a topic that has appeared as a feature within the past six to twelve months.

Editorial calendar. Find an editorial calendar if possible. It may be on the page for advertisers—you can search the site for "calendar" or drill down through the links. Editorial calendars set out the full year's editorial themes and dates for the magazine so that advertisers can fine-tune their ads to emphasize certain aspects that are covered editorially in a particular issue. You can use that same information to match your article queries to a proposed issue. Keep in mind that magazines work up to six months ahead in acquiring material (some smaller online publications might be able to publish with less lead time).

Comparing the websites of several magazines that are possible publishers for your proposed article or story will help you to get a feel for which are the best fit. The submissions guidelines page on the magazine's website will give you the details on how to proceed and also information on freelance rates and payment for accepted or commissioned articles. You can quickly find the submission guidelines for most publications by adding the word "guidelines" to your keyword search for the magazine title. The guidelines are also widely available in some of the online resources for writers described on the following pages.

GENERAL ONLINE RESOURCES FOR WRITERS

An invaluable source of information and encouragement for writers has developed on the World Wide Web. Magazines, ezines, newsletters, organizations, writers' resource sites, discussion groups, blogs, webrings, and other online community web pages bring together information from all over the Web and from the print world, too. Instead of going to your local library in hopes that you could find a copy of *Literary Marketplace* from the current decade (it's expensive, so libraries don't order every year), you can log on and search for the latest news and tips for writers.

PUBLICATIONS FOR WRITERS AND PUBLISHERS

Magazines for writers and for the publishing industry in general often have online versions that you can visit and then subscribe to if you wish. Trade publications tend to be more expensive than magazines for the individual writer, and your local library may have subscriptions to the main publications for the publishing business. Make friends with your reference librarians.

Booklist

www.booklistonline.com

Writers read *Booklist* for the reviews and articles by people who love books. The long-running journal is published by the American Library Association.

The Horn Book

www.hbook.com

A journal devoted to the field of children's and young adult literature, *The Horn Book* provides exceptional book reviews and articles by and about authors and illustrators.

Library Journal

www.libraryjournal.com

Keeps you up-to-date on what's going on in the library world, especially in the book reviews and articles on trends in what readers want.

Poets & Writers

www.pw.org/mag

An excellent resource for poets and other writers, "from inspiration to publication."

Publishers Weekly

www.publishersweekly.com

The premier trade magazine for the publishing industry, which offers free e-mail newsletters. Although a subscription presently includes both the weekly print version of the magazine and access to the online version, I prefer the online version in terms of usefulness and timeliness.

Writer's Digest Magazine

www.writersdigest.com

A monthly magazine that is essential for beginning and experienced writers alike. Articles cover a wide spectrum of writing-related subjects, including techniques for writing stories, articles, novels, nonfiction books, audiovisual materials, and speeches. Regular columns in the magazine cover news in the industry, fiction, nonfiction, submitting, and publishing. The publication carries interviews with well-known writers, information on subjects involving legal matters and material on the business of writing.

The Writer Magazine

www.writermag.com/wrt

Published for more than 120 years, this magazine offers articles, interviews, and a wide variety of online forums for discussion on the website.

ORGANIZATION AND ASSOCIATION RESOURCES

Just about every genre of writing has its own representation on the Web. Some organizations and associations are open only to published authors; others welcome new writers and associate members who are in the publishing, research, and educational fields. You can find these organizations and others like them by searching for "writers organizations" on Google or Yahoo! You'll also find hyperlinks to various organizations on writer-oriented web pages. Among the best and most established groups are listed below.

- **American Society of Journalists and Authors** (www.asja.org)
- **The Authors Guild** (www.authorsguild.org)
- **Horror Writers Association** (www.horror.org)
- **Mystery Writers of America** (www.mysterywriters.org)
- **Poetry Society of America** (www.poetrysociety.org)
- **Poets & Writers, Inc.** (www.pw.org)
- **Romance Writers of America** (www.rwanational.org)

- **Sisters in Crime** (www.sistersincrime.org)
- **Society of Children's Book Writers and Illustrators** (www.scbwi.org)

HELPFUL WEBSITES FOR WRITERS AND FREELANCERS

Websites for writers abound in cyberspace. Some are more serious than others and offer useful tips and contacts from working writers and editors. Others are great for inspiration and fun. The sites listed below are among the ones that I judged to be worth a visit, but you might want to search the Web yourself to see the hundreds of other sites out there.

About Freelance Writing (www.aboutfreelancewriting.com)

Dmoz Open Directory Project
(http://dmoz.org/Arts/Writers_Resources)

Funds for Writers (www.fundsforwriters.com)

Suite 101: Enter Curious (www.suite101.com)

Writer's Resource Center (www.poewar.com)

Writers Weekly (www.writersweekly.com)

Writing.com (www.writing.com)

Writing for Dollars Newsletter (www.writingfordollars.com)

Writers' web resources—both practical and inspirational— can also be found by searching for your favorite authors' websites. Established authors often post encouraging information and links for beginning writers on their sites, and there are blogs and online discussion groups that provide valuable information. Don't spend all your time browsing online, though—use some to get started on that new book or article.

BACKGROUND RESEARCH TIPS FOR WRITERS

All the techniques explored in this section are applicable to writers who are researching facts and flavor for stories, novels, plays, articles, books, reports, technical white papers, theses, and other forms of writing. The depth of the background research depends, of course, on the objective of the written piece—an article for the newsletter of a community group requires much less research than an article for the newsletter of a national association of professional engineers. That's not to say that the *standards* are different: You should be scrupulous in checking facts and quotations and in citing sources for both.

BRINGING PEOPLE TO LIFE

In this section we'll look at how to find the online details and background information that will help you to create and delineate people and their lifestyles, contemporary or historical, fictional or real. Creating believable, compelling characters is one of the most important skills for a fiction writer to develop. Portraying real people accurately and objectively is also a skill needed by journalists and other non-fiction writers, teachers of literature and social sciences, and anyone who summarizes the lives and accomplishments of people for the public eye.

Chapter seven described how to search for people using various search engines and telephone and e-mail directory websites. That's not exactly the type of search we're looking at here. We want to find out the details that make real people tick, the careers and lifestyles of the socio-ethnic group on which you plan to center your writing or other project. If one of your fictional characters is a Native American and you are not, how do you find the appropriate details to bring that character to life within his culture? If you're writing a magazine article profiling a Native American teacher, for instance, you need to find the background knowledge to place that individual in context. You can't merely read the novels of Tony Hillerman and call it research. You've got to find the places on the internet where people are sharing their experiences and perspectives on being a Native American in today's world.

Searching blogs and online discussion groups is one way to find their voices. Reading online magazines and newspapers focused on the Native American reader and writer is another. Better still, if you know where your story is set or where your character or subject has lived, you can search for the Native American communities in that city or state. The Native American experience in Arizona is as different from that in West Virginia as it is from that in Washington State. Use keyword and advanced searches to specify locations and interests. For example, a search on "Native American communities Seattle" quickly takes you to a web page for Red Eagle Soaring, a Native American volunteer youth theater group in Seattle. A search for the same keywords using "Minneapolis" as the location provides a website from the University of Minnesota Graduate School with detailed information on the large, urban Native American communities in the Twin Cities. That's the beginning of an entry into Native American contemporary urban culture. If the fictional character about whom you are writing is only a secondary character, online research may be sufficient.

Characters in fiction, as well as real peole in articles and nonfiction books, need to earn a living, which is part of their background stories. Internet research conducted on any of the subject directories described in chapter five will help you find information on any career—the employers, locations, wages, schedules, and daily grind of any particular industry or service. Just link to the "Business" or "Career" categories of a directory and you're on your way. Major job search sites such as Monster.com and Hotjobs.com can also provide useful articles on what's required and expected in different employment areas. It's also really interesting to read the bloggers' views of their current and past employment experiences.

Personal Web Pages as a Research Tool

When technology advanced to the point where ordinary people could create websites with user-friendly software, the online community started to become like a neighborhood. Families post travel diaries of their vacations and share photos with friends and relatives online. School district websites offer access to homework assignments for fifth-graders who forgot their notebooks at school, and teachers create classroom pages to display students' artwork and writing projects. Local cafés post their daily specials online. You may even have a website of your own that reflects your enthusiasms and interests.

The personal flavor of such websites provides an unusual resource for writers of fiction and nonfiction. We can get to know what's in the hearts and minds of perfect strangers—and the more we know about the human condition, the richer our works will become. The individuals who maintain personal web pages are *hoping* for visitors. They invest time and thought into what information and opinions they offer to the online community. It's a valued form of expression that has never been available before.

Because of the issue of privacy, I don't feel comfortable in pointing out specific websites for a sample search in this section. As a fiction writer you can base a character's physical description on a photograph found on the Web, but be careful not to use a name or an identifying piece of clothing or jewelry. Nonfiction writers may want to approach the owner for permission to use materials on a personal website, if the information will be useful in the writing project.

Personal websites tend to be less stable over time than commercial or institutional websites. I suggest you run a basic search on Google, Yahoo! or another large search engine for "personal websites" or "personal web pages" to get a list of results to evaluate. Some will be websites offering to create personal web pages for you, and some will direct you to lists of personal websites or to internet providers that host them. You'll probably get a couple of online dating services, too.

You can also combine the "personal websites" search with a topic keyword. If you find an entry on the results list that points you where you want to go, try clicking on the "Similar" or "More like this" options to expand your search.

HISTORICAL BACKGROUND

The best writing is rich in the detail that makes the story and people come alive. Using your online research skills and some creative thinking, you can find accurate and solid details on life in just about any period in history or any place in the world. The lengthy research process that used to involve sending letters back and forth to archivists, librarians, and experts—and pestering the interlibrary loan staff at your local library—can now be accomplished in a few good sessions at your computer.

Forward-thinking writers and researchers take full advantage of the modern technology of the World Wide Web to give them a view into the historical past. Access to documents, maps, photographs, journals, diaries, court records, and various other artifacts of the past has given users an almost endless bounty on which to draw—and more treasures are being added all the time.

Researching historical detail for my books (and to satisfy my own curiosity) is my favorite activity on the internet. Any excuse will do. I was making a batch of split pea soup the other day and suddenly I wondered how the hard dried peas are split so perfectly in half. Is there industrial pea-splitting machinery? How did farmers in the 1800s make split peas? And why did they bother splitting the peas at all?

A quick search online revealed that yellow field peas are a staple crop of Saskatchewan, and one of the largest Saskatchewan processors has a facility in neighboring province Manitoba that only handles yellow peas. I could easily call the company or e-mail them to ask what kind of machinery they use. But when I discovered on another agricultural website that peas began to be split in ancient Egypt, to make them tastier and more like lentils, my curiosity was satisfied.

Research Skills for Writers

There must be a way to husk the peas and split them by hand as well as by machine. That's enough for me at present. And now I know why the soup recipe was called "Canadian Yellow Split Pea Soup."

That little search may seem frivolous, but if I ever wanted to write a story about a restless young Canadian in 1905 who is stuck on a prairie farm near Saskatoon splitting peas for a living, I'd want to have details on the exact method he used. That's the level of authenticity I look for in historical fiction—and in biographies and historical nonfiction as well.

(As an aside, I should say that when I revise my manuscripts some of that meticulous detail has to come out. What I, as the author, need to know and what the reader needs to know at each point in the story do not always require the same level of detail.)

In the following sections we'll take a closer look at a few of the online resources that are available to the historical researcher. You'll be applying the same kinds of search techniques that you would use to search for information about the modern world. And you'll need to be just as vigilant about incorrect assumptions and faulty facts. Don't take everything you read and see on the internet at face value.

Adding Period Detail

Adding flavor to your historical writing or research project is done most easily with period detail—the clothing, etiquette, manner of speech, commonly used objects, typical food and medicines, and daily work of an identifiable period in history. You can find information on these elements in a variety of ways online.

          Mastering Online Research

One place to start is with a keyword search for "historical sites" in which you can specify the country if you know where you want to focus your work. If you're looking for detail on American life, you can search the databases at the National Park Service's National Register of Historic Places (www.cr.nps.gov/nr/). Locate the historic places or other landmarks in the state, area, or community in which you're interested, and the resulting description will give you a group of hyperlinks to websites related to that place.

One good example of the wealth of material available online is the website for Thomas Jefferson's home at Monticello (www.monticello.org). The site offers an in-depth multimedia tour, including 3-D models of the house and a narrated tour of the gardens and plantation. You can search within the website to find more specific detail, too. A search for "slave quarters" turned up hyperlinks that provided information from archaeological studies, historical descriptions, and even sketches of the cabins. The website also has links to academic research, document collections, slave biographies, Jefferson's books and other writings, and much more.

Writers can locate excellent information about life in specific time periods through the work of archaeologists who study the human past. As the CyberPursuits archaeology website says, "It is a science well suited for anyone who enjoys biology, botany, geology, chemistry, history, psychology, art, and solving a great puzzle." Writers and researchers can benefit from the serious work done by archaeologists at physical sites all over the world, and a good place to start is this website (www.cyber

pursuits.com/archeo/default.asp). You'll find great links that are easy to follow, organized by regions, topics, programs, and resources. The same website has an anthropology section (www.cyberpursuits.com/anthro/default .asp) that covers general, cultural, and physical anthropology, linguistics, and ethnology, the study of culture. It provides links to reference material, academic departments, libraries, museums, publications, organizations, and other endeavors. You can even buy a museum replica of a Neanderthal skull.

Searching for details on authentic clothing opens up the world of costume design, clothing history, and even the modern area of historical reenactments. A simple keyword search for "costume design" turns up a number of results for theatrical costume designers and a Wikipedia.com article that has a hyperlink to the University of Washington Libraries' special interest collections, one of which is a digital fashion plate collection. Organized by women's fashion styles into distinct chronological periods, the digital images are illustrations from the popular magazines and printed sources of the times. The Victoria and Albert Museum mentioned in chapter nine on page 247 also has searchable archives for fashion and textiles that are remarkably rich.

An unusual but interesting search area is comprised of the websites maintained by historical reenactors and the clothing designers who outfit them, who are generally called sutlers. A keyword search for "reenactors clothing" will net you lots of websites for many different time periods (often connected to a war, because it gives the reenactors something to do). Many of the sites give explicit instructions on the styles and the fabrics that conform to the authenticity required of serious reenactors, which can be very informative.

Do you wonder what the characters in your historical biography or novel might have eaten? Food research on the World Wide Web is lots of fun. An easy starting point is a keyword search for "reenactors food," since we've been discussing that topic. The search brings up a page on About.com on food and drink resources for reenactors, most of which is focused on the Middle Ages. The links provide recipes for brewing mead, medieval recipes adapted for the modern kitchen, and Jacobean dinner recipes.

Whether the time period you're researching is ancient Rome, colonial America, or eighteenth-century France, you can be sure someone has written something on the food of the times. The website www.foodtimeline.com is a rich resource to find out what people ate at different periods and places in history. The earliest written recipes (for meat-and-sauce dishes and barley-wheat bread) are found in Mesopotamia in the second millennium B.C.E. The timeline continues onward, with hyperlinks to recipes and other web resources for food throughout the ages.

A perhaps surprising web resource in which to look for period lifestyle detail is an online auction site, such as EBay.com. If you want to find out describable details on a common lamp in 1910, browse or search the "Antiques" category on EBay. The site has artifacts from an amazingly broad range of historical eras, including classical antiquities, maps, furniture, musical instruments, and rugs for sale—and you can browse for free. You can also conduct keyword searches on Yahoo! or Google for specific articles or tools that will bring up collector and antique dealer sites. These sites usually have detailed photographs and descriptions of the items.

When you are looking for general information on what types of furnishings, lighting, sanitation, and the like would be authentic to a particular time period and place, you might get the best results by searching an online encyclopedia, an informational site such as About.com, or even Wikipedia.org.

As your skills in online research develop, you'll find information and inspiration coming to you ever more quickly. Writers of all types have communications capabilities that would have amazed their counterparts in earlier centuries—even in earlier decades. But the standards of excellence for which writers strive don't change, and neither does our enthusiasm for the writing process.

CHAPTER 11
PERMISSIONS AND COPYRIGHT ISSUES

When you find some incredible statistical information, or a paragraph by a writer that says exactly what you mean, or an image that is just perfect for your project, can you merely copy it from the World Wide Web and use it?

The technology makes it so easy. But the U.S. and international copyright laws say "Nope—not without asking." Of course there are shades of gray in the answer to any such black-and-white question, and that's what we'll look at in this chapter. What is covered by copyright law and requires written permission to reproduce? What can you reproduce under the doctrine of "fair use"? How long do copyrights last? Is there material that is free for everybody? If you are only reading about a topic for your own personal knowledge and don't plan to use the information or images in any other way, then you are in no danger of violating copyright law. But if you want to write a book or article quoting from or drawing on ideas from another source, or if you want to create a website using images and text from other websites, or if you want to teach a course using some of the material, then you need to take note of the copyright issues.

Students who are writing research papers and essays for their classes may quote from copyrighted sources without requesting permission to use the material because their papers will not be published. Of course the quoted material must be identified and attributed to its original author to avoid any possibility of plagiarism.

The issues surrounding the copyright of published and unpublished materials have never been simple, even after Congress passed a law thirty years ago attempting to improve the regulations. Ever since what may be called "new media" became part of the picture, people have been scrambling to fit the existing rules to the new technology. Fortunately for our purposes, we can rely on the advice of a few respected authorities on the application of U.S. copyright law (which cooperates with foreign copyright laws) and the accepted practices in the publishing industry. Unless you're preparing to produce a multimedia extravaganza complete with music, song lyrics, art works, and readings of contemporary poems, what you'll learn here should be sufficient. (And if you are a multimedia producer, hire a good permissions consultant immediately.)

THE DOCTRINE OF FAIR USE

Before we get into the specifics of copyright laws, it would be good to address the concept of *fair use*. Copyright violations and plagiarism are taken seriously in today's litigious society (just search any newspaper archive for the latest plagiarism scandal or copyright infringement suit). On the other hand, writers and thinkers need to be able to build upon the work of others to support their own ideas and to add tangy bits of wisdom and information from those who have already published. That sharing of intellect and freedom of knowledge is part of the community of readers and writers, whether in print or online, and it must be preserved. From the concept of limiting the "absolutism" of copyright law, the doctrine of fair use evolved.

The *Chicago Manual of Style* (the most recent edition is the fifteenth, published by the University of Chicago Press in 2003) is the authority for writers, editors, and publishers about matters of punctuation, grammar, footnotes, and bibliographies. The venerable book also has a splendid and up-to-date chapter on permissions and copyright, and a clear, understandable discussion of what is called the doctrine of fair use. In an exercise of the fair use doctrine advocated by the University of Chicago Press, I am quoting here a couple of sentences from its *Manual of Style* (section 4.75), to be sure that you understand the limits clearly. According to the *Manual of Style*, the doctrine of fair use "allows authors to quote from other authors' work or to reproduce small amounts of graphic or pictorial material for purposes of review or criticism or to illustrate or buttress their own points. Authors invoking fair use should transcribe accurately and give credit to their sources. They should not quote out of context, making the author of the quoted passage seem to be saying something opposite to, or different from, what was intended."

I couldn't say it any better than that.

HOW FAIR USE HELPS YOU

The idea of fair use applies similarly to the use of print and online resources and is intended to allow people to share their work freely when the goal is to benefit the community as a whole. It's not recorded as written law but is a "rule of thumb" that people try to follow, using their judgment and common sense as a guide. Basically, you cannot use such a large proportion of a copyrighted work that its intrinsic value is endangered. If you reproduce an entire five-line poem, for instance, you've taken the whole piece away from the author without payment. If the poem is eighty lines and you quote only five of them in an article or book or web page that discusses such poetry, it could be considered fair use—you have not diminished the worth of the poem as it appears in the poet's published volume, and you may even have contributed to gaining new readers for the poet. Of course, you need to give accurate citation to the source of the poem, but you do not need to request written permission to use such a small portion of the work. If, however, those five lines were to be used for commercial purposes—as part of a Honda television advertisement, for example—it would be sensible to request permission, as there is a clear economic benefit to Honda, and thus the usage is not for educational, community, or review purposes.

Another of the criteria for assessing fair use versus plagiarism is whether you are using the ideas or text or images of someone else's work to stand in for your own efforts. If you want to publish a biographical sketch of Abraham Lincoln on your Civil War website, you can't simply copy and paste one from an online encyclopedia or website. You would either need to write a new biographical sketch yourself in your own words or else request permission to use the text of an article from the encyclopedia or other resource. If you wanted to include a couple paragraphs from a noted four hundred-page biography of Lincoln, however, you could do so with no qualms, because the amount of the quoted material is small in relation to the complete biography—of course, you would need to cite the biography as your source, with full publishing information and page numbers.

The use of ideas expressed in someone else's work is a more subtle question of fair use. If you are basing your arguments or discussion of a subject on the ideas or statistics that you've read in a work written by another person—whether in printed or electronic form—then you must credit the originator of those ideas in your own work. Copyright law protects the author against the production of derivative works, not to mention the ethics of pretending that someone else's original idea is your own. Do you recall the plagiarism lawsuits over the Harry Potter books? An American author claimed that J.K. Rowling had stolen the term "Muggles" and the physical appearance of a character named Larry Potter from works published in 1983 and later. U.S. courts in 2002 found in favor of Rowling and assessed fines against the other author for lying and doctoring evidence. In this case the accused was innocent. But in everyday, less sensational contexts, if you are using the groundbreaking studies on fat metabolism from a university research scientist to develop a new diet plan published on your website, give the doctor the credit for the statistics and for the original thinking. How you *apply* his work becomes your own original expression.

PUBLISHERS' GENERALLY ACCEPTED GUIDELINES REGARDING FAIR USE

When you submit a manuscript to a publisher and it is accepted for publication, the publishing agreement usually stipulates that you will obtain the necessary permissions and pay the usage fees for including any copyrighted pieces in your work. When you publish online, even if you are posting to your own website, there is no contract that holds you accountable. Again, that's where the doctrine of fair use holds sway. Online or in print, copyright still matters. So what guidelines do the publishers follow?

Most of the scholarly and trade publishers for whom I've worked as an editor and who publish my books use the same general "rules of thumb":

You may quote no more than 300–350 words from an individual book-length work before needing to request formal permission. That's a total—whether it's in one chunk or several widely dispersed through the work. A short story, article, or essay would have a proportionately smaller quota, about 100 words.

You may quote up to 4–5 lines of a single poem, unless those lines comprise most of the entire poem. If you quote a complete poem, you must request permission.

Song lyrics are iffy. The recording companies are highly sensitive to copyright issues, and using even one line from a song may require permission.

Quotations must be transcribed accurately from the original. You can't mess around with the original author's words, and anything omitted from the original in your quote must be replaced by an ellipsis (…).

Sources must be given for all quoted material, either in the text or in endnotes or footnotes, depending on the publisher's style.

Short quotations used as epigraphs at the beginnings of chapters or of the work itself do not usually require permission, but they do require citation of the author and work. That may also be extended to inspirational quotes used as added material in the margins of the text or web page, but not necessarily. A complete book or website made up of quotes from other people's work is not covered under the fair use doctrine.

If some of these rules and regulations tempt you to head for the hills, don't panic! Everything can be worked out in its own time. That's one of the cardinal rules of requesting permission to use copyrighted material—allow plenty of time. Rights and permissions departments at publishing houses are understaffed and overworked. If you can restrict your use of copyrighted material to only that which falls under the doctrine of fair use or is in the public domain, it's better for everybody concerned.

But sometimes your research does require that you use copyrighted material. How do you know who owns the rights to the work you want to use? Is it an individual or a company? Or maybe it's in the public domain—where can you go to look that up? Distribution of the work used to be primarily through print publication, whether in a book, magazine, or newspaper. In our modern world the distribution or publication can also be through posting of material on a website; through e-mails, blogs, and continuous RSS feeds; in audio files, video files, or online visual images; and all of the new communications venues being developed. It can be mind-boggling just trying to figure out who owns the copyright and whether you can legally use the material.

INTRODUCTION TO U.S. COPYRIGHT LAW

Copyright law was established to protect the rights of the author of an original work. (The term "author" refers to a writer, artist, composer, illustrator, performer, photographer, programmer, or producer—in other words, the individual who brings into existence any original work that can be publicly distributed in a tangible form.) The U.S. copyright law gives the author the exclusive right to reproduce the work, prepare new works based on that work (called derivative works), distribute copies, and publicly perform and distribute the work. The author also has the right to transfer that copyright to another party, such as a publisher, and the copyright is a form of intellectual property that is part of the author's inheritable estate at death. Most of the documents, graphics, images, audio, video, and other media files that you encounter on the internet are protected by U.S. copyright laws, even if they originate on non-U.S. websites. They are not free for borrowing without permission, in excess of the doctrine of fair use described above.

The World Wide Web used to be like the Wild West. On the frontier, marshals were few and far between, so a person's code of honor operated as the law: A cowboy wouldn't steal another guy's horse; if a stranger showed up at your campfire you shared the beans. But in recent years in the online world—which by its open nature does not have a marshal to enforce the law—the personal code of honor apparently bit the dust. Perhaps it was because of the anonymity of online contact; perhaps because of ignorance of the law: in any event, wholesale "borrowing" of copyrighted material, graphics, even software programs seemed acceptable. Downloading and swapping music files was perhaps the most flagrant violation of copyright law, and it brought the issue of copyright ownership and protection to public—and corporate and legal—attention (remember Napster?). Copyright law is now being enforced more seriously, particularly through litigation between major web corporations and publishers. Some sites on the Web remain open for anyone to share, as in the old days: Usually the organization or the loose group of "members" who maintain the site will make a point of stating that their material is free of copyright or usage restrictions. But other than those free sites, you can assume that everything else on the internet is protected under the copyright laws (unless it passed into the public domain after the copyright expired—more on that on page 295).

HOW COPYRIGHT LAW WORKS

When Congress passed the Copyright Act of 1976, many reforms were made to the existing federal copyright law. All the details aren't necessary here, but there are certain important changes that went into effect with the new law on

January 1, 1978. The most significant is the fact that an automatic copyright protects the author from the moment she makes a tangible piece of original expression—puts pen to paper or fingers to keyboard or clicks that digital camera button. The work does not have to be published or distributed in order to have copyright protected status; it simply has to be in existence. The rights to the work can be transferred to some other individual or entity, through a publishing contract or other sale or licensing of rights, without the necessity of prior formal registration of copyright at the U.S. Copyright Office.

The bottom line is: Even if you find a website without a copyright line at the foot of the home page, that content is not anyone's for the taking. Everything belongs to someone.

The revision of the law was also intended to extend the copyright protection further into the future for every author. Before 1978, the author was protected by two kinds of copyright law: common-law and federal. Common-law copyright gave the rights to the author from the moment of creation of the work until it was published, and if the book or letter or sketch was never published, that common-law copyright continued to govern the rights. That's why authors used to mail copies of their stories to themselves in sealed envelopes, assuming that the date of the stamp cancellation on the unopened envelope would prove their copyright protection. If you were to find a private letter in your great-grandmother's sewing basket from Teddy Roosevelt, it would be protected by this form of copyright law, until (and if) it was published. And the permission to publish would have to come from President Roosevelt—the author of the letter—or his legal heirs. Your great-grandmother was the owner of the letter, but did not own the right of reproduction.

When a work covered by common-law copyright eventually was published, its copyright was registered formally and copies deposited in the Library of Congress. The work was protected under the federal (or statutory) copyright law, which set a specific term of years for its protection: twenty-eight years after the publication date, providing that the appropriate copyright notice was published in the work. At the end of that time, the copyright had to be renewed by the author or the publisher, which extended the protection for another twenty-eight years. When the total of fifty-six years expired, the work would enter into the public domain, where it was free for anyone to use.

The change to a unified copyright law in 1978 did not diminish the copyright protection on works published pre-1978, which continued in effect and in some cases was extended. There are many exceptions to that rule, including some easing of the renewal requirement, which we do not need to go into here.

So, a quick review of how copyright law stands at the present time:

Pre-1923: In the public domain. All works published before January 1, 1923, are in the public domain, which means they are free to use. However, any newer material that accompanies the work, such as notes or introductory essays or bibliographies, would still be under copyright protection.

1923–1963: Protected for up to fifty-six years: For works published from 1923 through 1963, most copyrights are still in place, if they were renewed properly.

1964–1977: Protected for ninety-five years. Works published from 1964 through 1977 are protected for ninety-five years from the date of first publication. That covers just about everything now in print or online, including foreign publications, which are extended the same copyright protection as works published in the United States, through the worldwide Berne Convention, an agreement that countries would respect each other's copyright laws. The exception to the rule is any publication of the U.S. federal government itself, which is free of copyright restrictions on use. (That does not apply to publications of state or local governments.)

Post-1978: Protected for life of the author plus fifty years. Works copyrighted after 1978 are protected for the life of the author plus fifty years—again with a number of exceptions (for example, works created by joint authors are protected for fifty years after the last remaining author's death; and works that fall into the category of "works-for-hire"—work created as part of an employee's paid responsibilities or commissioned specifically as a work-for-hire in which the copyright was registered by the employer or commissioning entity—are protected for seventy-five years after publication or one hundred years after creation, whichever is the lesser time). Some authors allow their works to be published in journals, magazines, or online web pages but request that they retain the copyright to the work rather than transfer it to the publisher, online or otherwise. It can take some digging to find out who

Mastering Online Research

owns the copyright on those collected pieces, in order to request permission to use them.

For the nitty-gritty details on the copyright law, you can visit the website of the U.S. Copyright Office at www.copyright .gov. It's a very helpful site (a beautiful example of a web subject directory), and it's easy to find the circulars that the department has produced to explain the different applications of the law. They're available right on the site as PDF files that you can download.

We'll look further at the capabilities of this website when we discuss how to search for copyright status on a particular work, in the permissions section on page 300.

EXAMPLES OF ONLINE MATERIAL AND COPYRIGHT STATUS

The copyright rules may become clear to you if we look at one research topic and determine the copyright status of a few materials you might want to use. Briefly, we'll take a look at the typical copyright issues that would arise if you were conducting online research to write a book or article on a historical figure. As an example, we'll use George Armstrong Custer, the U.S. army officer who met his famous end at the Battle of the Little Bighorn in 1876. But keep in mind that the identical copyright issues would arise for a similar search on any well-known figure from the past. There should be plenty of material in the public domain and perhaps even more material under copyright protection, including images, private journals and letters, biographies, and autobiographies.

As in any online research, your best approach is to look for clues as to where the material posted on a website has been taken from. A website hosted by a Custer enthusiast contains photos of the Little Bighorn battleground in Montana. Many of the photos are recent ones taken at the site (the full color panoramas are a dead giveaway!). If you wanted to use any of those recent photos, you would need the permission of the photographer. This site's home page offers links to various other items of interest to Custer fans. There are no notices of copyright, but the nineteenth-century photos of Custer and his men and horses are in the public domain by now. If a website provides the sources of old photographs, you can search the Web to find more photos in the same archive or collection.

Like many historical societies and similar organizations, the Custer Battlefield Historical Museum Association maintains a website with valuable research materials: in this case, a fine chronology of Custer's life and career as well as other information and book reviews. If you wanted to duplicate this chronology, you would need to request permission from the association. (If the association had obtained it from another source, then the copyright is owned by that source and permission could only be granted by them, not by the museum association.)

Another website posts twenty-two pages of photographs of Custer, his men, and other Civil War generals and officers. The only credit appears on the first web page, stating that many of the photographs were "posted with the permission of Mark Katz, author of the book *Custer in Photographs.*" That statement should immediately signal to you that your next click should be on Amazon.com, to find out what the Katz book is and when it was published. Again, this technique applies to any subject or person that you're researching. This particular book turns out to be a 156-page hardcover by D. Mark Katz published first in 1990.

Armed with that information, if you seriously think you want to use any of those photographs in your own work, you should verify the book's information by doing a basic search on the Library of Congress website for the title of the book or the author's name. The Library of Congress database contains three editions of *Custer in Photographs*, including one published in 2001. Because Katz cannot copyright the photographs themselves (they are in the public domain by now), the copyright on his work pertains only to the organization and arrangement of the photos and to any newly created text or annotation. Katz and his publisher have no actual copyright ownership of the photos, so according to copyright law, you can use them; however, it would be courteous to include an acknowledgment to the Katz book.

In cases such as this, I would also strongly suggest obtaining a copy of the book from which you want to take public domain images, maps, or documents. Buy a new or used copy, or order the book through interlibrary loan, then read carefully through the Acknowledgments or Credits pages in the book itself, to further ascertain that no one claims copyright lawfully. If some pieces that you want to use do require permission, you'll have some clues from the credits of whom to contact with your request.

Using material from an autobiography or biography of a historical figure is often very useful, and the copyright issues depend on when the autobiography was published and in what form it is now available. Custer, for example, wrote his own book in 1874 titled *My Life on the Plains: or, Personal Experiences with Indians*. A searchable full text of the book is available online, in a newly scanned text copy. Since the book is in the public domain, you could quote portions of it without permission (although you should credit the source). If, however, you wanted to reproduce a page or two from an online facsimile edition that displays photographic images of each original page, you would need to request permission from the University of Michigan Library, which created the digital facsimiles to display in a series called "The Making of America." The facsimile edition is available to search and view online but any subsequent distribution in print or electronically would require permission. The copyright protection in this case applies not to the content of Custer's book but to the digital images created of the book.

All of these research sources were concerned with material that originated during the lifetime of the historical figure. But if recently published books are most definitely covered by copyright law, how can you use them at all? That question leads us to how to obtain permission from the publisher or copyright holder and how to cite online sources.

PERMISSIONS AND HOW TO OBTAIN THEM

As mentioned on page 295, works published before 1923 are now in the public domain. They can be used freely, posted on a website, adapted for a screenplay, and reproduced in any way—*citing the original source.* It's never okay to claim or imply authorship of a work that is not your own, even if it's in the public domain.

Some works published between 1923 and 1963 have begun to migrate into the public domain if their copyrights were not properly renewed at the end of the first twenty-eight years, but that's a rarity. The only way to be certain is to commission a search of the Copyright Office records, which is done at the Library of Congress in Washington, D.C. You can request a paid search to be conducted by the staff by completing an online request form; alternatively there are a number of copyright attorneys and other research services who will conduct the onsite research for a fee. I would suggest looking in a recent edition of *Literary Marketplace* to locate such a service if you're considering republishing or repurposing (using in another way) content from a work that you suspect is now in the public domain. If a copy of this annual guide to publishing professionals is not available in your library, you can search portions of the database online (literarymarketplace .com) for free or subscribe to the full database service.

HOW TO CONDUCT AN INFORMAL SEARCH FOR COPYRIGHT STATUS

You can conduct your own informal preliminary search online through the Library of Congress and Copyright Office website. It won't be definitive, but it might give you some idea of the status. Go to the Copyright Office home page at www.copyright.gov, and click on the link for "Registrations and Documents" under the heading "Search Copyright Records."You will find online circulars (government-issued reports) about how to search for copyright status, how to request a search to be made, and other useful resources. You can also type in www.copyright.gov/records to go straight to the records search page.

This brief search capability that the Copyright Office provides on its website might be the best way to go, at the start. Based on what you find, you can decide whether you need to order a paid copyright search. On your own, you can search the database for registrations of books, music, films, sound recordings, maps, software, photos, art, and multimedia. The search also includes all renewals. Click on the "Books, music, etc." selection for searching. You have a choice to search by author, title, copyright claimant, registration number, miscellaneous map index terms, and sound recordings, and a combined search that includes all categories.

An example of what information you can find from the Library of Congress that pertains to copyright is a search for a 1907 book by anthropologist Gertrude Lowthian Bell, entitled *Syria: The Desert and the Sown*. Bell was an Englishwoman born in 1868, the founder of the Baghdad Museum and came to be called "the female Lawrence of Arabia" for her efforts to bring Iraq into the modern world. The results from the author search for "Bell, Gertrude" include a couple of other Gertrude Bells—you must read the brief record to determine whether it's the correct author or another by the same name. The entry for a book entitled *The Desert and the Sown: The Syrian Adventures of the Female Lawrence of Arabia* by Gertrude Bell has a new introduction by Rosemary O'Brien. The book is a 2001 reissue of the 1907 original with a slightly altered title, and only the new introduction has been registered for copyright, as you can see in the record.

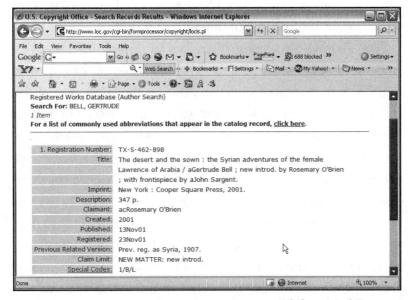

U.S. Copyright Office entry

The quantity of recent information in the Library of Congress record indicates that the 1907 Bell book is not a treasure waiting for rescue from the oblivion of the public domain. Indeed, there are several biographies of Bell and even a facsimile edition of the 1907 book that was published in 2002. The bottom line of this informal search, then, is that you wouldn't need to pay $150 per hour for the Copyright Office to search the status of this book. Obviously it's in the public domain because so many other publishers have brought out new editions.

LOCATING THE COPYRIGHT OWNER
AND REQUESTING PERMISSION

What if you want to use parts of a book that still has full copyright protection and your proposed usage would not fall under the fair use doctrine? You need to track down the copyright owner and request permission in writing.

Yes, it's time-consuming, often frustrating, and sometimes expensive to request permission to reprint materials in your new work, whether in print or online. But on the other side of the coin, if you create a stunning image on your website or you post the best poem you've ever written, you wouldn't want to see it on someone else's site the next week without even a note that the piece was created by you. Turnabout is fair play, someone said. (Okay, go find out who said that and then come back ...)

The trickiest part about requesting permission to use someone else's work is determining who legally controls the copyright *and* the right to grant permission. Commonly, even though the copyright is registered in the author's name, the book's publisher takes on the responsibility of granting permission and assessing fees. Permissions fees are generally split between the author and the publisher, according to the terms of each contract. A poet friend may tell you that you can use his entire poem on your website or in your article for a national writers' magazine, but if the publisher or rights manager of his poetry collection notices the piece, you could be in for trouble. The ideal practice in this case would be for your friend the poet to write to his publisher and request that they grant permission to you and waive all fees before you reprint his poem.

When you are attempting to track down the permissions grantor for a work that you located through online research, it might require a couple more steps than if you selected a 1,000-word excerpt from a printed book. If you are lucky, the author and title and publishing information for the work are posted online. (Dream on ...) What I usually do is take what information is available, even if it's only the author's name, and go to Amazon.com or the Library of Congress to search for the full information. If it's a recognizable publisher who is still in existence—even if only as an imprint of a conglomerate—I then go to the publisher's website to search for their permissions request guidelines. These days most large publishers make it easy for you to request permission online, although others still demand a hardcopy permissions request form and samples of the manner in which you plan to use the materials.

For instance, if you wanted to reprint an article for educators from the Scholastic Publishing website in your local school district's online newsletter, you would need to request permission. Going to the main Scholastic.com home page, you don't see any link to "permissions" or "rights management," but you know they must have such a department somewhere in their organization. Try entering the keyword "reprint rights" in the search box on the main page. Within a click or two, you will see the web page entitled "Terms of Use," and if you scroll down through the legalese, you'll find a paragraph that gives the address to which reprint permissions requests must be sent. That wasn't so hard, but it took a few steps and some thinking. You could also start by searching for "Terms of Use," which may be a document that only applies to use of the publisher's website or software but also may contain reprint permission information.

Other publishers have a form online that you can complete for permissions requests. The respected publisher W.W. Norton & Company, for example, posts its permission requirements online. You need to go to www.wwnorton.com (you can find this URL by using the Google search engine), clicking on "Contact Us," and then clicking on the directory listing of "Rights and Permissions." That will take you to the hyperlink for the permission request form. Because Norton publishes many anthologies, there is a special caution to the requestor to ascertain who holds the copyright to the specific piece by examining the credit lines and acknowledgments in the book from which the excerpt is requested. That's a helpful tip—those pages of acknowledgments and permissions at the back of a book or on the copyright page aren't just taking up space for the fun of it.

Permissions Form - Windows Internet Explorer

http://www2.wwnorton.com/area4/permissions.htm

File Edit View Favorites Tools Help

W.W. NORTON & COMPANY

Search Our Site   How to Order   Technical Support   Contact Us   About W.W. Norton

technical Support

PERMISSIONS FORM

Please complete this form to request permission to reprint copyrighted material from a Norton or Liveright publication. Incomplete forms cannot be processed and will be returned to you. If you are requesting permission to reprint material from two or more of our books, complete one form per title. Please note that we cannot grant permission to reproduce material that we have reprinted in our book by permission of another rights holder. It is your responsibility to determine the correct copyright holder using the credit lines and acknowledgments in the book, and to apply directly to them for permission. You may also fax your request to 212-790-4369.

Note: Required fields are in **bold**.

Name		Company Name	
Address		City	
State		Zip	

| Phone | | | | Fax | |

Email Address

Book from which you would like to excerpt material

- ○ Norton
- ○ Liveright
- ○ Other

Author/Editor

ISBN   Book Title

Copyright line
(please supply
from the
copyright page of
book you are
using as your
source)

Page(s) on
which the
excerpt
appears

Title of
selections(s)   Total number
of pages

Total number of
words/lines   Total number of
illustrations

The above material will be used in the following publication.

Title   Author/Editor

To be published   Publication
by   Date

Format
- ○ Hardcover
- ○ Paperback
- ○ Electronic
- ○ Other

Number of
Pages

First Print Run   Price

Territory
- ○ North American
- ○ Worldwide English
- ○ Other

Other Notes:

If you are editing the material in any way, you must submit the edited text for our approval. Please allow a minimum of 6-8 weeks for processing. Requests will NOT be processed on a rush basis.

[Submit Form] [Reset]

Online permissions request form

INFORMATION YOU NEED TO PROVIDE

Most publishers request similar information from anyone asking permission to reuse portions of a copyrighted work. Usually, you need to specify the exact title and author of the original work, and the specific page numbers where the passages appear. They may want to see the way in which the material is being used, asking for a copy of the text surrounding the quoted passages. If the material is being printed in a publication, the rights holder will want to know the title, publisher, date of publication, approximate number of copies being printed, whether hardcover or paperback, and the probable list price. All these factors determine the amount of the permissions fee that the rights holder will specify.

Similar questions will be asked of requestors of permission for internet publication, although those are only now being formulated. If you are not expecting a monetary gain from the publication in which the reprint material appears (for instance, the school district newsletter), make certain to include that information with the permission request. It may substantially lower the permission fee.

SPECIFIC CONCERNS

The permission rights granted are very specific. Some may be limited to a one-time use of the material. That's not so great if you want to use your own piece containing the excerpted material in any other way. Most permissions experts suggest that you request permission to use the excerpted material with nonexclusive world rights in all languages, and for all editions of the work in all media. We don't need to go into more specifics than these, because you will need to address the issues for each individual request.

If this all seems too overwhelming, you can obtain assistance in securing rights and permissions through an organization called the Copyright Clearing House (www.copyright

.com) for a fee or through freelance permissions consultants (check for them in *Literary Marketplace*).

PERMISSIONS FOR IMAGES

Images, illustrations, and other artwork have copyright protection as well, and it may take even more effort to determine who can grant permission for reproduction. Before the 1978 revision of the copyright law, the right to license reproduction of an artwork generally was assumed to belong to whoever owned the physical work of art. After 1978, the artist or photographer or illustrator was granted the copyright from the moment of creation of the work. If the work was sold or given to another owner, the rights of reproduction did not go along with the sale, unless otherwise negotiated. Therefore, a publisher of a book (in print or online) may not have the capacity to grant permission to reproduce the artwork—you would have to obtain permission from the artist or other copyright holder separately. Similar restrictions apply to unpublished materials such as manuscripts, letters, journals, even e-mails.

What other complications can arise in the permissions process? For a deceased author or artist, you would need to ascertain who has inherited the copyright. For a work published by a company that has since closed its doors, you would need to make a good-faith effort to locate whoever controls the rights to its books, by trying to locate the publisher on the internet and sending a request to its last known address.

Sometimes the books are sold to another publisher, with all rights. A large publisher acquiring a smaller one normally takes over its backlist of books and thus controls the rights.

Other small publishers simply fold their tents and steal away. And in the case of books that have gone out of print, the rights almost always revert to the authors or their heirs. You need to make an effort to find them, too. The last resort, after all else has failed to locate a copyright holder, is to use the piece with a disclaimer stating that all efforts have been made to request permission, and if anyone does hold the copyright to the work, ask them to please come forward and identify themselves.

The copyright laws and permissions guidelines apply to images of all kinds, just as they do to text materials. Redrawing a map that has been created by another artist, without making substantial changes, is a violation of copyright. Posting a photo on your website that you've downloaded from someone else's site without permission is a violation. Adding copyrighted songs to your home page without permission is a violation. If you are not trying to sell the images or make money from displaying them, it's questionable whether you will be brought to account—unless you're using the Nike logo or another recognizable commercial image. Still, it's best to follow the generally accepted doctrine of fair use and request permission for any usage that exceeds those parameters.

In chapter nine we discussed the techniques for searching for online images and digital audio and video files and explained in more detail about the ownership of such files and how to arrange for their legal use. The rules governing new media are still changing as the World Wide Web grows up.

HOW TO CITE ONLINE SOURCES

If you are doing lots of your research online (and we hope you are, at this point), you will want to capture the information necessary to accurately and fully cite the source of your information, whether in an online web page or in a print document. Even if you aren't planning to publish or distribute the results of your research, for your own protection you ought to have a complete citation for all quotations and web data that you have used. You never know when you might need to substantiate your research; and given the ephemeral nature of the Web, sources can disappear.

There are two excellent online sources of information on how to cite the web documents that you have used in your research.

"How to Cite Electronic Sources"

www.memory.loc.gov/learn/start/cite/index.html

This guide to the Library of Congress's American Memory collections provides instructions and examples for citing entire websites, cartoons and illustrations, films, legal documents and government publications, maps, newspapers, photographs, sound recordings, special presentations such as timelines or family trees, and primary historic texts such as letters, pamphlets, and other written materials. Examples of correct citations are furnished for both major style structures, the *MLA Handbook*, sixth edition (published by the Modern Language Association) and the *Chicago Manual of Style*, fifteenth edition (published by the University of Chicago Press). The guide is well worth the ink and paper to print out a copy for your easy reference. At the very end are some hyperlinks to additional websites relating to citing source information from the internet.

Online! Citation Styles

www.bedfordstmartins.com/online/citex.html
This website is hosted by Andrew Harnack and Eugene Kleppinger, the authors of *Online! A Reference Guide to Using Internet Sources*, which was published by Bedford/St. Martin's in 2003. Study their recommendations for citation style, which cover various popular and academic style requirements.

When you find material on a website that you know you're likely to keep and possibly use, make a record of it—copy the information into a document on your computer or keep accurate notes in hard copy—with all the pertinent information. If you've got the facts, you can put it into any citation style at a later time. If any source questions ever come up, you will be happy that you made the effort.

The most basic information to capture is the following:

- Author's last name, first name, middle initial, if given, (and the same for all authors); if no author, use the site owner
- Title of the site
- Editor of the site, if given
- Electronic publication information available, including version number, date of electronic publication (original posting), and latest update
- Name of sponsoring institution or organization
- Electronic address or URL
- Date of your individual access

It's possible that your own book or magazine publisher, teacher, or professor may have a preferred style for citing internet sources, but when you've captured all the information, it's easy enough to rework it for style.

In the next chapter, we'll look at how to determine when you've completed your search for information. All good things must come to an end—so you can start new ones.

CHAPTER 12

CONCLUDING YOUR RESEARCH

As you might guess from the title of this chapter, we've nearly completed the practice of online research skills. But in order to answer the question "Are we done yet?" we'll need to look at how much research is enough and when it's time to move on. It's an individual decision, of course, but we can use a few guidelines to help us.

When I was telling people about the plan for this book, most of them said, "Oh, I need that book!" Many immediately followed with, "Will it tell me how to *stop* researching?" None of those people were trying to avoid finishing the project they were researching—they simply had a hard time knowing when to say "Finis." I think people feel a real reluctance to put the brakes on an activity they enjoy and that is so stimulating to the mind. There's also that terrible fear that you might miss something really important if you declare an end to the research. And doing research on a favorite subject can become a lifelong pursuit for some people.

HOW DO YOU KNOW WHEN YOU HAVE ENOUGH RESEARCH?

So when is the right time to say "Enough research already!" and get on with your writing or reading or begin another research project? That's a hard question. Murphy's Law of Research states that "Enough research will tend to support whatever theory" (the corollary: Stop before you find some stuff that doesn't). It's similar to Hiram's Law that if you consult enough experts, you can confirm any opinion. Both of these recommendations are given tongue-in-cheek, of course, but I'm always surprised at the people who follow them.

Seriously, finishing the research on any work project, or even a just-for-fun search, is a hard declaration to make. There are always more opinions to consider, more websites to visit. It's an admission of confidence in yourself to make the statement that you now know enough about a subject to proceed to the next step—whatever that step is. This may be difficult. Many of us have been raised to believe in authority figures who will tell us the rules. Teachers, managers, facilitators, doctors—we look to those in charge to determine the parameters of the work, the beginning and ending of the test or the workday or the brainstorming session. But that doesn't apply if you are involved in an activity as open-ended as internet research. You need to hear your own vote of confidence in your work.

So here are some basic questions to ask yourself about the completeness of your research. Don't agonize over them; just answer with your gut feeling.

- Do I know enough about the subject now to explain it clearly to someone else?

- Did I discover facts and interpretations that I didn't know before I started my research?

- Did I obtain information on each of the important events, discoveries, or milestones of my subject, within the time period I chose to research?

- Am I happy with the amount of detailed source material I found?

- Do I have a sufficient selection of images to inspire me or to illustrate my work?

- Is there a part of my subject I avoided handling because it made me uncomfortable or anxious? Do I need to include that information for balance?

- Do I have source citations for everything I copied from websites?

- Have I checked at least two or three reliable sources to confirm facts and to resolve ambiguities?

- Have I begun to encounter the same repeating results on every new search I run?

- Is there another research project that I'm looking forward to beginning when this one is finished?

- Are there some side journeys I didn't have time to take, and would they significantly add to the completeness of my research?

- Did I turn over every single stone? (This is a trick question. You're supposed to answer "No," because it's not humanly possible to examine every related piece of information in the billions of pages posted on the World Wide Web.)

Mastering Online Research

If, after answering these questions, you are comfortable with the amount, accuracy, and depth of information you've acquired—and with the idea of the final project having your name attached to it—then call it confidence and say you're done.

However, if you didn't learn anything new about your subject, and you're not excited at the prospect of sharing your research with others, then you had better return to the keyboard until some spark on a website lights your enthusiasm. Maybe you can find a different angle on the topic that will inspire you—or switch to a new topic altogether. If you have avoided an area of concern that will affect the balance and objectivity of your research, then get back to work. That's not responsible research.

HOW LONG SHOULD RESEARCH TAKE?

Online researching must have some rough guidelines for the time you could reasonably be expected to spend in the research phase—doesn't it? In all of my research, I've never found a standard answer. When you pay for a professional legal research firm to search court records, there might be a ten-hour minimum to conduct a thorough search. A genealogical researcher might charge by the half-hour, and you can decide how much time you are willing to pay for. But when you are doing the research yourself, it's entirely up to your judgment as to how thorough the research needs to be and how quickly it can be accomplished.

If you are researching a topic just for enjoyment and your own knowledge, you may never want to say you've reached the end. My interest in Irish history goes on and on, for instance, even though I've already completed the research for one Irish historical novel (published in 2005) and two as-yet-unwritten sequels. But I'm still drawn to searching the online research world for all things Irish—although I confine it to my spare time. You might have topics you enjoy researching without any focused plan to use the material you find. At some point your research may solidify into a project—and then you might declare an end to that phase of research for that particular project.

RESEARCH PHASES

In considering the amount of time spent on online research, I find it helpful to divide the process into four phases, even though a specific number of hours would be difficult to assign to each phase.

- general research necessary to identify the scope of the resources available online and the kinds of web resources that may be most useful

- targeted research to give you the facts, figures, and documents you need to support the topic or thesis on which your project is based

- still narrower research, to add flavor, expert opinions, and pithy quotes, and to fill in any last missing bits of information

- double-checking of facts and verification of sources

There's an axiom that says that work expands to fill the available time. I find that to be especially true in doing online research—so much fascinating information is circling around out there. At the same time, if you have a firm deadline for finishing a project, you need to set time limits for your work. It's a matter of professional discipline and of developing a sense of perspective. If you've captured sufficient information—which is balanced, accurate, and timely—to give you what you need to start the next part of your project, then move on from the research phase. As you're working along on your project, you might discover a hole that needs filling or another viewpoint that ought to be represented. No problem. You can do a little more digging on the internet, with a tightly targeted search to find precisely what you need.

Take your cue from the software development engineers— they aim for 95 percent accuracy in any program before it's released. Spending the time to track down the 5 percent of the computer code that might need tweaking isn't efficient use of their time—those programming bugs will make themselves evident as the software is tested and can be remedied as they appear. For someone who has been trying to achieve 100 percent perfection most of his life, it's a novel idea. But it's actually smart thinking.

TIPS FOR TIGHT DEADLINES

Researchers and writers frequently have to work against tight deadlines. And if you're a freelancer for whom time is money, or you are trying to squeeze your research project time in between a full-time job and family obligations, you really have to make every moment count. Nothing can help with outright procrastination, but here are a few suggestions for speeding along your research without sacrificing quality.

Narrow your search. Target your searches as closely as possible to what you actually need to cover in the final project or written piece; avoid spending time on broad general searches.

Quick scan. Review the results lists quickly by scanning the URLs to see who is sponsoring the site. Click on only the most solid choices—universities, libraries, news media, reference sources. Don't waste time on the oddities.

Save for later. Bookmark pages that look as if they might be extremely useful, rather than taking the time to read them thoroughly as you search. You can go back to them later.

Multitask. Keep several browser screens open at the same time (or use the "Tabs" feature on Internet Explorer and Mozilla Firefox to keep track of open screens). You can leave the search results open in one screen while you visit other websites, and you can compare text and websites across open screens as well.

Focus. Unless your research involves commercial advertising and business, ignore all the ads and banners on the periphery of your screen.

Ignore distractions. Practice mental discipline in focusing on your research topic. Forget about checking the online weather report or your online auction bid. Get the job done.

Document. Beware the tendency to copy chunks of text from a website to your own research files in a hurry. Take the time to carefully note where the text has been taken from—it will save you time and aggravation later when you're fact-checking or reviewing the copyediting queries on your piece. Mark clearly what text is copied, to prevent unintentional plagiarism.

Research. Scan online encyclopedias and other general reference sources to determine what is considered "general knowledge" of a topic. You may not have to start your research at the most basic level if you can build on established fact.

Print for later reading. Print pages of online research that may not be available to you at a later date, such as current articles from newspapers that require payment to access their archives. Many newspapers will also permit you to e-mail a copy of the article to yourself.

E-mail. Use e-mail to contact interview sources or other individuals you find on the Web. Make sure your request or question is respectful and clear. A source may be willing to dash off a quick e-mail reply to you, if you make it easy.

EVER ONWARD

When deciding how much research is enough, keep in mind the law of diminishing returns. Those unexplored side journeys may be fun to do for your own edification, but if they're not essential to your subject, leave them for now. You can always return to fill in little holes in the research if you discover any. If your research is finished, find a new research interest to start on tomorrow. Or go shopping online for a present to reward yourself for your successful effort.

As a final tip, I'll share with you my personal motto: "Ever Onward" (or if you enjoy classical languages, you can use its

Latin form, *Semper Procedamus*). It applies to most situations in life and work, I've found.

I truly hope you've learned some useful techniques and approaches to mastering online research during our journey together. Expanding your knowledge is a never-ending journey, of course, and as the technology of the World Wide Web advances, you'll grow in capabilities along with it.

Ever onward!

GLOSSARY

Advanced search: A search that looks for keywords that are joined with other query requirements that you specify, such as the words being in a particular order, or language, or appearing on a particular kind of site.

Algorithm: A proprietary mathematical/logical formula that analyzes the data retrieved from a search in order to determine relevance ranking for display of results.

Basic keyword search: An online search that will find results for simple words and phrases.

Blog: An online personal journal or commentary, posted by individuals or organizations and usually allowing responses from other readers; short for web log.

Blogosphere: The loosely organized online community of those who write and read blogs.

Bookmark: The feature on a browser that allows the user to save the URL address of a website in order to return to it at a future time (also called Favorites).

Boolean: An application of logic known as Boolean operators to filter the search and provide more accurate results by modifying and connecting the search words in specific relationships. Boolean operators include: AND—The Boolean logical operator that instructs the search engine to find documents that contain every one of the keywords you have specified. NOT—The Boolean logical operator that tells the search engine to ignore the word or words following the operator in an advanced search. OR—The Boolean logical operator that tells the search engine to find documents in which at least one of the keywords appears.

Browser: The program application that allows you to access and interact with the internet by interpreting the HTML or XML code and assembling it for viewing on your screen.

Browsing: Moving from one website to another through the use of hyperlinks, either through manual searching or through subject directory links; also called drilling down.

Cookies: Small programs placed via the internet on a computer hard drive by a website to allow tracking and delivery of information to that website (often for marketing and advertising purposes).

Data packets: The bundles of information (data) sent back and forth between web servers using TCP/IP technology.

Database: Records of information (data) stored in a computer-readable format.

Deep Web: Website data that is not able to be found by webcrawlers or search engines; also called the Invisible Web, Dark Web, and Hidden Web.

Directory: See Subject directory.

Domain: The unique name that identifies an internet website and the organization that registers the website, as identified at the top level of the URL address by name and by type (e.g., commercial, government, educational, etc.).

Download: To transport data through an internet connection to your computer or mobile device.

Drill down: To search through multiple successive layers of hyperlinks to find information on web pages.

File extension: The designation of the file type of a document, which appears at the end of the document name; also identifies the type of domain hosting a website (e.g., .com, .gov, .edu).

Filter: Search parameter that will restrict the results of an online search to eliminate certain kinds of data (e.g., adult content sites) and include other kinds (e.g., events within a specified date range).

Hits: The results of an online search; also, the number of visitors to a website.

Home page: The initial page displayed on a website, which usually contains links for navigating the site.

HTML: HyperText Markup Language, the language in which much web content is written; it contains a system of tagged elements that are universally accepted.

HTTP: Hypertext Transfer Protocol, the method by which data is transferred on the internet, on the foundation of TCP/IP protocols.

Https: The transmission of data over a secure network, indicated by the "s" at the end, used for financial information, purchases, and other security-sensitive transactions.

Hyperlink: Internet link that connects one web location (URL) to another, within one website or from one website to another.

IP address: A unique computer location, which is a series of numbers that indicate the site's location on a network and even on a specific device such as a server or desktop computer. This IP address anchors the delivery of the information sent back and forth between web servers.

Keywords: Words that describe most specifically what you want to find, used in a search query.

Links: See Hyperlink.

Metasearch engine: A search engine that runs the query on a group of other search engines and then sorts and displays the best and most relevant results from among them all (also called megasearch engine).

Metatags: Specific keywords that are placed in the website's coding, and which describe the site's content and include terms that are likely to match a high level of search queries.

News aggregator: A website that brings together data (news, weather, other current information) from a number of different websites and displays the top ranking results on one page, by category.

"On the fly": A dynamically generated web page constructed of information and graphics brought together specifically to meet the requirements of a programming script. It does not exist as a complete page of HTML or XML until the host computer follows complex programming commands to retrieve and process the data before displaying it online as a page.

Portal: A website whose purpose is to display hyperlinks to various other websites arranged by category of interest; also called a gateway because it provides broad access to the World Wide Web.

Protocol: The rules and applications that facilitate transmission of information over the internet.

Proximity: A search feature that retrieves results based on how close together your chosen search terms appear in the website.

Query: The string of keywords to which the web search engine matches results; also the computer-readable instructions that retrieve results from a database search.

Ranking: The order in which search engine results will be displayed, as determined by an algorithmic formula.

Record: A single piece of information stored in a database.

Relevance: The closest match of the search query to the search engine's retrieved results; also called relevance ranking.

Results list: A list of hyperlinks and brief descriptions of web pages that match your search criteria, displayed on the search engine's results page.

RSS: Really Simple Syndication, a method of delivering continuously updated information from online publishers directly to your computer or mobile device.

Search engine: The programming application that directs the search and returns its results; a search engine stores information gathered from multiple websites in a database and then indexes it for future retrieval by a search query.

Search site: The operating website that owns or licenses the search engine software, such as Google.com.

Search string: The keywords or query on which a search engine conducts its searches.

Search system: The algorithmic methods used by a particular search engine; also, the choice of search method by the researcher, either a basic keyword search or an advanced search.

Servers: Computers dedicated to handling the traffic of data packets traveling back and forth on the internet.

Spider: See Webcrawler.

Sponsored results: Search results that are paid for by advertisers, separate from the results that the keyword search returns by the usual methods.

Stop words: Specific words that are excluded from search engines because they are used so frequently in a language that the search would be slowed (e.g., *the, and, it*).

Subject directory: A website that is a hierarchically organized collection of subject categories, containing hyperlinks to relevant websites evaluated and selected by human editors.

TCP/IP: Transmission Control Protocol/Internet Protocol, the data transfer program that makes everything on the internet work.

Toolbar: The display of buttons and icons at the top of a browser or document screen that simplify using its features, which are also accessible by drop-down menus or keyboard commands.

URL: Universal Resource Locator, the internet address of a website including its domain name, which conforms to a specific internet protocol allowing access to the website.

Web browser: see Browser.

Web log: see Blog.

Web page: A page of content displayed on the Web, composed of text and image files and hyperlinks, which has no standard length.

Webcrawler: A robotic (automated) web browser that retrieves data from millions of web pages by following links from one site to another.

Webmaster: The individual who maintains a website and is responsible for keeping the hyperlinks active and the content updated.

Website: A group of files organized into pages displaying text and images on the Web.

Wildcard: A symbol, such as an asterisk, that stands in for a character or characters in a search string.

XML: Extensible Markup Language, a coding language that has broader applications in facilitating user access of information on the internet than HTML, although it uses similar tagging elements.

INDEX

Google Custom Search Engine, 135
Google Earth, 186, 191
Google Labs, 59
Google Maps, 188
Google News Archive search, 77
Google Scholar, 77, 212
Gopher, 32
Government websites, suggested,
149-151
Grolier Online, 142

H

Hacken, Richard, 155
Hart, Michael, 140
Health and medicine websites,
suggested, 153-154
HighBeam Encyclopedia.com, 142
History websites, suggested, 155
Hits, 11, 325
Home page, 9, 325
evaluating website by, 96-98
HTML, 6, 18, 66, 70, 124, 324, 326,
327, 329
creator, 144
document text, 56, 213
language display, 65
HTTP, 17-18, 326
Https:, 326
Hyperlinks, 5, 9, 118, 135, 145, 325-330
identification shortcut, 124-125
image search and, 225
See also Links; Subject directories;
Webrings
HyperText, 18
HyperText links, 9
See also Hyperlinks; Links
HyperText Markup Language, 6, 326
See also HTML
HyperText Transfer Protocol, 18, 326
See also HTTP

I

Image files, 224
formats, 228
See also Images, online
Image searches, 229-241, 246-248
Google, 224-225, 229-232, 238,
240, 242
results interpretation, 230-234
Yahoo!, 224, 238-239, 242
See also Image websites; Images,
online; *and specific search
engines*
Image websites
commercial, 243-245
low-cost, 246-248
See also Image searches
Images, online, 225-228
copyright issues, 233, 235-238
fees, 237
file size, 227-228
image clarity, 225-226
model releases, 238, 243
permissions, 232-233, 243
saving, 234-235
See also Copyright law, U.S.; Fair
use, doctrine of; Image files;
Images, online
InfoSpace, 83, 84, 92
Internet
connections, 10-11
history, 6
overview, 4-7
researching on, 12-16
terms, 7-11
Internet Archive, 250-252
Internet Explorer, 9, 14, 80, 204,
206, 320
"Favorites," 25, 202
managing bookmarks using
toolbars, 26, 27
RSS feed reader, 16, 202, 203
tabbed browsing feature, 14
URL display, 17

Internet Movie Database (IMDB), 145
Internet Protocol address, 8, 17
    See also IP address
Internet Public Library Reference
    Ready Reference, 145
Internet service provider (ISP), 5, 8, 20
    See also specific internet service
        providers
Intranet, 35
Intute, 140-141
IP address, 8, 9, 17, 326

K

Keyword searches. *See* Searches,
    basic keyword
Keywords, 11, 326
    for basic searches, 40-44
    See also Searches, basic keyword
Koll, Matthew, 30-31

L

Law websites, suggested, 155-156
    FindLaw.com, 156
    Lexis-Nexis, 146, 156
Librarians' Index to the Internet,
    143-144
Libraries
    search engines, 215-216
    searchable databases/publica-
        tions available in, 136-138
    websites, 143-145
    See also Library of Congress
Library of Congress, 137-139, 295
    audio files, 249
    copyright records search, 301, 302
    Gateway to Library Catalogs, 144
    Prints and Photographs division,
        247
    SONIC, 249-250
    State and Local Governments
        site, 150
    THOMAS, 150
    website, 137, 216, 255

Links, 9, 326
    See also Hyperlinks
Log-in, website, 115-116
LookSmart.com database, 82, 83, 87
Lycos.com, 81
    image search, 240
    people search, 171-172

M

Mac computer
    feed reader, 204
    saving images, 235
    users, 5, 209
Mamma.com, 91-92, 153
    Deep Web Health Search, 91-92,
        153-154
    Desktop Search, 92
    image search, 241
Map subject directories, 191
Maps, using for research, 165-167,
    188-191
    See also Ask.com; Google Maps;
        Perry-Casteñada Library Map
        Collection
Mashups, 135
Metacrawler.com, 92
Metasearch engines, 12, 81, 241, 326
    using, 83-92
    See also Clusty.com; Dogpile.com;
        Mamma.com; Metacrawler.com;
        Webcrawler.com
Meta-tags, 11-12, 34, 35, 326
Microsoft. *See* Internet Explorer;
    PowerPoint; Vista; Windows;
    Windows Live; Windows Live
    Academic
Modem, 10
Mozilla Firefox browser, 9, 14, 204, 320
    RSS feed reader, 16, 203
    tabbed browsing feature, 14
    toolbar, 27
Msn.com, 81, 85, 86, 88, 241
    home page, 121-122

using keywords, 40-44
using queries, 36-38
See also Boolean operators;
  Searches, basic keyword;
  Searches, phrase
Searches, basic keyword, 13-15,
  38-46, 118, 130, 165, 323, 328
  with browser open to web page, 44
  images, 225
  people, 171
  tips, 40-44
  See also Keywords; Truncation
Searches, phrase, 48-50
  See also Quotation marks in
  searches
Searches, proximity, 56
  See also Proximity
Security
  keeping computer's up-to-date, 16
  website, 116-117
Servers, 8, 18, 328
Social bookmarking, 28
Sources, keeping track of valuable,
  24-29
  See also Bookmarks; "Favorites"
  file
Spam, 34-35, 112
Special operators, 56-57
Special search areas, accessing.
  See Academic scholarship, access-
  ing; Deep Web; Ezines; News re-
  sources/sources; Online groups;
  RSS feeds
Spiders, 32, 125, 328
  See also Webcrawlers
Sponsored results, 15, 85, 328
Sponsorship, website, 93, 96, 98-99,
  105
Spyware protection, 97, 117
Statistics websites, suggested,
  162-163, 191
Stemming technology, 41-42
Stop words, 50-52, 328

Subject directories 5, 12, 87, 118,
  135, 329
  academic, 119, 125-131
  advanced search capabilities, 119
  Best of the Web, 122-123, 252-253
  commercial, 119, 120-125
  image search and, 225
  keyword search capabilities, 119
Switchboard.com, 83

T

TCP/IP, 18, 325, 326, 329
Toolbar, 329
  bookmarks, 26-28
  installing, 27-28
Transmission Control Protocol/
  Internet Protocol, 18, 329
  See also TCP/IP
Tree, 121, 123
Truncation, 41
TVlink Film and Television Website
  Archive, 145

U

Universal Resource Locator, 9-10,
  16-17, 94, 329
  See also URL
University of Virginia hypertext
  collection, 141
URL, 9-10, 16-24, 71, 94, 124-125,
  129, 324, 325, 326, 329
  country designations, 22
  dynamically generated, 23-24
  image files and, 230, 232
  structure, 17-18
  suffixes, 18, 22-23, 94-95
  understanding, 19-21
  updating, 110

V

Verizon, 8
Vertical organization, 122
Victoria and Albert Museum, 247, 282
Video files, 224, 249, 250

special search features, 135
See also Windows Live Academic; Windows Live Search
Windows Live Academic, 212
Windows Live Search, 82-83
Wireless network, 11
See also Wifi
Wireless router, 11
WiseNut.com, 81-82, 88
Open Directory Project and, 126
World Wide Web, 8
creator, 144
errors, 108
Writers, background research tips for, 275-284
character development, 275-277
historical background, 278-284
personal web pages as tool, 277-278
Writers, general online resources for, 271-274
organization and association resources, 273-274
publications for writers and publishers, 271-273
websites for writers and freelancers, 274
Writers, market research for
book proposals, 259-267
magazine articles, 267-271
Writer's Market online, 269
WWW Virtual Library, 144

X

XML, 18, 66, 201, 203, 324, 327, 330
language display, 65
XML feeds, 15, 157

Y

Yahoo!, 14, 28, 37, 41, 44, 52, 57, 58, 76, 77, 78, 85, 86, 87, 165, 193, 194, 206, 210, 240, 241, 273, 284
advanced image search, 242
advanced search features, 52, 56, 59, 61, 63-66, 73-78
audio search, 250
Boolean operators, 53, 81
custom search engine, 135
customizable news pages, 199-200
"Directory," 120, 165, 264
e-mail, 112
image search, 224, 238-239
My Yahoo! feed reader, 203
news alerts, 200
online groups, 210-211, 265
Open Directory Project and, 126
people search, 169-171, 174, 180-181
search box, 35, 57
search results list, 24
special operators, 56-57
sponsored results, 15
stemming technology, 41-42
toolbar bookmarks, 26-27, 28
URL, 21
video search, 224, 250
writer's market research, 268
See also Yahoo! Babel Fish; Yahoo! News; Yahoo! Travel
Yahoo! Babel Fish, 147-148
Yahoo! News, 159
Yahoo! Travel, 188, 192, 215
YouTube.com, 172, 199, 249

Z

Zillman, Marcus P., 214, 220

Mastering Online Research